FROMELLES
1916

ABOUT THE AUTHOR

Paul Cobb's grandfathers both fought in the Great War – one served in the Royal West Surrey Regt and the other was commissioned in the Dorset Regt. Both were wounded on the Western Front in 1917 but survived. He first visited the battlefields in France and Belgium in 1969. He has published a number of articles on the First World War in the journal of The Western Front Association and has been its Membership Secretary and Vice Chairman. Paul was the winner of the inaugural 'Spirit of Aveluy Award' for a thesis on the Royal Flying Corps. He lives in Lechlade in Gloucestershire.

FROMELLES
1916

PAUL COBB

TEMPUS

To the memory of Randall King

28.6.1956–13.3.2002

First published 2007

Tempus Publishing Limited
The Mill, Brimscombe Port,
Stroud, Gloucestershire, GL5 2QG
www.tempus-publishing.com

British Library Cataloguing in Publication Data.
A catalogue record for this book is available from the British Library.

ISBN 978 07524 4174 0

Typesetting and origination by Tempus Publishing Limited
Printed in Great Britain

Contents

	Introduction	7
	Foreword by Col Terry Cave CBE	9
1	Lawyers, Bakers and Drapers	11
2	An Adequate Supply of Guns	15
3	Into a Stream of Lead	23
4	Sending Fritz Iron Rations	31
5	Annihilating Fire	41
6	I'll be Alright	49
7	Some Ghastly Sights	53
8	Twisted Heap of Khaki	59
9	Destruction and Havoc	69
10	Conspicuous Gallantry	77
11	The Final Stages	87
12	A Fearful Price	95
13	Casualties	105
14	Captivity	117
15	First View of Heaven	125
16	Bitter Legacy	157
17	Better Than I Expected	165
18	The Dismissal of Harold Pope	181
19	Remembering	193
	Appendix A: Order of Battle	203
	Appendix B: Artillery Details	209
	Maps	215
	Bibliography	221
	Archival Sources	225
	Notes	229
	Acknowledgements	245
	List of Illustrations	247
	Index	249

Introduction

Ask any person in the street to name a few places associated with the Great War of 1914–1918 and the answers, if any, are likely to be 'the Somme' or 'Passchendaele'. This is not at all surprising since, for so many people, these stereotyped, muddy foreign fields represent common belief of what the First World War was actually about.

In July 1916, while the Battle of the Somme was raging in Picardy, there was just such a battle that would fit this popular image of a First World War battle. The generals behind the lines planned an impossible task for the troops, the rain fell on a battlefield pitted with shell holes, the infantry climbed out of their trenches and advanced against enemy machine guns before the whole affair ended in a bloodbath with no new ground captured.

To describe the attack at Fromelles on 19 July 1916 in these terms would be to adopt a simplistic view, but elements of it are not so far from the truth. In 1915 Lieutenant-General Sir Richard Haking had been an influential figure in a remarkably similar attack on Aubers Ridge which had been repulsed at great cost. A year later he was to try again but this time his troops would be two new divisions, one fresh from England and the other from Egypt where it had been put together with a mix of veterans of the ill-fated Gallipoli campaign and enthusiastic volunteers sent out from Australia after a few weeks' training. Their objective on 19 July would be to attempt to deter the Germans from transferring resources to the Somme, where the joint Anglo-French offensive had been underway for a fortnight.

The battlefield was indeed damaged by shellfire, but in addition it was low-lying land typical of the wet Flanders plain and, of course, gunfire had destroyed the drainage ditches that are such a common feature of this area. The enemy lines, however, were not as damaged as might have been expected despite the best efforts of the array of artillery brought forward to prepare the ground for the infantry. That day the enemy were well prepared and well organised.

What unfolded in the fields below the village of Fromelles was to be a remarkable story of blundering in the planning process but immense gallantry by troops largely inexperienced in battle. The legacy of the day remained, shown in the disparaging names given to certain generals and the tag 'a 19 July man' to men who survived this ordeal. It left a very bitter taste, but the entire tragedy of that day has until now been overshadowed by the much better-known fighting at Pozieres which started a couple of days later and which was a significant part of the Somme offensive.

This account will help visitors to the area to understand why there are so many graves with identical dates, why there is a memorial bearing the names of 1,299 missing soldiers, and why 'Fleurbaix' and '19 July' meant so much to that generation. It will help modern generations understand the experience of hundreds of volunteers who willingly left their homes to assist the 'mother country'. It will also provide a clear understanding of why commemoration of the battle is so strong in the locality so many years later.

Foreword by Col Terry Cave CBE

As I write this we are in the first few days of 2006, the year that is the ninetieth anniversary of the Battle of the Somme. Undoubtedly there will be, on 1 July, services commemorating the opening day of the British offensive. In the following months there will be many visits and pilgrimages made to various parts of the battlefield, but I wonder how many will remember Fromelles! The Australians will, for sure, for there is a small memorial park near the VC Corner cemetery commemorating a disastrous attack on Fromelles by their 5 Division, in concert with the British 61 (2 South Midland) Division, on 19–20 July 1916, an attack that resulted in some 7,080 casualties of which just over 5,500 were Australian. Although Fromelles is well to the north of the Somme battlefield, the aim of the attack was to 'fix' the German forces in their sector and dissuade them from sending reinforcements down to the Somme. Despite the bravery of the attacking troops the operation failed to achieve its aim. But the fact is that it was a battle that need not, should not have been fought, the result of hasty planning involving two divisions that had just arrived in France, divisions which, in the words of the Official History, 'lacked experience and training in offensive trench warfare'.

'Yesterday evening, south of Armentieres, we carried out some important raids on a front of two miles in which Australian troops took part. About 140 German prisoners were captured.' Thus GHQ's official communiqué of 20 July 1916 described the battle. This bland announcement, which reflected GHQ policy at the time of concealing unpleasant news from the British public (it certainly didn't fool the Germans), angered the Australian troops who had fought in an action in which their division had suffered the highest casualty figure sustained by any BEF division throughout the whole war in a single day's action, other than the 6,380 of the 34 Division on 1 July. Nor did it go down well back in Australia when the true facts emerged; there were many who regarded all GHQ communiqués thereafter with a deal of scepticism. To Australians this attack was a significant event, the first major operation on the Western Front involving their troops;

their official historian, Bean, devoted 120 pages to it, the British official historian, Edmonds, only fifteen. In the welter of the Somme battles in progress to the south, Fromelles has slipped from the British consciousness and has become a forgotten, overlooked battle – until now. With this book, which has taken up years of research, Paul Cobb has provided a comprehensive, detailed account of the battle in which he has made good use of official documents, correspondence, letters, war diaries, casualty returns and much more, as the lengthy bibliography reveals. We also have a report on the contentious dismissal of Harold Pope, one of the Australian brigade commanders, by his divisional commander – not on the usual grounds of incompetence but, and this is surely unique, on grounds of alleged drunkenness, and on his fight to clear his name.

If you visit VC Corner cemetery today, a cemetery with no headstones but two mass graves and with a wall at the rear on which are inscribed the names of the 1,299 Australian dead with no known graves, you can look across the flat fields on which they died and where, when Bean visited the scene in November 1918, the remains of many attackers still lay in No Man's Land. This is their story and this is a tribute to their memory.

Terry Cave
Worthing
January 2006

1

Lawyers, Bakers and Drapers

In early 1916 French army commanders urged the British High Command to launch an offensive to ease the burden on their sector of the Western Front. The location selected was the front occupied by the British Fourth Army. Weeks of intense preparation culminated in the Battle of the Somme – a 'big push' that would last 143 days. The first day, 1 July 1916, resulted in some 60,000 casualties sustained within a few hours of the infantry attack commencing. The next couple of weeks proved to be marginally more successful but to impede German resistance it was necessary to stop redeployment of resources from further north, in particular the Lille–Lens area.

A number of trench raids had been carried out in other sectors but an instruction was sent to the commanders of the First, Second and Third Armies to renew their efforts so that German units on their front might remain in position. An additional requirement was that the artillery should be economical with ammunition to ensure that the main offensive on the Somme would not be deprived of sufficient firepower.

The manpower supply on the Western Front would now also be improved. In Egypt, after withdrawal from Gallipoli, two Australian divisions had been divided and strengthened to make four divisions and another, the 3 Division,[1] had been formed in Australia. Sailing to Marseilles from late March 1916 onwards, these troops had made the long journey by train to northern France and were now ready to take part in offensive operations.

Sir Douglas Haig, commander-in-chief of the British forces on the Western Front, had also ordered the other army commanders to draw up plans for more substantial attacks in case the Germans were overwhelmed on the Somme. An optimistic appraisal of the Somme offensive was provided on 12 July by Lieutenant-General Sir Launcelot Kiggell,[2] Haig's Chief of Staff, who stated that 'steady progress is being made', though he did acknowledge that 'heavy rains, and consequent difficulties of ground, in addition to the strength and depth of the enemy's defences, have rendered rapid progress impossible and have enabled the enemy to gain time to recover from his first confusion and disorganisation – which were considerable'.[3] Kiggell was 'confident of breaking through… in the near future and inflicting a heavy defeat'.

General Sir Herbert Plumer, the very capable GOC Second Army, had made the requirement for seeking suitable locations for offensive action quite clear to his corps commanders on 3 July, but repeated it two days later when it was learned that the 13 Jager Battalion had been moved to the Somme vacating their position in the line opposite II Anzac Corps. Until now this corps had consisted of the New Zealand Division, and the 4 and the 5 Australian Divisions, the latter having only very recently arrived in northern France. Lt-Gen Sir Alexander Godley, the corps commander, now lost the 4 Australian Division, which was being sent to the Somme in readiness for the fighting around Pozieres.

More raids gallantly executed by the New Zealand troops were believed to have had negligible effect. Action on a far larger scale where enemy reserves were limited thus appeared to be the only real opportunity to meet Haig's requirements. Plumer's Second Army discounted an attack in the Messines Ridge area – this sector's turn would come in a spectacular way in June 1917 – or Ypres, where circumstances were not yet suited to an attack on the scale required by Haig. At the southernmost extremity of the Second Army, where it had joined the First Army at a point in the low-lying fields below the village of Fromelles, the Germans held their front line far more lightly than elsewhere on this army's front. The source of this plan, according to Australian historian Charles Bean writing in Reveille[4] in June 1931, was General Sir Richard Haking,[5] GOC XI Corps, who had 'suggested to his Army Commander that there existed on his front a prominent German salient, the "Sugar Loaf" near Fromelles, which offered, in his opinion, a favourable chance of capture'. Haking's view does not take into account the events in May 1915.

This very location below Aubers Ridge, in May 1915, had witnessed a singularly unsuccessful attack, a pincer movement on the enemy line, at the same time as the French attacked in the Vimy Ridge area. It was a disaster and cost three divisions some ten thousand casualties. Haking's new scheme, proposed to General Monro, was for a joint Second and First Army breakthrough in the Aubers Ridge area. With so many divisions committed to the Somme offensive, Haig's divisions to undertake any operation on Aubers Ridge were likely to include troops new to the Western Front. The two destined to carry out Haking's plan were the 61 (2 South Midland) Division and the 5 Australian Division.

The first of these, the 61 Division,[6] was a second-line or reserve division that did not exist until 31 August 1914. While the formation was based in Northampton it was part of First Army, Central Force; in April 1915 the 1 (South Midland) Division, the corresponding first-line imperial service unit, left Chelmsford bound for France, and so the 2 (South Midland) Division moved to Essex as part of Third Army, Central Force. In February/March 1916 the division moved to Salisbury Plain and preparations for warfare in France and Flanders intensified. Their GOC, Major-General Colin Mackenzie, was appointed on 4 February 1916, Brigadier-General A.F. Gordon of 182 Brigade on 13 February, followed by Brig-Gen C.G. Stewart (183 Brigade) and Brig-Gen C.H.P. Carter (184 Brigade) on 3 and 7 May 1916 respectively.

The battalions within the division recruited from an area of England around Birmingham, the Malverns, the Cotswolds and the Chilterns. For example, 2/5 Btn, Gloucestershire Regiment was formed in early September 1914 as a second-line battalion of 1/5 Gloucesters by Lt Col the Hon A.B. Bathurst and was designated as a Home Service Battalion. Like so many new units, membership overwhelmed the supply of uniforms and for a while its recruits wore a square of white silk inscribed '2/5th Glosters' to indicate that a man had joined up. Recruits came from a variety of backgrounds; 2/5 Gloucesters claimed that its personnel included 'members of Parliament, lawyers, bakers, accountants, drapers, musicians, conjurers, butchers, sugar magnates, farm labourers and artisans of every sort'.[7] Similarly, 2/8 Royal Warwicks recorded that a large number of their new soldiers came from Saltley College and from Birmingham Tramways.[8]

On 24 May the division left for France from Southampton aboard HMT *861*, landing the following day at Le Havre. The Laventie sector was to provide their first taste of the front line in France and Flanders; eight casualties in the first week was a mere hint of things to come. Laventie, the main base of 61 Division at this time, was described by Major Christie-Miller as 'not a wholly wrecked town but had been a good deal knocked about. The church had been demolished and a convent or school adjoining it with a good many buildings but there was quite a sprinkling of fairly complete houses.'[9]

While Mackenzie's division was preparing for the Western Front the formation of the 5 Australian Division was also underway, not in their home territory but midway to Europe, in Egypt.

With the evacuation from the Gallipoli peninsula completed the AIF could now concentrate upon its recuperation and expansion in Egypt. The 1 and 2 Divisions had returned from the Dardanelles, and in Egypt they joined the 4 and 8 Australian Infantry Brigades plus several thousand reinforcements. These fresh troops, mainly infantry and Light Horsemen, were to expand the two existing divisions into four, the two new ones being numbered 4 and 5 Divisions; the 3 Division was already being created in Australia. As well as the infantry battalions, other parts of the division were also formed including the artillery, the engineers, medical services and transport. A commander was on his way from Australia, Major-General the Hon James Whiteside McCay.

Despite the attractions of foreign parts, for some Egypt was a desolate spot. Robert Fulton, now in 53 Btn, wrote to his sister: 'we are in a very lonely part of the globe at present. We are in the trenches in Egypt, defending the canal. It does not take much defending either, I have not seen a Turk yet, and I don't think we are very likely to either'. With the urgent need for troops on the Western Front, the transfer started of a substantial part of the Australian Imperial Force from Egypt to France. The long transfer from the desert to the green fields of Picardy started with a train journey, a 150-mile trip from Moascar to Alexandria taking at least eight hours. The majority of the 5 Division left Egypt between 16 and 23 June 1916; some of the ships put in at Malta, but all eventually arrived in Marseilles where the troops disembarked wearing their new uniforms designed for cooler climates.

From Marseilles it would require about thirty trains to move the men and a couple of dozen to transport the equipment to their destination many miles to the north. Paris was 530 miles away and the railhead at Hazebrouck was a further 150 miles. The scenery along the way contrasted vividly not just with the deserts of Egypt but also with some of the more barren parts of Australia. The 53 Btn, known as 'The Whale Oil Guards', had their journey recorded by the Roman Catholic Chaplain Fr J.J. Kennedy, who wrote:

> ...our eyes feasted on the loveliness... beautifully cultivated farms, magnificent chateaus, serpentine rivers, castled crags, gray old towns with their old-time cathedrals and abbeys, picture succeeded picture and out-rivalled it in beauty... the towns... were old and historic; Avignon, once the refuge of exiled Popes, Tresancon, Orange, and many other places of interest. Everywhere along the way the people cheered us and blessed us.[10]

The 8 Brigade eventually detrained at Morbeque on 26 June, the 14 at Thiennes four days later and the 15 Brigade at Steenbecque on 27 June. McCay's division was now located close to Mackenzie's, and as Haking's plan to relieve the troops fighting on the Somme gathered momentum, the severest of tests approached.

2

An Adequate Supply of Guns

On 8 July at a conference of his corps commanders, Sir Charles Monro (Army Commander) stated that the battle of the Somme was 'progressing favourably'[1] but an operation was required on the front held by the First and Second Armies near Laventie. Monro instructed Haking to develop his plans on the understanding that his corps would go into action in conjunction with one division from the neighbouring Second Army as well as some additional artillery. On this same day the 4 Australian Division was instructed to move south to the Somme but was ordered to leave behind its artillery. At this time Haking's XI Corps was holding the line from south-west of Cambrin (south of the La Bassée Canal) to Laventie, the point where the First and Second Armies joined. If the attack was to go ahead, it presented the possibility that Haking could lose the same battle twice.

Considering the lack of success of British attacks on the Western Front in 1915 and thus far in 1916, Haking's enhanced plan, that he put to Monro the following day, was ambitious. His scheme was intended to capture a section of the Aubers–Fromelles ridge a mile or so behind the German front line from which the British had withdrawn in late October 1914; the attack would be a two-division assault on a front of 4,200 yards. Monro rejected it. According to Brig-Gen Harold Elliott (OC 15 Bde)[2] in an address to the RSSILA,[3] 'Monro, however, turned down this proposal in favour of an attack in the Vimy Ridge Sector, later carried out by the Canadians, as being more likely to be of use to Haig, being much nearer the Somme'.

Circumstances soon caused the resurrection of a variation of Haking's plan. Progress in capturing enemy-held territory on the Somme had been slower than expected and a number of German battalions had arrived on the Somme from the Lille area. The General Staff was of the opinion that an 'artillery demonstration' for a period of some three days on a front of 15,000 yards on the First and Second Army fronts would convince the Germans that a significant offensive was about to be launched.

On 13 July Monro informed Haking that the GOC Second Army would place a division at the disposal of the First Army for an offensive operation in the Picantin area on the boundary of the two armies. A senior officers' conference took place that day at Chocques. In attendance were Haig's deputy chief of the general staff, Major-General Sir R.H.K. Butler, accompanied by Major H. Howard, Major-General Sir G. Barrow and Major-General C. Harington,[4] chiefs-of-staff of the First and Second Armies respectively, as well as the army commander Sir Charles Monro and Colonel Wilson of GHQ First Army. It was agreed that each army could provide not only sufficient artillery for a demonstration but also three divisions, two from the First Army and one from the Second Army, for infantry participation in a scheme based upon Haking's plan. Haking would be in charge of the whole operation.

Butler then met Sir Herbert Plumer at La Motte-au-Bois (II Anzac Corps HQ) at 4.30p.m. where Plumer expressed his overall approval of the scheme. A further conference[5] was held attended by Plumer, Godley, Harington, Franks,[6] Gwynn,[7] Howard and Butler to discuss some of the detail. It was agreed that the divisional artillery of five to six divisions was to be collected at the junction of First and Second Armies; wire cutting would commence on the morning of 14 July with whatever guns were available and others would join the bombardment once they had moved into position; and the infantry attack was to take place about 17 July 'with a view to seizing and holding the German front system of trenches'.[8]

A First Army order (No. 100) issued on the 15 July confirmed the overall purpose of the action:

> …to prevent the enemy from moving troops southwards to take part in the
> main battle. For this purpose the preliminary operations, so far as it is possible,
> will give the impression of an impending offensive operation on a large scale,
> and the bombardment which commenced on the morning of the 14th inst. will
> be continued with increasing intensity up till the moment of the assault.[9]

As well as the troops moving into the front trenches on 12 July, Major-General McCay[10] was also taking over the accommodation occupied by his predecessor in a chateau in Sailly-sur-la-Lys a short distance behind the front line. On the morning of the 13 July[11] he travelled to La Motte-au-Bois to be informed that no sooner had they settled into their new positions than his division was to be placed on loan to Haking's XI Corps of the First Army. McCay seemed pleased that his division, so recently arrived in France, was about to become the first Australian division to participate in a significant action on the Western Front.

McCay was given details of the plan for an attack on enemy lines in fulfilment of Haig's instructions. The plan at this stage was to assault and capture approximately 6,000 yards of the enemy's front line lying below the northern slopes of Aubers Ridge; the north-easternmost point was opposite the site of a religious settlement (now identified by a monument by the side of the lane) marked as 'La Boutillerie' on trench maps, while the extreme right of the proposed battlefield was to be the country lane running between the hamlets of Fauquissart, on the British side of the line, and Trivelet on the German side.

Initially three divisions were allocated for the attack. The 5 Australian Division and the British 61 (2 South Midland) Division were to be joined by the British 31 Division; the latter occupied the section of line from La Cordonnerie, to the right of the Australians, to a point opposite the Sugar Loaf Salient, located on the left of the 61 Division. This operation was deemed within the capability of all three divisions but none were believed to be of sufficient strength or capability to be sent into action on the Somme. The Australians were freshly arrived from Egypt, the 31 Division had already received a mauling on the Somme, and the 61 Division was a recently arrived second-line Territorial division which had already lost a number of its men through transfers to other divisions.

At this juncture the chosen day was 17 July, but no sooner had McCay been informed of this than Haking discovered to his dismay that only two divisions' worth of artillery (4 and 5 Australian Divisions) had been allocated to him by the Second Army rather than the three he was expecting. Three further factors compounded his predicament: the shortcomings in training and battle experience of the Australian gunners, the fact that the 5 Australian Division had no trained 2-inch mortar personnel, and a much reduced supply of shells. Consequently, the front was reduced to a section running from the Fauquissart–Trivelet road to Delangre Farm. This narrowing of the front appears to be the basis of the corps commander's opinion that he had adequate artillery.

The width of the battlefield was now about 3,500 yards, and with the 39 Division taking over from La Bassée Canal to Oxford Street (map reference S.5.c.5.4), the pivot of the attack was now to be a point opposite the Sugar Loaf Salient. The 5 Australian Division would occupy from this point to La Cordonnerie Farm on their left, and the 61 Division would adjoin the Australians opposite the Sugar Loaf Salient and extend to their right to the Fauquissart–Trivelet road. Consequently, the 31 Division was to be pulled out of the line and transferred to the right of the 61 Division. Further changes were necessary to the left of the Australians in response to their sideways move towards the Sugar Loaf Salient, filling part of the ground previously occupied by the 31 Division. On their left was the New Zealand Division, which moved its right-hand boundary towards the Australians. To fill the remaining gap between the New Zealand and Australian units the British 60 Brigade (20 Division) was transferred from the Ypres Salient for the duration of the attack, though this brigade would take no part in the action apart from providing covering fire.

On 14 July the order was issued[12] allocating Australian artillery for the forthcoming battle. Further instructions followed in Corps Order No. 57, which detailed more artillery dispositions as well as the programme for each day leading up to 17 July when the attack should have gone ahead. So far as the threat of return fire of German guns was concerned, any known battery positions were to be shelled prior to the infantry attacking and during the battle. However, the intended three-day bombardment further south as far as the Hohenzollern Redoubt was reduced to selected targets in the 39 Division area.

Co-operation with the Royal Flying Corps (RFC) was also specified. So that the position of the infantry could be plotted on maps, attacking troops' positions in the enemy's trenches were to be notified to the RFC by means of flashing mirrors and flares one hour after the assault and thereafter at hourly intervals during daylight. Made available for the battle were 10 Squadron, 1 Bde RFC and 16 Squadron, 2 Bde for 'tactical reconnaissance, artillery work, liaison, photography and local protection of Corps machines'.[13] The 10 Wing RFC was also to provide an offensive patrol from 4.15a.m. until dark each day during the build-up and during the battle itself, around Illies and Beaucamps behind the German lines. This same wing was also to provide one aeroplane with a full plate camera and supply photographs for a Photographic Section RFC stationed at XI Corps Advanced HQ. Finally, No. 10 Kite Balloon Section was brought into the rear area for observation purposes.

Communications were to play a significant part in the battle. The Australian signal company had arrived in Marseilles on 25 June and by 30 June was in Blaringhem in northern France. As early as 4 July Capt R.A. Stanley and four men reported to Croix du Bac to open a signals office; on 12 July they moved to Sailly-sur-la-Lys, taking over the signals office vacated by the 4 Australian Division. Their preparations[14] continued over the next couple of days as provision and testing of cables to new positions progressed along with the installation of jamming sets and arrangements for a carrier pigeon service.

The difficult reorganisation of the various units holding the front line and the relief by fresh troops were exacerbated on the night of 14/15 July by two unwelcome intrusions. At 9p.m. on 14 July the 61 Division released a cloud of gas, which drifted across and along the German front line but then continued in an arc into the face of 60 Bde causing a number of casualties – as did shelling by the Germans in retaliation. On 18 and 19 June, 1,500 gas cylinders had been brought into the trenches; this gas was supposed to be released in the Neuve Chapelle and Fauquissart sectors on 15 July whilst the relief of battalions took place, but between 16 and 19 July every available 61 Division soldier not detailed for the assault was employed in removing these cylinders. By the time the assault finally went ahead on 19 July, only 470 cylinders had been removed, the men being too tired to remove any more.

Brig-Gen Elliott listed, in his 1931 paper to the RSSILA in Canberra, the retention of gas cylinders in the front line as one of the 'blunders' of the battle. Ellis noted in the divisional history[15] that 'it was imperative… that these should be removed before any heavy enemy artillery action occurred, and this work entailed a severe strain on their infantry working parties as well as occasioning considerable congestion in the saps leading to the front line'. Fortunately no cylinders were damaged during the battle, though one gas-related incident did occur on the day before the battle when the German gunners dropped 'several HE shells in our front line… one onto a gas cylinder in A Coy which of course burst and with an enfilade wind spread gas down the line instantly causing between 70 and 80 casualties including one officer, Lt Pitcher, and some of our best NCOs. In addition Capt Church and CSM Arthur Brown got a slight dose but did not report sick.'[16] Both men became casualties in the battle.

The second inopportune incident for the British proved a most fruitful excursion for the 21 Bavarian Reserve Infantry Regiment. At 9.15p.m. the real purpose of the retaliatory bombardment became clearer as it moved to the left of the intended front of the attack around Cellar Farm, where the line was held by the 58 Btn waiting to be relieved by the 6 Btn Oxfordshire and Buckinghamshire Light Infantry (OBLI). This position, along with Mine Avenue and Cellar Farm Avenue plus communication trenches and breastworks in the front line, received a very heavy pounding causing extensive damage. In conjunction with this bombardment, a raiding party led by a Leutnant Harder caused heavy casualties when it entered the Australian trenches, which were more heavily populated than usual due to the relief of the Australians. The OBLI lost ten men killed and a further nineteen wounded, light losses compared with the Australians who had forty-two killed, 118 wounded and a further four missing.

The timing was ideal for the Germans as, apart from capturing a Lewis gun and inflicting so many casualties, they learnt that the 5 Australian Division was now in the line in place of the 1 Australian Division; the departure of the 4 Australian Division had not been detected by the enemy. The price paid by the Bavarians was ten killed and twenty-two wounded. Even though they interrogated prisoners taken in the raid it appears unlikely that the Germans knew that an attack was imminent, and it was the start of the British artillery's registration on German targets and wire-cutting on 16 July that alerted German staff officers to the possibility that some offensive action might be about to start. From their vantage points on Aubers Ridge the Germans had also observed newly positioned field guns just behind the British front line. German opinion varied over the motive for the increased gunfire, some thinking that it was simply in response to the German trench raid, others believing that an infantry assault on the Sugar Loaf Salient was likely.

Doubts over the soundness of Haking's plan were further fuelled by a visit to 15 Bde's sector by Major Howard, one of Haig's staff, on 14 July. Elliott did not hesitate to show Howard the 400-yard-wide stretch of No Man's Land opposite the Sugar Loaf Salient over which his troops would have to advance. Howard concluded that the proposed attack was destined to be another appalling disaster and presented his report to Haig and Harington. On 15 July they approved the plans for the attack, but noted on Howard's report 'except that infantry should not be sent in unless an adequate supply of guns and ammunition for counter-battery work is provided'. This comment was noted by General Butler, who met the commanders of First and Second Armies and their chiefs of staff at Chocques on 16 July. Butler put the commander's position on adequacy of resources to paper in a secret memo[17] dated 17 July, in which he stated that the operation would proceed 'provided as always that General Sir Charles Monro is satisfied that the conditions are favourable, and that the resources at his disposal, including ammunition, are adequate for both the preparation and execution of the enterprise'.

Haking stated that he considered that the available ammunition and other resources at his disposal were sufficient to enable the operation to succeed; Monro also expressed his satisfaction that Haking's plan should proceed. In addition, Butler indicated that information on the redeployment of German units gained by GHQ suggested that the need for the operation to commence on the 17 July was no longer so rigid. Even with Monro's support it was suggested at this conference that the attack could be postponed or even cancelled. The British Official History[18] states that Butler informed Generals Monro, Plumer and Haking that 'there was now no urgent need for the XI Corps operation: Sir Douglas Haig did not wish the attack to take place at all unless the commanders on the spot were satisfied that their resources were, in every way, adequate'. However, the 'Commanders present were unanimously against a postponement. The troops were worked up to it, were ready and anxious to do it'; moreover, it would damage the confidence of the troops if the operation was cancelled. Haking 'was in particular most emphatic on this point'. It was agreed that the attack would continue but, even if the opportunity arose, 'it was not the intention to embark in any more extended operations however inviting'.[19] Notwithstanding any reservations expressed at First Army HQ, times were agreed for the commencement of the final bombardment – 4a.m. on 17 July – and the infantry assault – 11a.m.

During the afternoon of 16 July another factor emerged to burden operations – the rain – and the prospects did not look at all favourable for the coming 24 hours. The weather reports[20] for 17 and 18 July were similar, but locally around Fromelles the mist hung over the battlefield preventing the observation of the fall of shells. For 19 July, the weather was recorded as being 'fair generally… misty especially at night… cold at night'.[21]

The first casualty of the weather was to be the artillery, which needed to observe the bursting of their shells as part of the process of registering their guns on selected targets. Butler was acutely aware of the weather's potential to hinder this preparatory work, and so he returned to Chocques in order to gain information to make a more informed judgement. Monro was not present, but it was made clear to Lt Col S.H. Wilson (Monro's GSO1 – Operations) by Butler that the army commander had full discretion either to cancel or to postpone the attack for reasons of the weather or any other cause. Haig was informed of Butler's statement and gave his approval to this action by the deputy chief of his staff.

Following the postponement of the attack, Haking wrote to the troops of the two divisions informing them of the reasons for the delay:

> As you know we were going to have a fight on Monday, but the weather was so thick that our Artillery could not see well enough to produce the very accurate shooting we require for the success of our plan. So I had to put it off, and GHQ said to do it as soon as you can. I then fixed 'zero' for Wednesday, and I know you will do your best, for the sake of our lads who are fighting hard down south.[22]

Despite these setbacks, Haking remained confident that the afternoon of 16 July and the following morning would be adequate time for registration and practice before the battle itself got underway. Furthermore, at a conference that day he told his divisional commanders the 'the narrow depth of the attack should make it possible, with the ammunition available, to reduce the defenders to a state of collapse before the assault'. The rain that afternoon did not abate and the hour designated for the start of the final seven hours' bombardment approached. By 4a.m. the following morning the rain had eased, but heavy mist lingered over the fields delaying this bombardment for four hours. Subsequently, when conditions had still not improved, another postponement of three hours was agreed. At 8.30a.m. on 17 July Haking sent a despatch which appears to contradict some of the assurances he had been giving to his senior officers and shows that he knew about some of the deficiencies among the gunners and infantry. He commenced by saying that 'it is with great reluctance that I am compelled to advise the postponement… owing to weather conditions', continuing, 'some of the heavy artillery batteries that were sent to me have never fired out here before'. He alleged also that the infantry 'are not fully trained' and 'do not appear to be very anxious for the attack to be delivered'. For General Monro, on the other hand, cancellation of Haking's entire scheme seemed to be the preferred course of action.[23] Haking also pressed Monro to inform him whether he wanted the same timetable to be implemented the following day using the same troops, stating that this would 'minimise any loss of morale'. In addition, at 6a.m. on 17 July, advanced XI Corps HQ opened at Sailly-sur-la-Lys – a sign that Haking was not realistically expecting a postponement or cancellation.

Monro agreed to delay the assault until at least 19 July, and even this date would be dependent upon more favourable weather conditions prevailing. The opportunity was taken by the Australian division to return one of the battalions assigned for the assault per brigade to billets in the rear area, and to place the other assaulting battalion in the reserve lines. At the same time Lt Col A. Jackson (58 Btn) departed and was succeeded by Major C.A. Denehy, formerly of 57 Btn.

Fortunately for the gunners the improvement in the weather continued, enabling them to obtain the range of the enemy's positions, but their frustration had been noted in the war diary – 'fire totally unobserved owing to fog'.[24] A clue to the difficulties facing the gunners is given in Major Christie-Miller's papers[25] in which he comments that 'the OPs on Rue Tilleloy were heavily pounded by the enemy on 18th and more especially on 19th and that any fire control depending on these must have been far from efficient. The gunner officers who flocked to these OPs suffered heavy casualties. The wires in working order must have been few and far between.'

In the front line, troops completed stocking engineer's stores, delivering ammunition and bombs, as well as having a meal and snatching a few hours' sleep when the opportunity presented itself. The final seven-hour pre-assault bombardment that had been delayed by the adverse weather conditions was ordered to commence. This time Haking fixed the start time at 11a.m. on 19 July; the infantry would assault that evening at 6p.m.

3

Into a Stream of Lead

The area of the Fromelles battlefield was very flat from the left-hand point of the proposed attack across to the extreme right, for some distance behind the British lines, and for 600 yards behind the German line until the ground started to rise towards the ridge. It was also criss-crossed by drainage ditches, made necessary by the high water table in these low-lying fields. Along the sides of some of the ditches remained rows of willow trees, or in some cases their shell-shattered stumps. The prominent feature of the immediate battle area was the Layes Brook, the main drainage channel running from south-west to north-east, bisecting both the British and German front lines near the Sugar Loaf Salient; today it can be easily identified a few yards to the north of VC Corner.[1] The origin of the name 'Sugar Loaf' itself cannot be ascertained, but was probably bestowed upon the remains of a farm building, long destroyed, which had left a white smudge on the fields. Behind the German lines, gentle slopes led to the top of Aubers Ridge 500 yards beyond. Although only 30 feet above the battle area, in Great War terms this was a significant piece of high ground offering views across the British front and rear areas. The facility was enhanced even further by observation posts, such as the one constructed inside Fromelles church tower and another which can still be seen today in the main street of Aubers.

The tower in Fromelles was visited by Brig-Gen H.E. Elliott (OC 15 Brigade) in 1918. He wrote that it

> had been turned into a solid cube of concrete, except for a stair so narrow that only with difficulty could a normally built man ascend it. At its head near the ridge pole it terminated in a loophole for an observer, who, with a telescope could, with perfect safety to himself, count every sentry in our lines. He also had an extensive view across our back areas, and could at once detect any preparation for attack.[2]

In view of the high water table, digging trenches was a fruitless exercise. Consequently both sides had constructed thick breastworks of earth, timber and the ubiquitous sandbag. 4473 Pte W.H. Downing,[3] serving with 57 Btn, noted in *To the Last Ridge*:

> …there were no trenches, but solid breast-works of beaten sandbags revetted with iron and timber, fortified with concrete slabs or 'bursters'. These were from 20 to 30 feet thick, and seven to ten feet high. There was no parados. A fire step was in every bay and a sand-bag block-house used as a dugout.

Loopholes were provided for sentries keeping a watchful eye for activity in opposing lines. As well as positions for machine guns created in each front line there were provided, especially in the case of the Germans, well-concealed positions for snipers attentive to any soldier who might either recklessly or unwittingly expose himself to this unseen peril. The British official historian, Capt Wilfred Miles, noted, 'as little fighting had taken place in the region for the past fourteen months, the Germans had had ample opportunity to strengthen their breastworks defences, which now included many machine-gun emplacements constructed of concrete, well sited and concealed'.[4]

As the British desire in 1914–1918 was to be on the offensive and to move the front line forward, positions were regarded as short-term accommodation and therefore often lacked substantial shelters, though there were plenty of dugouts of various standards along the front. The Germans, on the other hand, had dug in with the purpose of holding their front line, usually on higher ground, until such time as the Russians had been defeated on the Eastern Front and resources could be transferred to the west in readiness for an offensive on a large scale that would push the Allies back to the sea and force them to capitulate. In order to hold the front line with relatively few men, to defend it in depth and to enable a reasonably comfortable existence in these inhospitable conditions, a number of dugouts had been prepared, supported by prefabricated timber structures. These were later augmented by concrete blockhouses, many of which may be seen nowadays on the battlefield. Pumping systems were installed to remove surplus water, electric power was provided for lighting and there are accounts of some dugouts being equipped with home comforts such as wallpaper and beds! As with the deep chalk dugouts on the Somme, these shelters offered reasonable protection from British bombardments, after which the German troops would emerge ready to resist an enemy attack.

By July 1916 the German expertise in the use of concrete had already been put to good use in the Aubers Ridge area,[5] but the concreted works that existed at the time of the assault appear to have been limited mainly to platforms for trench mortars and roofs for dugouts; one or two more substantial structures did exist further back, however.[6] The 8 Brigade's summary of the battle noted the 'trench mortars on concrete pods behind the island traverses in excavations in the parados. One very large mortar on a concrete platform; all these were destroyed'.[7]

At intervals along the breastworks were sally ports to allow access to and egress from No Man's Land for attacking troops or trench raiding parties. Beyond the breastworks were stretches of barbed wire wound around screw pickets and tossed into inextricable webs by shell fire. Amongst the wire and on into No Man's Land were uncultivated crops and long grass in fields pitted by shell craters, all of which provided useful cover for nocturnal raiding or listening activity; also lying amongst this agricultural detritus was the further debris of war such as items of equipment and human remains, in particular from the May 1915 attack. Downing noted this latter feature: 'graves of Englishmen lay everywhere; the dates on the little crosses had almost faded since "December 1914", "February", "May", "October 1915". Most of the graves were nameless'.[8]

Trailing back from the British front line were communication trenches constructed alongside hedgerows and farm tracks, utilising ruined farm buildings. These routes, also prone to flooding, were necessary for the movement to the front line of stores, weapons, ammunition, men and the vast array of material necessary for the conduct of war. In the return direction came troops collecting further loads to be brought forward, soldiers relieved from front-line duty making their way to the rear for a welcome break and wounded and dead being evacuated. Light railways brought ordnance as far forward as possible before transfer to waiting troops. In the line occupied by the Australians, for example, there were five communication trenches. In the 8 Bde sector there was Cellar Farm Avenue, which was passable, and Mine Avenue, which was impassable due to being partly blocked by mud and flood water. Similarly, Brompton Avenue in the 14 Bde sector was also flooded along part of its length but was of some use. This was the sole communication trench in this brigade's sector and would create a serious impediment when troops moved forward in readiness for the assault. On the Australian right, Elliott's men had the benefit of the serviceable trenches of Pinney's Avenue and VC Avenue.

No Man's Land varied from 100 yards on the extreme left to a maximum width of 400 yards opposite the Sugar Loaf Salient narrowing again to 200 yards on the right of the sector occupied by the 61 Division. The 'salient' opposite the junction of the 61 Division and the 5 Australian Division, the Sugar Loaf Salient, and the adjacent area certainly had the potential to create considerable difficulties for the attacking troops – so much so that a detailed description[9] was made by Capt S.B. Pope (II Anzac Corps) in preparation for Haking's attack. The issue of the width of No Man's Land was recalled by 'Pompey' Elliott in 1926 when he wrote to Charles Bean, commenting most favourably on Bean's draft chapter on the attack at Fromelles and in particular the part played by 15 Brigade. Elliott referred to a booklet prepared by the French staff and issued to AIF officers on arrival in France and Flanders, summarising their experiences of trench warfare to date. According to Elliott, 'one of the axioms… was that such an attack could not possibly succeed if the enemy's front trench was distant more than 200 yards from the "hop off"'. He continues by saying that this principle had occurred to him too, but that owing to his 'loyalty to the higher command… I had to carefully conceal my feelings and even my thoughts on the subject'.[10] However, the width of No Man's Land to be crossed by the infantry emphasised the utmost importance of a satisfactory artillery bombardment in order to minimise the dire effect of well-placed German machine guns. Secondly, a salutary lesson had been learned from the bloody experience of British battalions on 1 July 1916 on the Somme, when the interval between the bombardment ceasing and the arrival of British troops on the German wire had been sufficient for German troops to leave the sanctuary of their dugouts and man their parapets with devastating effect. To overcome this severe threat to success, Haking impressed three things on the officers present at the 16 July conference:[11]

1. To keep the artillery fire on the wire and parapets of the enemy and not over them. The zone of attack was narrow in depth and with the ammunition available the artillery should be able to reduce the defenders to a state of collapse before the infantry assault took place.
2. The assaulting infantry, both the charging line and the support line, to be deployed in No Man's Land in time to rush forward at the exact moment fixed for the assault.
3. The vast importance of impressing on the men that they must rush forward together immediately the officers gave the signal.

The Germans were formidable opponents. Their 6 Bavarian Reserve Division was one of a number of reserve divisions raised in 1914 and composed of a mix of fully trained reservists and untrained recruits. It had occupied the sector around Fromelles since March 1915, having already by then participated in the First Battle of Ypres. Commanded by General von Schleinitz, it consisted of two brigades, the 12 and 14; the 12 contained the 16 and 17 Reserve Infantry Regiments and the 14 was made up of the 20 and 21. In each regiment there were three battalions, each consisting of four companies, and each company was supplied with six machine guns. Each battalion had a strength of 776 men. The infantry were supported by the artillery of two divisions, the 50 Reserve Division on their right and the 54 on their left, and they had the benefit of observers on Aubers Ridge. Their arrangement was as follows: opposite the 61 Division from Fauquissart to Tilleloy was the 17 Bavarian Reserve Infantry Regiment, astride the Sugar Loaf Salient from Tilleloy to Petillon was the 16 Bavarian R.I.R.,[12] from Petillon to Cordonnerie was the 21 Bavarian RIR, and beyond Cordonnerie towards La Boutillerie (the original left-hand flank of the assault) was positioned the 20

Bavarian RIR. Only a relatively small number of German troops were positioned there, the principle being that more troops could be brought up with rapidity to resist an attack. Just one battalion per regiment held the front area, the other being divided between the 800 yard line and strongpoints dotted along the line, with the remainder on Aubers Ridge.

However, their defences were more robust. Their front line included seventy-five shelters built into the parapet protected by nine to twelve inches of concrete, and sixty of them remained intact after the bombardment. The earthworks to be demolished by the gunners, according to troops after the battle, were estimated to have an eight-foot-high parapet which varied in thickness from three to twelve feet and a parados some seven feet high. After the battle, Lt Col Cass (54 Btn) submitted a detailed commentary on the German positions opposite his battalion in which he commented on the number of machine gun positions, most of which were destroyed by British artillery. Around ten yards further back were more dugouts which appeared to be used as headquarters of section officers, signal officers and the like; these had about five feet of earth for a roof and were sunk four feet into the ground, giving an internal height of six feet or so. All the German dugouts were well constructed using stout timber; the revetments of the trenches were also strong timbers with small mesh wire netting and vertical walls. The trenches, however, were narrow and awkward for evacuating wounded men. Cass even noted that the latrines were on a pan system.[13]

Reports of the accommodation discovered by troops clearing the German line were published in the *Sydney Morning Herald*:[14]

We found the enemy's trenches well built. The commanding officer's dugout was spacious and well furnished. The walls were papered, and the larder well stocked. A good collection of French wines and Scotch whisky was at hand. Dugouts were lit up with electric light. They had electric stoves and bells.

Private soldiers probably knew few details of the coming attack, and apart from whatever information company commanders passed on to their men, Lt Gen Haking's message[15] was the only overview provided. The order read:

It has been ascertained that the enemy is moving his troops from our front to resist the attacks of our comrades to the South. The Commander-in-Chief has directed the XIth Corps to attack the enemy in front of us, capture his front system of trenches, and thus prevent him from reinforcing his troops to the South.

Two divisions are about to attack the enemy's line of trenches along a front of 4,200 yards.

I wish all ranks to understand the plan of attack, and I trust them not to disclose it to any one.

There will first be a heavy bombardment the day before along a front some seven miles to the South of the attack. By this bombardment I hope to induce the enemy, who is very weak in artillery, to move some of his batteries in that direction.

This bombardment will be continued on the morning of the attack, whilst our guns along the front of our real attack will be getting the exact range of the enemy's trenches without attracting undue notice.

When everything is ready our guns, consisting of some 350 pieces of all descriptions, and our trench mortars, will commence an intense bombardment of the enemy's front system of trenches. After about half an hour's bombardment the guns will suddenly lengthen range, our Infantry will show their bayonets over the parapet, and the enemy thinking we are about to assault will come out of his shelters and man his parapets. The guns will then shorten their range and drive the enemy back into his shelters again. This will be repeated several times. Finally, when we have cut all the wire, destroyed all the enemy's machine gun emplacements, knocked down most of his parapets, killed a large proportion of the enemy, and thoroughly frightened the remainder, our Infantry will assault, capture and hold the enemy's support line along the whole front. The objective will be strictly limited to the enemy's support trenches and no more.

This order to be read to all troops taking part in the attack.

[Signed] R. Haking
Lieut-General
Commanding XIth Corps
16.7.16

The main details of the attack were well known in the estaminets behind the lines. There was much talk of German spies passing messages to observers on Aubers Ridge, though in reality the pattern of artillery activity and the movement of men and material seen by the enemy from their observation posts in Fromelles church or in Aubers itself was sufficient to tell them that an attack was imminent. W.H. Downing related his version of the spy story:

All this was known to pseudo-refugees, to spies, to cowardly franc-tireurs in the villages behind. Enemy airmen observed the white and coloured cloths spread in order and in design in fields, like washing left to dry, according to the custom of the blanchisseuses of Flanders. Fields were ploughed lengthwise, crosswise and diagonally. White horses were depastured in particular fields. Even the genuine inhabitants knew more about the attack than we.

Secrecy was commented upon by Capt W.H. Zander (30 Btn),[16] who recorded that 'even the Mademoiselles asked when it was coming off…'. There were plenty of other signs too, also noted by Zander:

Dumps sprang up here and there – the Bosche couldn't have helped seeing all these preparations for his planes were over often enough and spies seemed all over the place. Even the farm where we were billeted in had a girl who we understood was under observations as a suspected spy.

Pte Tom Brain, serving in 60 Btn, told a similar tale[17] concerning a farmer who had four horses of different colours and used to vary the ploughing team so that a different combination would appear day by day, thus arousing the troops' suspicion that he was sending a coded message to German observers. Tom claimed that the farmer was a spy and so the troops shot him and took his horses! Major Christie-Miller, 2/1 Bucks, also commented on spies,[18] believing that 'a good percentage… were included in the population. There were more pigeons than we liked seen flying towards the Hun lines.'

The veracity of some accounts needs to be treated with caution, especially those related many years after the war. Charles Bean wisely left a sticker[19] on many records contained in the AWM archives advising readers to take care with such accounts. The events of the coming days would certainly provide plenty of material for the survivors to write about, but in the meantime further preparatory work was still to be conducted.

4

Sending Fritz Iron Rations

The artillery's wire-cutting efforts were monitored by patrols during the night before the battle, and found to be partially achieved in front of the 8 Bde, unsuccessful in the 14 Bde's sector and not capable of being adequately assessed in front of 15 Bde due to German troops being positioned partway into No Man's Land by the Sugar Loaf Salient. Similar patrols sent out by 61 Division reported that the enemy line appeared to be lightly held. The morning and afternoon of 19 July provided the artillery with further opportunity to fulfil this task. The artillery programme is shown in Appendix B.

One change to the plan for the final bombardment was made in acknowledgement of the Australian gunners' inexperience. Whereas the 61 Division could be relied on to maintain a barrage on the German second line, the Australian batteries were now required to move from bombarding the German front line to the longer-range targets beyond the frontal area. Accounts confirm that the German breastworks were being badly damaged by shellfire, though in contrast, and most importantly of all, the apex of the Sugar Loaf Salient was virtually intact.

The trench mortars were also at work. Sapper W. Smith in 14 Field Coy recalled, in an article in *Reveille*:

Our trench mortars were busy sending Fritz 'iron rations', battering down his parapets and wire, and racking his nerves. The large mortars – which were worked by Canadians – were sending over football bombs – each weighing 60 lbs. – at the rate of eight to ten per minute, while the 'Stokes mortars', under Lt McNab were firing a three-inch cylindrical bomb [weighing about 12 lbs] at the rate of fifteen to twenty per minute. These mortars naturally attracted a lot of enemy fire, and our parapets in their vicinity received a severe battering, and we sustained a large number of casualties.[1]

At 2.35p.m. orders were given for increased bombardment of the Sugar Loaf Salient, but the request for greater efforts to cut the wire in front of Elliott's brigade was made far too late, less than an hour before zero. Capt Zander, 30 Btn, confirmed the artillery activity:

> It seemed as if all the artillery in France was helping us… About midday the barrage started… the Hun didn't seem to be retaliating much, a little shrapnel came our way but not doing much damage… further ahead we could hear the occasional crumps of his 5.9's but as we were not very near them we didn't worry.[2]

Inevitable retaliation came swiftly on Picantin Avenue and Bond Street communication trenches. From 1.30p.m. shelling on the 61 Division front became heavier; 5.9-inch guns fired on Bond Street again, as well as on artillery observation posts in Rue Tilleloy. Between 4 and 5p.m., wire cutting batteries in the 61 Division sector were heavily shelled.[3] The two RFC squadrons, 10 and 16, working in co-operation with Haking's two divisions, had attempted to report the positions of German batteries but had been frustrated by the weather. On 16 July 2/Lts E.C. Winkley and G. Leckie noted that the enemy's guns near Aubers were very active but they were unable to spot flashes on account of the mist. On 19 July 2/Lt C.E.W. Foster and Lt A.P.D. Hill (flying BE2c 4325) reported 'heavy mist… impossible to see target' and, later, that flash spotting was again patchy due to the mist.[4]

While the artillery prepared the ground for the infantry assault, the troops were being concentrated in their appointed positions, fully equipped for the task facing them. The assaulting battalions were relatively lightly burdened with a rifle, rations, ammunition, a supply of grenades and empty sandbags which could be filled when required to make fortified positions once the enemy line had been occupied; on occasions a sand bag might also make a handy body bag for any unfortunate soldier on the receiving end of a shell. In the Australian lines many soldiers went into action wearing their wide-brimmed felt hats, as steel helmets had not been issued to all those about to go over the top; this was probably the only instance on the Western Front when large numbers of Australians wore them into action.

The plan required troops to leave their positions and cross No Man's Land to the part of the enemy line directly opposite or as close to this target as possible, taking into account gaps in the wire and changes in direction due to harassing fire. In the centre, the Sugar Loaf Salient was to be approached by troops of the 184 Bde on the right and the 15 Bde on the left, the large gap between the two brigades being covered by machine gun fire until, in theory at least, the attacking infantry merged and thereby denied the machine-gunners an arc of fire. On the Australian side the responsibility for provision of this barrage would fall upon the

15 Australian Machine Gun Company[5] using the Lewis Gun, weighing 26lb and supplied by a drum containing forty-seven rounds of .303-inch ammunition. In total, this gap directly opposite the apex of the salient was to be covered by five Lewis guns and four Vickers machine guns positioned adjacent to Bond Street (the army boundary). Whilst the capture of the Sugar Loaf Salient should have been accomplished by 184 Bde and 15 Bde, Brig-Gen H.E. Elliott, in his report after the battle, mistakenly stated 'this work was in the objective allotted to 184th Brigade'.[6]

When the 5 Australian Division machine gun units were formed in early 1916, each infantry brigade was provided with a company consisting nominally of six officers and 200 other ranks.[7] The company in 15 Bde commenced briefings on their role in the forthcoming attack on 14 July, and had their numbers expanded on 17 July by the addition of '17 reserve gunners and 10 ammunition carriers from 57th and 58th Battalions'.[8] On 16 July Capt S.W. Neale issued attack orders to each section, and the following extract illustrates the task set for one section under 2/Lt Fitzgerald:

> You will assemble at and attack the enemy trenches where the River Laies cuts parapet near it to the right of VC Avenue. You will leave shortly after the fourth line of infantry gets into the enemy's trench. You will make use of sap leading out of our lines to advance.
>
> Ammunition – every man will carry 170 rounds. 2,600 will be carried in belts with guns, also 2,000 in boxes. No. 1 and 2 will carry one belt of ammunition. The NCO will also carry both boxes.
>
> Direction – You will direct fire on Delaporte Farm and if 15 Bde is not in touch with Brigade on its right one gun must be specially detailed to guard that flank. On entering enemy's trenches you will at once push forward to first line.
>
> Rations – 1 day's iron rations and 1 day's ordinary rations will be carried. One man will be detailed to go back to dump to direct ammunition carriers to the guns.
>
> Casualties – commandeer any infantry to fill belts if short of ammunition.

Similar orders[9] were issued to 2/Lts McCracken, Saunders, Whelpton and Elliot. In order to keep the machine-gunner well supplied, special instructions were issued to the NCO in charge of the ammunition and store dump:

> You will make yourself acquainted with the saps leading from our firing line to the enemy's lines.
>
> You will send forward by ammunition carriers who will be sent forward by 2/Lieut Dight filled belts of ammunition and any equipment asked for.
>
> Each section will send back one man to guide these carriers to the guns failing this, in case guide is put out of action, you will show ammunition carriers route across No Man's Land namely by the saps;

You will have one man with you. He will send ammunition forward to you at your depot to be established as mentioned below.

Should the attack begin late in afternoon you will establish after dark an ammunition dump in enemy's trenches; where a communication trench meets the old enemy's firing line you will go forward yourself and the man left behind will be held responsible that you are supplied with ammunition etc during the night.

Should the attack begin early in the day you will go forward through the saps that will be under construction and establish a dump near its junction with old German firing line. In such case Cpl Trevan in charge of Pinneys Ave dump will take an ammunition carrier with him, leaving him at the junction and then go to the left to get in touch with our left guns. He will then decide on a suitable depot in the vicinity of such gun.

During the night the belt filling machine and MkIV tripod will be carried across.

You will send forward firstly the filled belt boxes then ammunition in boxes.

You will see that all dumps where our ammunition is, is well marked 'Machine Gun Ammunition'.

The achievements of the trench mortar batteries in 5 Australian Division on 19–20 July should not be underestimated. A week or so before the battle there was no Divisional Trench Mortar Officer so Capt G.H. Wilson, OC X5A battery was appointed to this position with Lt W.H. Hind as his second-in-command. Shortages of trained personnel extended to the batteries themselves; X5A, for example, had only five men who had been trained in the use of the mortars. Training was provided at Sailly-sur-la-Lys under Capt Miles and Major Sir John Keane, who had responsibility for all trench mortar batteries in the Second Army.

Capt Wilson had been summoned to Corps HQ for instructions and then drew up plans for going into battle. Ammunition was ordered and a party of 150 men of 5 Pioneer Btn were placed at Wilson's disposal. By working at night, positions were rapidly prepared for the batteries and two guns were placed in each bay. The three Australian medium trench mortar batteries (firing 'plum puddings') to be used were X5A (8 Bde), Y5A (14 Bde) and Z5A (15 Bde). One heavy battery, V5A (firing 'flying pigs'), was also allocated to the divisional front, as were a number of trained Canadian troops. One, Capt W.J.R. Richardson, was slightly wounded on the night of 18 July while supervising the preparations of the batteries.

Most of the wire cutting and firing at known machine gun posts was completed on the morning of 19 July, when the batteries withdrew having sustained three casualties. However, on the following morning men of X5A battery were pressed into action carrying forward boxes of Mills bombs, having been hastily trained in fusing them by four regimental sergeant majors from 8 Bde. Two men, Bombardier A.S. Wiles and Gunner S. Power, enthusiastically pushed a truck up and down a trench railway, taking bombs forward and bringing wounded men back.[10]

As well as preparations by the gunners, the three Field Companies, Australian Engineers (8, 14 and 15) were still very active.[11] The 8 Field Company, commanded by Major Vernon Sturdee, had left Mudros on 6 January 1916, spent several months in Tel el Kebir, crossed to Marseilles arriving on 25 May, and then travelled north to Abbeville before arriving in billets in an old school in Fleurbaix on 7 July. The 14 and 15 Field Companies landed in France four days after 8 Field Company; the latter came to the area behind the lines on 9 July, a week after 15 Field Company. At the same time Lt Merkel and 2/Lt Buchanan, along with six other ranks, went to Bac St. Maur[12] to take over RE stores and workshops where, due to a lack of transport, two motor lorries were sent by the New Zealand Division to enable stores to be moved.[13] By the time of the battle, 15 Field Company was based in the former RE yard in Sailly-sur-la-Lys[14] and was commanded by Major Harold Greenway.

With the battle approaching, all three Field Companies were heavily engaged in general trench work and the movement of stores. The 14 Field Company, under Major Henry Bachtold, spent the four days leading up to 19 July providing an RE dump on the Rue Petillon and delivering as many engineering stores as possible to the front line,[15] utilising along part of the way a tramline constructed on the night of 17 July by the 5 Pioneer Btn. In view of difficulties encountered by the infantry using the communication trenches, 14 Field Company checked one of them, Brompton Avenue, on 15 July. Out of a total length of about 1,050 yards, 350 yards were found to be revetted and duckboarded; the remainder was dug but was now impossible to pass through, and in some places the avenue was flooded to a depth of four feet.[16] It took a Herculean effort by working parties to lay duckboards and make sandbag revetments along the section from the 300 yard line and the firing line.

Major Christie-Miller's papers provide some idea of the amount of material moved by carrying parties. He noted 'hundreds of preserved rations and tins of water, thousands of Mills Bombs, wire and picquets in profusion and… an abundance of trench mortar ammunition, heavy, medium and light… a respectable carrying load for a couple of battalions for a couple of nights'.[17]

The 15 Field Company were set the job of establishing dumps at Rifle Villa, the intersection of the tramline with VC Avenue and at the forward tramline terminus; the delay in the start of the battle enabled them to complete their task. A more hazardous activity carried out by this company's No. 3 section was supervising wire cutting by the infantry while their No. 2 section made wire-crossing mats and trench ladders further back at Sailly-sur-la-Lys and at Bac St. Maur.

Once this work had been completed there was no respite for the engineers. The sections of 8 Field Company, in preparation for the next phase, were arranged as follows: No. 1 was to assist 31 Btn to consolidate the German trenches which they were to take; No. 2 was in reserve to keep the communication trenches and tramline clear and to help dig a communication trench across No Man's Land; No. 3 was to assist 32 Btn to hold any German trenches they captured; and No. 4 was to dig a firing line across No Man's Land using A Coy, 30 Btn as a working party.[18]

In the middle sector, 14 Field Company had one section with two attacking battalions, two sections detailed with two infantry companies to dig communication trenches, and one section looking after the dumps and pushing up stores to the front line.[19] The 15 Field Company's arrangements were:

No. 1 section under Lt Noedl was made responsible for
    communications across No Man's Land, with one company of 58
    Btn provided for digging parties.
No. 2 section, led by Lt McCloughay, was employed at the RE yard in
    Sailly-sur-la-Lys and Bac St. Maur.
No. 3 section, consisting of Lt Mallarky plus one NCO and five
    sappers, was provided for each of 59 and 60 Btns in each of the
    third and fourth waves of the attacks. Their role was to assist in
    consolidation of positions won and to convey gun cotton charges
    (already made up) for any demolition tasks, which would be the
    responsibility of Lt Mallarky.
No. 4 section under Lt Evans was to be in charge of all supplies of
    engineers' stores, to transfer dumps to the most forward positions
    won, to supervise carrying parties and to see that correct material
    was sent forward. This section also provided a band of ten sappers
    who could be called upon as necessary to immediately assist where
    required including the placing of demolition charges.[20]

The 5 Divisional Pioneer Btn distinguished itself by constructing a trench railway during two nights' strenuous work. This greatly assisted the movement of stores, and 495 CSM J.H. Gaylor (DCM), 3039 L/Cpl S. Eddington and 3260 L/Cpl A.E. Landaman (MM) were recognised in the awards after the battle. Three fatal casualties were also incurred by the Pioneers.

Another noteworthy unit was the 3 Australian Tunnelling Company (ATC), commanded by Major L.J. Coulter. It was part of a 1,200-strong mining battalion formed in Australia in October 1915 which had arrived in Hazebrouck on 8 May 1916, where the unit was divided into three: 1, 2 and 3 Tunnelling Companies. Two sections, 1 and 2, joined the Second Army in Belgium in the Ypres sector whilst the 3 was allocated to the First Army. This latter unit moved to Laventie where it relieved the 255 Tunnelling Company, RE. Another unit, comprising thirty men from each company, was also created and adopted the name 'Australian Electrical and Mechanical Mining and Boring Company', colloquially known as the 'Alphabetical Company'.

Mining had long been a feature of warfare in the Great War, and in the Ypres sector work was already well in hand to create the mines that would be blown on 7 June 1917 under Messines Ridge. Apart from picks and shovels, these engineers had drilling machines, hydraulic jacks, pumps (essential near Laventie) and lighting systems, along with duckboards, corrugated iron and all the other items necessary to undertake their onerous task. For safety reasons, white mice and canaries were part of the team.

The geology of this northern part of the Western Front was difficult to work, and the saturated sand around Fleurbaix caused significant problems, but once into the clay the engineers had an easier task. In the area to be occupied by the 3 Tunnelling Company, near La Cordonnerie, the 173 and 181 Tunnelling Companies, RE, had been active in 1915 and 1916 and on the evening of 19 July the work of the tunnellers in this area came to fruition when a 1,200-pound mine was blown at N.10.d.1.8. This location was in No Man's Land ahead of La Cordonnerie but no trace of a crater remains today. In addition, a group of engineers in No Man's Land was observed by the enemy who shelled their position in Rhondda Sap in front of 184 Bde. The 3 ATC was in Rhondda Sap to work a 'pipe pusher', a Barrett hydraulic forcing jack to push pipes filled with ammonal into the ground parallel with the surface at a depth of around five feet. When detonated the charges would create a trench several feet deep. Retaliatory shell fire had damaged the wires used to detonate the pipes but the engineers succeeded in mending them and blowing the charges, thereby forming a trench that would provide cover for troops moving out into No Man's Land and for those falling back to the British line. In the course of this work Major Coulter and six men were wounded, but Coulter would be awarded the DSO for his work during the attack. Other awards to the tunnellers would be an MC to Capt Alexander Sanderson and DCMs to Sgt Kirby and to Cpl Street.

With the greater part of their preparations completed, the engineers, like the infantry, now awaited the order to go out into No Man's Land. Mixed start times were stipulated in 5 Australian Division Order No. 31, which explicitly said that 'Brigade Commanders will fix the time for their first wave to leave the front trench according to their distance from the enemy's line'.[21] Meanwhile, units in support moved forward. The 57 Btn, fresh from a night's rest in billets in Sailly-sur-la-Lys, was in position by 5.35p.m.[22] Later in the evening A and B Coys under Capt Marshall moved firstly to the 300 yard line at 8p.m., and then to the firing line at 5.55a.m. on 20 July; C and D Coys replaced them in the 300 yard line. After the battle they assisted in the recovery of the wounded. Two men, 4583 Cpl W. Saunders and 1914 Pte J. Duke, were subsequently awarded the Military Medal.

One 55 Btn soldier, 3762 Pte Bert Bishop, later prepared an account of his experience of the battle. Originally using the pseudonym Soldier Solomon, he wrote whilst in billets in Bac St. Maur:

It was to be grim work, and it didn't seem fair to him that they should be given such a job right away. As yet his division knew very little of real warfare, and they were to be put into this stunt against German troops who most likely knew all there was to be known about trench fighting.

His account was later published as *A Private's View of World War I*. H.R. Williams, 56 Btn, was also making preparations. He later wrote:

After our midday meal, and having deposited our packs in the Q.M. Store, we stood about and watched the bombardment on our front. We entered an estaminet, and found the place crowded to overflowing. Madame and her assistants were hard pressed to cope with the rush. The men were in the best of spirits… and the women of the estaminet knew the details as well as we did.

Williams and his mates then went back to their billets where they collected extra ammunition and rations while the NCOs had wire-cutters fixed to their rifles. More kit was collected: 'each man carried a pick or a shovel and several sandbags. Water-bottles were filled, ammunition cleaned, gas helmets inspected. We fell-in in the school-yard, children gazing at us with a look of awe… About 5p.m. we moved forward.'[23]

On the morning of the battle Elliott wrote again to his wife Katie. He told her that at six o'clock the battle would commence, but whilst it would be 'nothing like what is going down on the Somme… in other wars it would be a very considerable battle indeed'. He continued, assuring her that 'I have taken every precaution that I can think of to help my boys along'.

Others had more leisurely preparations. W.H. Downing recalled:

They lay in a mill on the outskirts of Sailly… they woke with the birds, reminded of friendly magpies in the morning. Here were only twitterings under the eaves, but at least it was a cheerful sound, pleasant on a lazy summer morning when the ripening corn was splashed with poppies, and the clover was pink, and the cornflowers blue under the hedges. In Sailly they listened to the chatter in the estaminets. At the mill, old women and very small girls were selling ginger-bread and sweets with cognac in them, sitting on stools, gossiping among themselves.[24]

In contrast, Major E. Lister, a gunner, wrote:

Am feeling very tired… haven't had any sleep for 3 or 4 nights. Last night we were in action all night and when not in action we are replenishing our ammunition under cover of darkness. We are in action here quite close to our front line and often experience being under Bosche machine gun fire.[25]

By early afternoon, infantry movements were proceeding to plan when German shelling increased dramatically on the communication avenues and support lines. At 3p.m., as the bigger British guns joined in the barrage, the Germans responded by multiplying their efforts, causing a limited amount of damage. In anticipation of an attack the two reserve battalions of the 6 Bavarian Reserve Division brought ammunition to the front line on 18 July, and the following morning a battalion of 20 Bavarian RIR was moved from the rear area to Fournes, some three miles behind the line, ready to be pressed into action if required.

Later in the afternoon the sector occupied by the 8 Bde was subjected to very heavy shelling, which was compounded by shells intended for the German positions falling short; among the wounded was Lt Col F.W. Toll (31 Btn). At 4p.m. the four waves of the 31 Btn were in position despite the afternoon's setbacks, and observers in the battalion reported heavy damage to the German positions although some sections of barbed wire were still intact. At 4.50p.m. shells were again falling short, landing on the Australian parapet, and an urgent request was made to the gunners to move the barrage ahead. This did not happen; the situation worsened causing very heavy casualties. At 5.10p.m. a very urgent wire was sent asking for a lift of 100 yards; the situation subsequently improved, but the support lines around Cellar Farm were again under an enemy barrage, their guns also searching to the north for British batteries. Toll stated in his report that 'just prior to us launching the attack, the enemy bombardment was hellish, and it seemed as if they accurately knew the time set'.[26] At four intervals (3.25p.m., 4.04p.m., 4.29p.m. and 5.21p.m.) the British bombardment was reduced then resumed more heavily than before, provoking heavy shelling from the Germans. Fortunately by 5p.m. German gunfire had reduced, giving a brief respite of half an hour before troops of the 61 Division started moving out into No Man's Land. About this same time the third and fourth waves in the 14 Bde sector were compelled to move forward across fields rather than using communication trenches, which were blocked by other troops on the move or abandoned stores or had been damaged by German shells.

Even before the battle started in earnest, Elliott reflected upon the harm being caused to his troops in a letter home to his wife:[27]

My poor boys are getting pretty badly knocked about. Capt Mair[28] who was a Dentist was killed yesterday his legs being blown off by a shell and three other officers were wounded and a number of men. Poor fellows – some of them were a dreadful sight after the bombardment of the trenches…

One of the most prolific letter-writers in the AIF was Lt J.G. Ridley MC, who served as a sergeant in 53 Btn on 19–20 July. Ridley's letters provide a useful record of his observations, wounding and subsequent recovery punctuated by outbursts of religious fervour: Ridley was a committed Christian and later became a Baptist minister. He recalled:

> What an afternoon it was – the shadow of the coming charge made us fall quiet and thoughtful, thinking of home and loved ones and the days of life that were passed but thoughts were broken by the thunder of that awful bombardment and the scream of shrapnel as it passed over us… trench was now packed with men and I could hardly move round to give my orders… the din was terrible – the shells would burst above and then swish and down came the hail of lead and iron dealing awful wounds.[29]

Troop movements were observed by the Germans, who responded by calling down a heavy bombardment on the British and Australian reserve lines. They were joined by artillery batteries belonging to the 50 Reserve Division located towards Armentières and the 54 Reserve Division situated further south near Neuve Chapelle. This fire by the enemy posed a huge threat to the infantry as it could break up the assault before it really started. However, despite causing a lot of damage, the enemy's guns were probably insufficient in number to halt an oncoming attack by two divisions. The British gunners themselves did not go unscathed; a number of field guns had been brought up to within 3,000 yards of the enemy's line and their observers stationed themselves in damaged houses along the Rue Tilleloy, which runs parallel to the north side of the 61 Division's sector. Although their guns received only minor damage, several dumps of shells were hit and many gun crews became casualties.

Between 2 and 4p.m. on 18 July the Germans shelled Rue Tilleloy and the Berkeley Hotel observation post, also in Rue Tilleloy, which was destroyed. During this shelling Major G.P. Linorea (B300 battery) was killed, Major S.R. Field (B306) was wounded, Lt Martin and three telephonists (D306) were killed, Major A.D. Boyd (O Bty RHA) and Capt Archer-Houblon (32 Bty RFA), both of 8 Division, were wounded, and Capt Parsons of the same battery was killed.[30]

5

Annihilating Fire

Orders for the deployment of infantry had been issued. As the attack was intended to be limited to 100 yards or so beyond the German front line, two battalions of each brigade were felt to be adequate, other troops being used to carry stores to the front line and beyond in support of assaulting lines leaving the remaining troops to relieve the initial waves in the captured enemy line. Not only would the Australians be attacking over the same ground as the 8 Division had fought in May 1915, they would also be fighting the same German opponents – 6 Bavarian Reserve Division – who had defended the line a year earlier.

Among the infantry units in the front line there was considerable imbalance between the numbers of troops available for the forthcoming attack and the length of line being held. Mackenzie's 61 Division had been reduced in strength by about one third and their frontage extended to 1,500 yards; the Australian Division, in contrast, held 2,000 yards of the line and their infantry units were at full strength. Before the original planned date for the attack some of Mackenzie's battalions were moved out of the line; the 2/1 Bucks Btn history, for example, records that the 'Battalion was withdrawn on the 15th July, and marched back to Lavantie, where preparations were begun for the attack'. It goes on to state that 'the Oxfords and Glosters were in support and reserve near Sailly and at Estaires, and moved up... to Bacquerot Street and to some strongpoints in the vicinity'.[1]

In the Australian sector each brigade would occupy just over 600 yards, and thus each assaulting battalion was allocated 300 yards. According to McCay's calculations, this allowed his troops to be two yards apart; there were therefore sufficient troops to create four waves, with each battalion providing two half companies, amounting to 200 men, in each wave. The first wave was to move across No Man's Land to the enemy wire where they would lie down ready to attack once the artillery bombardment had ceased; the three following waves were to be spaced at intervals of 100 yards. Holding this number of men in the front line was not only impracticable but also foolhardy, considering the sighting of the lines by German observers.

The men to form the first and second waves had to be in position in the front line three hours before the assault commenced, while the remaining two waves were to be in the reserve line ready to move forward in sufficient time to enter the front line very soon after the second wave had departed. Behind them the troops transporting stores were to be ready to advance behind the fourth wave. Further troops would also move forward to hold the front and reserve lines, while the remaining troops of each brigade would stay in the rear. Once in the German front line, the first wave would remain there and the second wave would leapfrog it and capture the German second line. McCay had instructed that enemy communication trenches were to be blocked to impede German movements; the exposed flanks of Australian troops in the German front lines were to be barricaded for protection. The plan also required the digging of two trenches by each brigade across No Man's Land to facilitate the movement of ammunition and bombs as well as providing a degree of cover for troops returning to their own line.

Ordinarily all available sources of firepower would also be taken forward by the infantry to offer them a better chance of capturing and consolidating a position, but at this stage of the war the troops were ordered to zealously protect Vickers machine guns and Stokes mortars in order to prevent them from falling into enemy hands; they were only to be taken into the enemy's lines once it was believed that positions were securely held. Lewis guns, however, were to be brought up after the fourth wave of infantry.

To provide information to senior officers, flares would be lit to signal to aircraft, and red flags shown to communicate with artillery observation officers. Raymond Page, 14 Field Coy, recalled that 'some troops reached their objective and flags were waved as a signal of their arrival and were observed by those watching for them, but quickly disappeared'.[2]

XI Corps papers also show that some thought had been given to the next steps should the initial assault prove successful. These plans, to be enacted after consolidation of the new front line, would be decided by Haking and his divisional commanders and might include the following:

1. the capture of advanced hostile posts in front of our new line, probably by night after an intense bombardment before dark;
2. the capture of the enemy's trenches from the Fauquissart–Trivelet road to the Birdcage [M.30.a.5.4];
3. possibly the capture of a more advanced line towards Aubers Ridge.[3]

Both divisions moved into their battle positions. For six Australian battalions this meant not only their first contact with the enemy on the Western Front but also their first occupation of the front line. The remaining six battalions had marginally more experience – two days and nights in the trenches – by 14 July. It was at this point that the width of the assault was reduced, and the time allowed was quite short considering that such movements in a front-line zone were unfamiliar to the men of these brigades. Nevertheless, over three nights, 14, 15 and 16 July, the changes were effected, commencing with the 1 and 3 New Zealand (Rifle) Brigades replacing 8 Bde which returned to Fleurbaix. The middle Australian brigade, the 14, was relieved by the British 60 Bde and they fell back to Bac St. Maur. The 60 Bde also occupied part of the line held by the 15 Bde, and by the morning of 16 July just the 57 and 58 Btns of 15 Bde remained in the front line. The 15 Bde now occupied, for a short time, the entire length of front line from which all three Australian brigades would subsequently attack. On the third night, 16 July, the 15 Bde concentrated its men in the section of the line directly opposite the Sugar Loaf Salient, thus allowing the 14 Bde to move in on their left and the 8 Bde to come into the line between the 14 and 60 Bdes. Consequently, by dawn on 17 July the Australians were finally in the intended positions for the attack planned for that day, subject to other factors being favourable.

Whilst the Australians could probably afford a limited number of casualties early on as they were at full strength, the establishments of the battalions in the 61 Division were not so strong and similar treatment meted out to them by the German gunners could have proved a very serious impediment to achieving a successful outcome. These British troops, like the Australians, were completely inexperienced on the Western Front, though Bean's comment about them being 'of much slighter physique than the Australian' was unwarranted. Fortunately the 61 Division's artillery displayed great proficiency, particularly on the right where the German breastworks had been very severely damaged and the troops occupying these positions incapacitated. As a ploy to draw more enemy troops within the arc of fire of the British guns a common Great War tactic was used, as described in the Bucks Btn history:

> On the afternoon of the 19th lifts to barrage lines were ordered for the Artillery for certain periods, varying from four to ten minutes, during which the Infantry in the trenches were to show their bayonets and steel helmets over the parapets, and officers were to whistle and shout orders with the view of inducing the enemy to man his parapet and thereby incur heavy casualties.[4]

The troops of Brig-Gen A.F. Gordon's 182 Bde were therefore able to leave their trenches and move forward against very little opposition. The 2/7 Warwicks were able to deploy in No Man's Land with very little loss and they were only 50 yards from the enemy parapet when the guns lifted and they rushed the line without delay and rapidly took the enemy trenches, the German survivors being overwhelmed before they could resist.

In support, the 2/8 Warwicks had a rather different view of the action. H.C. Chidgey wrote in the unit history:

The Boche riflemen and machine gunners having retired to their strong concrete shelters, where they remained in safety during the bombardment, emerged as soon as the barrage lifted and blazed away with rifles and machine guns at the advancing British troops. One German machine gunner was alleged to have fired 14,000 rounds in the course of the day. Certainly the hostile fire was very deadly, and many fine fellows fell in No Man's Land.[5]

The Germans estimated that two hundred British troops entered their line and then moved on to the second line, killing or capturing the garrison. Once it was realised that the Warwicks had succeeded in penetrating their line, German artillery shelled this position in an attempt to force them out. An attempt was made by the British troops to bomb their way along the German line but a swift and decisive counter-attack prevented any progress.

To their left were 2/6 Warwicks, whose objective was the section of German line to the right of the Wick Salient occupied by 11 Company, 17 Bavarian RIR commanded by Leutnant Reichenhardt. As early as 14 July 2/6 Warwicks had lost Capt Forbes who was sent to work with B306 Battery; the battalion also supplied a number of men for working parties in the days leading up to the attack. On 16 July they received 'sudden orders', according to their war diary, to go to the trenches (N.13.c.3½.4½ to N.13.c.9.0 to the right of the Wick Salient), and this movement was completed by 9p.m. in readiness for an attack on the salient. During the night, finding that their supply of ammunition was inadequate, working parties were organised to bring supplies from reserve dumps at Hougoumont and Strand Trench. Later in the night a message informed them that they would attack at 11a.m.

Fortunately the adverse weather allowed the industrious Warwicks to rest until the morning of 19 July, when A and C Coys returned to the trenches leaving B Coy in support and D Coy in reserve. A conference was held by the CO attended by various officers, and following hard work by the carrying parties sufficient ammunition was in position by the time the artillery opened fire at 11a.m. In the Warwicks' trenches the waiting troops were subjected to German shelling from 1p.m. for about one hour, after which the barrage moved back to the reserve lines for two hours; the war diary records a remarkably low number of just eight casualties in this period.

At 5.31p.m., according to the war diary, 'men started to file out through sally ports for the offensive on the Wick Salient and formed four lines in No Man's Land composed of A and C Coys'. The assault, though, did not go well, for 'immediately they left the trenches the enemy shelled very heavily and all officers were killed or wounded'. From here the troops advanced to 'within 80 yards of the Wick Salient' when they were hit by heavy shelling and 'at the same time the German trenches became alive with men and a large number of machine guns opened a heavy fire on them mowing down the advancing lines'. B Coy which followed suffered the same fate as the other two companies; the war diary claims that two platoons reached the enemy parapet but achieved no further success.

Another criticism made by Elliott in his Canberra speech of 1931 was the use of the sally ports (exits made in the breastworks). Major Christie-Miller recorded that in 61 Division 'we were forbidden to go over the top of the trench and narrow and inconvenient sally ports were ordered by higher authorities to be used. This of course necessitated forming up in No Man's Land before zero as of course it would be impossible to deploy a battalion in an instant through low and inconvenient sally ports through which men in attack order would crawl slowly'.[6]

D Coy moved two platoons up to the front line, but any hope of launching a fresh assault was thwarted by further German bombardment; postponement to 8.10p.m. was agreed. Survivors of the first attack would also be withdrawn under cover of a barrage put down on the Wick Salient. This succeeded, but the 8.10p.m. attack was delayed until 9p.m.; subsequently it would be totally abandoned. At 9.45p.m. the 2/6 Warwicks received word that the 2/5 Warwicks would relieve them. This was achieved by 1a.m., with the exception of a few men from D Coy who remained to recover the wounded from No Man's Land.[7]

According to their regimental history, German troops in this sector set up three machine guns amid the wreckage of their breastworks as the Warwicks closed in, repelling this attack as it was on the brink of succeeding. Major-General Mackenzie acknowledged the ability of the enemy in his report:

> The 6th Warwicks were within 80 yards of the German trenches, when the guns lifted, and the front lines had reached the wire, when machine guns, handled with great bravery from the top of the German parapet, open upon them with great effect. The supporting Company, however, was close up, and advanced gallantly, carrying the leading company forward, and a few men are reported to have entered the German trenches. Nine officers and 220 men, however, had been hit and the attack failed.[8]

The parapet here was not damaged to the same extent as it was to their right, where the 2/7 Warwicks had 'advanced with great dash' according to Mackenzie's report;[9] some accounts even state that it was intact. The combination of a good defensive position and well-managed machine guns brought this attack to a halt, and groups of men who made a fresh attempt to reach the enemy line were rapidly cut down. A third company which had left the brigade's line to reinforce the assault was stopped in No Man's Land by machine gun fire.

The 2/7 Warwicks certainly captured the German trenches opposite, and an observer reported[10] that ten minutes later they were in the support lines. Remarkably, it is estimated that only four men were wounded getting this far, though when Lt Col Nutt sent a machine gun company and other infantry forward to support this breakthrough they were enfiladed by machine gun fire and suffered heavily. The 2/7 Warwicks found the German breastworks badly damaged, estimates of enemy dead varying from 200 to 400. Then one of the misfortunes of war occurred: sixty German prisoners were sent back across No Man's Land but they were mistaken for a counter-attack and half were killed by 61 Division machine-gunners.[11]

The centre British brigade, the 183 (Brig-Gen C.G. Stewart), had been shelled while they awaited the command to attack and the 2/6 Gloucesters lost over fifty men. At 5.30p.m. they moved into No Man's Land and were immediately fired upon, incurring many casualties. It was known that the sally ports were likely to be covered by enemy machine-gunners, and yet the timbered underground passages leading out into No Man's Land, constructed by the 1/3 South Midland Field Company, Royal Engineers, were not used. Nevertheless, a party of 2/6 Gloucesters did reach the German front line to the left of the Wick Salient, but they were unable to hold a position for very long and Lt Col F.A.C. Hamilton of 2/6 Gloucesters was wounded while directing his men.

The 2/4 Royal Berks were the troops of 184 Bde (Brig-Gen C.H.P. Carter) who were given the task of advancing towards the Sugar Loaf Salient, where they would meet 15 Bde men. They incurred some 140 casualties while preparing to move forward,[12] as did the 2/1 Bucks. Whilst noting Elliott's angst on this point, 61 Division Order No. 32 dated 18 July explicitly stated that 'it is vital for the success of the attack that the whole of our assaulting line is deployed in No Man's Land as close to the enemy's parapet as possible during our bombardment'.[13] These two battalions had been in position in the front trench since 9a.m. and had incurred casualties during the morning. The A Coy of the Bucks Btn,[14] commanded by Capt H. Church, had already suffered seventy-eight casualties the previous day owing to a shell from a British gun falling short onto a gas cylinder and bursting it in their trench.[15] Men from the reserve plus a newly arrived draft were brought in to fill the ranks, but it was nevertheless much understrength by the time zero hour arrived.

It is unlikely that the troops attacking the German positions were in any way fresh and rested. Major Christie-Miller observed, 'it is a fair general statement that practically none of the troops detached for the attack had a decent night's rest from that at Richebourg on the Wednesday [a clear week] before the attack'.[16]

In spite of their casualties the 2/1 Bucks moved forward towards their objective, leaving their trench not by the sally ports but by using Rhondda Sap. This had been constructed by the 3 Australian Tunnelling Company, which exploded a 'pipe-pusher'[17] at the fourth attempt in order to lengthen the sap in the direction of the German parapet. Its length was about 220 feet and it was some six feet deep. A couple of other similar devices were exploded on the 183 Bde's front for the same purpose and for the evacuation of the wounded. This sap provided adequate cover, but once troops emerged into the open their advance was soon halted by machine guns located in the Sugar Loaf Salient which had clearly not been sufficiently damaged by artillery, as well as by the hail of shrapnel directed on them. According to their unit history, 'at 6p.m. with a cheer the four waves leaped up and assaulted the enemy's trenches. The advance was described by an officer of the RFC, observing for the Artillery, as magnificent. Not a man was seen to waver...'[18] However, German machine-gunners found their targets and inflicted even more casualties on these two weakened battalions.

The problems faced by 2/1 Bucks were compounded by German machine guns covering the sally ports. As the battalion advanced 'the fire brought to bear was annihilating, hardly a man if any reached the enemy parapet – it was said that one man L/Cpl Stevens of D Coy was seen to reach it'.[19] Casualties included the 2/4 Royal Berks CO Lt Col Beer, who was killed.[20] A small party, amongst them Captain H. Church of 2/1 Bucks Btn, somehow reached the Salient itself where they found the wire uncut; there were rumours that they even managed to enter the German front line. This was recorded in Maj-Gen Mackenzie's report, in which he said that 'Captain Church... was killed on the slope of the parapet... but a number got into the Sugar Loaf'.[21] He also wrote that this was 'substantiated later by eye-witnesses of the 15th Australian Brigade', though it is doubtful how close any survivors of the latter brigade actually got to the Sugar Loaf. By the end of the fighting on 20 July, the Bucks Btn, which had gone into action with 20 officers and 622 other ranks, had sustained a total of 322 casualties.[22]

By 6.30p.m. Divisional HQ was in possession of reports that 2/7 Warwicks were holding the German line, that the attack on the Wick Salient had not succeeded and that some troops were in the Sugar Loaf.[23] Many men, including those who were wounded, lay in No Man's Land waiting for darkness to cover their withdrawal. The options open to the divisional commander were clearly limited. At 7p.m. Major-General Mackenzie assessed the position of his brigades, and in accordance with corps instructions he instructed the artillery to bombard the line where attacks had been frustrated. Half an hour later Haking's order to get the 184 Bde to extend their hold on the Sugar Loaf Salient and join with the Australian 15 Bde was received; as no men were in the Salient this order was worthless. All three brigades were ordered to organise a second attack, and one of the two reserve battalions which had been moved up to brigade reserve in each section was placed at the disposal of the brigadiers to support this attack. Around this time word was received that 184 Bde did not have a single man in the Sugar Loaf. Later in the evening attempts were made to start another assault but to no avail. The corp's records,[24] which express the belief that at least one company of the Bucks Btn was holding the Sugar Loaf Salient, subsequently admit that early reports of infantry successes in gaining possession of parts of the enemy line 'had been too optimistic'. The 61 Division's assault had come to a halt.

6

I'll be Alright

The Australian battalions' departure from their front line was staggered to take into account the variations in width of No Man's Land. Two battalions of 15 Bde, 59 and 60, were ready for the assault, having replaced 57 and 58 Btns as a consequence of the delay in the start date and the time of the attack. The 59 and 60 Btns went out at 5.45p.m. (6.45p.m. according to 59 Btn's war diary),[1] two minutes ahead of the 53 bn, while the other 14 Bde battalion started at 5.50p.m.; the 31 and 32 bns in the 8 Bde on the extreme left went over the parapet at 5.53p.m. The artillery bombardment continued until 6p.m. so that the assaulting troops might be able to cross No Man's Land with minimal return fire coming from the enemy who, it was hoped, would still be sheltering in their dugouts.

Communications, particularly once troops had been committed to the attack, were a further impediment.[2] Runners were available to carry messages but were targets for marksmen as they struggled across difficult terrain, as well as frequently coming under shellfire. Even when the message was successfully delivered the information it contained might well be out-of-date. Signallers were also employed, but in exposing themselves to send a message they too would attract rifle fire. Pigeons were another option, though they had to be carried forward with all the other paraphernalia of battle; it is recorded that during the attack at Fromelles pigeons were reaching the divisional lofts in seventeen minutes. Field telephones and a network of lines had been put in place in the lead-up to the battle to augment existing telephone links, but they were very vulnerable to shell fire or, where strung along the sides of trenches, to accidental damage by passing troops laden with equipment. Signals from aeroplanes were not always reliable; Lt Col Caddy recorded at 8.15p.m. on 19 July that 'one of our aeroplanes dropped six white lights in pairs, directly over 49th Battery: signal not understood'.[3]

Brigadier-General Elliott, having given encouragement to his men just before they went over the top, had moved back a few hundred yards to Le Trou Post (G.36.d.8.7), adjacent to what is now a very picturesque war cemetery. At

5.50p.m. staff at Brigade HQ could hear German rifle fire; five minutes later a machine gun located in the Sugar Loaf Salient joined in, in defiance of the shells falling around. A heavy shrapnel bombardment was hitting 15 Bde's front and reserve trenches, causing casualties among the waves preparing to support those that had already gone out. The divisional report on the battle notes that they were 'struck with machine gun fire after going 50 yards. It pressed on some 300 yards when it was brought to a standstill'.[4]

Once the British barrage lengthened its range at 6p.m., German infantry very quickly took up positions on their battered parapet, and at Brigade HQ the sound of greatly increased rifle fire was quite audible. This continued until 6.15p.m. when it slackened, and this was interpreted as a sign of successful entry by 59 and 60 Btns into the German front line. The Right Group of the Australian artillery noted as early as 6.35p.m. that there was no sign of an assault on the Australian right.[5] Still, in the absence of any confirmation of such an achievement, Elliott reported at 6.30p.m. that his brigade's troops had made a successful attack.

This was not the true position, however, especially as far as the 59 Btn was concerned. Lt Col Harris' men had started well enough, climbing over their parapet and passing through the ruins of a farm and orchard a short distance out into No Man's Land; their passage had been made easier by the good work done by patrols before the battle in preparing passages through the wire and bridging ditches in their path. As they advanced past these ruins enemy fire increased, and as, erroneously, they moved closer towards the Laies Brook they came under machine gun fire from the Sugar Loaf Salient, which by now was slightly to their right flank instead of being straight ahead. The 60 Btn to the left was faring better and crossed the Laies Brook. As 59 Btn was stalled, 60 Btn moved on, reaching the German wire before being halted. From observations by artillery officers at 6.09p.m., it had been noted that Elliott's infantry were certainly part way across No Man's Land. At 6.34p.m. and 6.40p.m. further reports stated that although these troops were still advancing they were only halfway across No Man's Land, which was 400 yards wide at this point. Other waves followed the first but found few men alive and capable of advancing. Many dead were found and plenty of wounded; other survivors were sheltering in shell holes, ditches or in any other place that might offer some protection.

3239 Pte Algernon Bell, 59 Btn, was wounded very early in the attack and was determined to regain the line by his own efforts if necessary. He recorded in his diary entry for 19 July: '7 o'clock at night, big chance. Wounded in arm and leg, going to try to crawl back to trenches tonight'. Private Bell's fortitude almost paid off; he did reach safety and was evacuated, but died of wounds five days later and is buried in Boulogne Eastern Cemetery.[6] Not surprisingly the war diary entry of 60 Btn for 19 July is scant, but it does claim that the 'advance continued to within 90 yards of enemy's trenches… it was believed that a few of the battalion entered enemy trenches'.[7] The 59 Btn account, meanwhile, clearly states that the attack did not penetrate the enemy trenches as it was held up by intense rifle and machine gun fire about 100 yards from the German front line. [8]

The artillery observers were soon proved correct when Major Herbert Layh returned to the Australian front line under instructions from Lt Col Harris (59 Btn). Layh confirmed that his troops, who were on the extreme right flank of the Australian attack, had not been able to progress any further than midway across No Man's Land. A group of wounded men from the 60 Btn also returned about the same time and brought much better news, stating that they had fought their way into the German first and second lines and moved to a position fifty yards beyond the second line. Moreover, they also reported that 14 Bde had achieved similar success. Having assessed the situation with this allegedly more reliable information Elliott instructed Major Layh to inform his CO that the 59 Btn must continue their assault in order to achieve the same success that the 60 Btn apparently had secured. Shortly afterwards Elliott sent another officer into No Man's Land, Lt D.B. Doyle, to contact Major G.G. McCrae, commander of the 60 Btn, to appraise him of the situation. It seems that Doyle was unable to find McCrae who, along with many other officers and men of his battalion, was already dead. [9] Some time later Doyle returned to his own lines and reported to Elliott that he had made contact with Major Layh, who had informed him that the 59 Btn were unable to make any further advance.

McCrae's second-in-command also became a casualty, and this event was subsequently described by Elliott as 'the greatest individual loss the Brigade has suffered since its formation'. [10] Major T.P Elliott (no relation to his brigadier), a highly rated officer aged just twenty-two, was struck in the chest by a bullet and soon died of his wound. [11] Tom Elliott was another of Brig-Gen Elliott's highly regarded officers, and 'Pompey' had asked him to transfer from 7 Light Horse to 60 Btn, which he did on 12 March 1916. He had been responsible for much of 60 Btn's preparation for the attack, including making soldiers out of 'raw and, in many cases, unpromising material'. After the battle his brigadier wrote, 'his early death thus unfortunately terminated what promised to be an exceptionally brilliant career'. [12] His letter home a few hours before the battle proved to be his last. 'Just a line to let you know all well... some operations are pending... I'll be alright'. [13]

Brig-Gen Elliott issued orders for the 59 Btn to remain where they were in order to provide some foothold in No Man's Land should Gen McCay decide to commit another battalion. Meanwhile, Lt Col Harris had been wounded and Layh was temporarily in command. Troops remaining in front of the enemy line were rallied by their officers and made further attempts to reach their objective. Some were said to have reached the wire, and one group led by Capt Aubrey Liddelow is stated to have reached the German parapet before withdrawing to the shelter of shell holes to plan their next move. Tragically, Capt Liddelow did not survive the day. The battalion adjutant, Lt H. Wrigley, was wounded, as was Lt J.H. Smith, the signalling officer. Like so many that day, Smith did not live to see the conclusion of the battle. Once Layh received Elliott's orders he instructed his men to dig in.[14] It is also recorded by the gunners that the Germans were using a searchlight and directing it ahead of the Sugar Loaf Salient, but no infantry war diaries comment on this feature.

As the infantry left their lines, 15 Field Company, under Lt L. Noedl of No. 1 section, left Pinney Sap to dig a communication trench. Noedl was wounded soon after 6p.m. but remained with his men, directing their work for some three hours until relieved by Lt McCloughay.[15] Lt Noedl's men performed a remarkable task, completing around 220 yards of trench some three feet six inches deep of which in excess of fifty yards was duckboarded. For his outstanding leadership that night Lt Noedl was awarded the Military Cross. Not everything went to plan; it had been intended that VC Avenue would be used for inwards traffic and Pinney's Avenue for outwards movements, but with men diverted elsewhere control of VC Avenue became difficult until a party was placed there by Major Greenway and Lt Dawson of the 58 Btn. Even then the sap became blocked by shellfire and a party of pioneers had to be found to reopen it. Similarly, the tramline was put out of action on several occasions by artillery fire, and it took much good work by Lt Evans, L/Cpl Bowman and Spr Blows to organise repairs to keep movements going with the minimum disruption.[16] However, this work was to no avail, as 15 Bde would be unable to capture their objective during the coming night.

7

Some Ghastly Sights

In the 14 Bde sector, 56 Btn, commanded by Lt Col A.H. Scott DSO, was allocated to be in reserve. They had taken their positions by 4p.m. on 19 July along the line from Rue Quesnoy to Rue Bastille. At 6p.m. they moved to Rue de Quesnes where their Battalion HQ was established. Major Simpson then led A and B Coys to the 300 yard line between Pinney's Avenue–Brompton Avenue and Brompton Avenue–Mine Avenue, accompanied by six Lewis guns. The successful deployment of these guns in the enemy line by 14 MGC would make a significant difference to the brigade's ability to hold their positions. Very soon, enemy shellfire began to take its toll and five men were killed and thirty wounded.

Before the battle had started 14 Bde encountered difficulties; some of their troops moved forward across open fields as the communication trenches in their sector were congested. Not only did they suffer from the effects of German gunfire but they also had their formation disorganised in the wire protecting their own 300 yard line. Part of the rear waves (C and D Coys under Major Sampson and Capt Arblaster)[1] of the 53 Btn, the right-hand assaulting battalion, also veered to their right and found themselves in Pinney's Avenue, believing that they had reached the front line. The first wave of this battalion (half of Capt Thompson's A Coy and Capt Murray's B Coy),[2] meanwhile, left the breastworks at 5.43p.m. and moved to a position in front of the German wire, where they came under the same harassing machine gun fire from the Sugar Loaf Salient that caused so many casualties among the 59 and 60 Btns.[3] In addition, at 6p.m. when the barrage moved beyond the German front line they were faced by rifle fire from German infantry manning their parapet. This impeded the right half of the first wave of the 53 Btn; the remainder of this battalion, and the entire first wave of the 54 Btn, were able to enter the German front line, which had been bombarded with great accuracy. According to some accounts, the speed of arrival in this trench enabled them to take the Bavarians by surprise, many still taking refuge in their dugouts. A contrary view is given by Major S.W. Evers MC:

As soon as the Hun saw the attack… it did not take him long to teach us how murderous enfilade machine gun fire can be, caught out in the open with 150 yards still to go. There was nothing for it – down in the grass we got and crawled forward about 100 yards, till we came to the edge of the clearing in front of the enemy wire. The extra bandoliers and other gear we carried had, by gravity, found their way like heavy bellies underneath us as we crawled.[4]

In readiness for hand-to-hand fighting, men of 53 and 54 Btns had been issued with 475 knobkerries![5] Possession was taken of a couple of machine guns, and as the wave moved on to the next line a few men remained behind to deal with the German occupants.

As the last minutes had ticked away, Sgt Ridley, 53 Btn, described his feelings:

It was awful. My thoughts I can hardly explain, my heart thumped with fear and my face must have been white. Now I was to lead and show an example to 20 men who carried three guns. I can never forget it – I prayed and all my hope was in 'Him'. At last the time was drawing near, I drew my revolver and placed my whistle in my mouth…[6]

Ridley goes on to describe the advance across No Man's Land:

I blew my whistle, gave a shout of 'forward'… I dashed out along the railway line [trench railway]. I had only gone about 50 yards when I tripped and fell. 'Hard luck' exclaimed some of the 55th thinking I was shot but I sprung up and rushed on… rushed bang into barbed wire… I heard the bullets smacking the ground about me. Picking my way through the wire made me go slower and I thought of the awful position I was in. 'Oh! God help me' were the words I uttered. At last I was free…[7]

In accordance with orders both battalions pressed forward, searching for the second line of breastworks clearly marked on their maps. No such trench was found. They went through long grass in the abandoned fields, at intervals crossing more ditches and occasionally encountering German soldiers. After going some 300 yards it was decided that the maps must be flawed and that they should halt; sandbags were filled and defensive positions prepared in expectation of counter-attacks.

Where shellfire had damaged drainage channels or created craters, now water-filled, more obstacles were placed in the paths of advancing troops. After gaining the German front line Sgt Ridley attempted to move further forward, climbing 'over the parapet… suddenly, splash! I was up to my chest in muddy water in a hollow. Dead men and wounded lay about the ditch in all directions, an awful scene in an awful war. I turned to the right holding my revolver high to keep it clear of the water.'[8]

At the time of its formation in Egypt, 53 Btn, in addition to 'Whale Oil Guards', acquired the nickname the 'War Babies'. One of them, Robert Fulton, like many others at Fromelles, had enlisted as recently as 19 July 1915, but there were others with even less service. 2751 Sapper Albert Findlay, 14 Field Coy, did not enlist until 13 September 1915 at the age of 22. He sailed with 7 Field Coy for Egypt and was transferred to 14 Field Coy at Tel el Kebir on 18 March 1916; he survived the war and lived until 1949. Robert Fulton left Australia on HMAT *Port Lincoln* on 13 October 1915, bound for Egypt as part of 11 Reinforcements to 2 Btn. By 22 May 1916 he was in A Coy, 53 Btn. Fulton and many others saw just a few hours service on the Western Front before being killed in action in unknown circumstances.

This assault by 53 Btn was recalled by Lt Ron Crank in his manuscript entitled *A Short History of 53rd Battalion AIF (Whale Oil Guards)*. Crank wrote, 'we attacked in the late sunlight of a summer's day over a straight 350 yards, criss-crossed with deadly machine gun fire'. He claimed that the first 200 yards were taken at 'a jog trot, as the extra gear we all carried and the distance, prevented faster progress'. However, with 150 yards to go the German infantry fired on them, causing Crank and the men around him to drop into the long grass and continue their advance by crawling. As the Germans stood behind their parapet firing at the Australians, they made an easy target for the infantry. Crank levelled his 'sights as steadily as possible, I fired and at the same time felt a hit like a mule kick as a bullet hit my hunched shoulder'. Crank was certainly not alone and recalled that 'Lt Stan Robertson, just near, got hit next'; fortunately, Robertson also lived to tell the tale.

Not all troops in this sector advanced in full view of the enemy. H.R. Williams, 56 Btn, used one of the shallow communication trenches, as he described them in *The Gallant Company*. Immediately upon leaving the trench they encountered casualties. Williams wrote, 'Here we saw the first dead... we halted in the support trench and took shelter against the parapet... a lot of dead were in the trench. Here we sustained our first casualties... the concussion of the exploding shells and the smell of the high explosive are still vivid in my memory.' True leaders were being noticed amongst the mayhem: 'Company Sergeant-Major Dykes... walked along the duckboards cool as an icicle'. The Germans gunners continued to add to the carnage; their shells 'blew great craters... Some of the wounded lay in pools staining the water with their blood. Dead men, broken trench-material, shattered duckboards that tripped us as we passed...'[9]

The trench mortar crews were incurring casualties. About half an hour into the infantry assault another of the highly rated young officers from Duntroon was killed. Clive Hopkins had been educated at Warrnambool High School before securing entrance to the Royal Military College, from where he graduated in October 1914 as Cadet No. 52 (second intake).[10] Along with many of his contemporaries he was sent to Egypt, and was initially attached to 13 Btn, 4 Bde. After the battle Capt Hopkins was buried in a nearby cemetery, and the original grave marker placed there was soon replaced with an ornate white cross with a shield bearing his name and the lettering '14th Bde Hqr AIF Killed in Action 20th July 1916'. The inscription disguises his leadership role in the battle, but the new cross demonstrated the high regard in which he was held.[11]

Shells falling short were causing casualties for the brigade. According to Capt Knyvett, once they discovered that many of the shells bursting among them came from behind they contacted their gunners:

> Our first message… was very polite "we preferred to be killed by the Germans, thank you"… two of our officers being killed, our next message was worded very differently, and we told him that "if he fired again we would turn our machine guns on them". I was sent back to make sure that he got the message… this battery did not belong to our division.[12]

Those men securing the line were in for a surprise. They discovered not the basic earthworks to which they were accustomed but skilfully constructed dugouts strengthened with concrete and timber framework, covered with soil to absorb the impact of shells as well as to conceal their position from aircraft. Galleries had been built off some of the passages to provide living quarters and storage for ammunition. Lt Col Cass, CO 54 Btn, made his temporary HQ in one of these rooms. It was, he wrote:

> reached by steps and had a passage for light to a window. It was strongly built and had an upright about 12" x 12" in the centre supporting a rafter of somewhat similar thickness. The ceiling appeared to be flat sheet iron papered with wallpaper. The walls were papered and even decorated with gold moulding similar to picture frame moulding. It had table, armchair, heating stove, electric bell, electric light, acetylene gas lamp similar to bicycle lamp. In it were stored from 10 to 20 thousand rounds SAA, many flares, gas helmets and a special type of rubber bag with cast iron cylinder probably for oxygen…

This was clearly indicative of the Germans' intention to hold this line for a long period. A similar report was made by the neighbouring 8 Bde:

> Dugouts are numerous and built in island traverses; there are four or five steps down to the floor of the dugout. Heavily timbered, steel roofs, duck boards on the floor and a well sunk in each to drain off water. Good pumping plant with a very large diameter hose is used to drain dugouts. All dugouts were fitted with electric light.[13]

A pumping system kept this accommodation dry and some of these tunnels remain beneath the battlefield, some having been opened and drained for investigation by members of a local history society.[14]

Cass also recorded in his report that 'the trenches were easily captured and two m.g.s in addition. Our men followed the fleeing enemy for about 600 yards.'[15] The section of 53 Btn that had been delayed in No Man's Land was able to catch up and continue their advance, in conjunction with their second wave which also caught them up. However, the next two waves of both battalions drew the attention of some very accurate machine gun fire, which killed not only Lt Col I.B. Norris, CO of 53 Btn, but also his adjutant Lt Moffitt.[16] Major V.H.B. Sampson, also of the 53 Btn, was killed around the same time. This caused command in the German lines to fall upon Capt Charles Arblaster, since Major O.M. Croshaw,[17] Norris' second-in-command, was on special duties maintaining liaison between battalion and brigade as well as supervising the movement of ordnance to the assaulting waves. Likewise the 54 Btn lost its second-in-command, Major Roy Harrison.[18]

Behind the 53 and 54 Btns, the 55 Btn moved into action in their role of consolidating the line by bringing forward supplies of bombs, ammunition and sandbags. Pte Bert Bishop provides a vivid description of the ordinary soldier's experience of undertaking this task:

A messenger came along with orders for the ammunition and water parties to get busy on their jobs – the first and second German lines were in our hands. With the rest of his platoon Solomon strapped two tins of water over his shoulders, grabbed a box of bombs and went down the communication trench into – hell.[19]

His description was well justified; the first wounded men he met as he crossed No Man's Land was 'a big man… stripped bare from the waist up. Solomon felt sick as he saw a great hole in the back of his shoulder, a hole which would have held a man's two fists'. This was only the start. Behind this wounded man came 'stretcher bearers carrying poor huddled heaps of broken humanity covered by a blanket. A man crawled by on hands and knees, gibbering foolishly, with blood flowing from his nose, ears and mouth.'[20]

Meanwhile the construction of a shallow trench across No Man's Land in the 14 Bde sector was underway, under the supervision of Major H. Bachtold, Lt J.S. Ferguson and Lt H.W. Fry of 14 Field Company. This was one of two trenches per brigade originally planned, though this was subsequently modified to just one in this sector.

A first-hand account of the experience of 14 Field Coy was prepared in 1934 by Sidney Donnan, serving in No. 1 Section under Lt J.S. Ferguson. The initial forward movement 'with the tape drum and other tools… was too far for me, and I decided to walk the last quarter and hang the consequences'. Lt Ferguson had already been hit in the neck and Sapper Saunders was staunching the flow of blood. Ferguson was compelled to return to the rear 'accompanied by 50 men who apparently had had enough'.

Donnan made one trip back to collect bombs and on his return was informed by Major Bachtold 'that we had to get a trench across No Man's Land under any circumstances'. Using the drum of tape, Donnan laid out a zigzag route for the new trench and any available men were pressed into digging. At one stage a group of German prisoners arrived under escort:

> They were terrified and jumped into the trench being constructed. Belaboured with anything handy to the diggers they jumped out again. One big chap made a dash for the German side and the escort chased him amid much barracking and advice what to do with him. He overtook the German and had to bayonet him. He made three lunges altogether but the German had a sensitive stomach and avoided by doubling up and grabbing the bayonet or end of the rifle. Eventually he went peacefully away with the others.[21]

This work, which was started immediately the infantry attack commenced, was completed and duckboarded by daybreak. The total length of the trench was 195 yards, which incorporated twenty yards of a German sap filled with bundles of barbed wire and another twenty-five yards of a ditch. The 150 yards that were dug were achieved by 120 infantrymen and forty engineers, with another three dozen infantrymen (56 Btn) carrying duckboards and sandbags; these men had been arranged by Major Bachtold, OC 14 Field Company, Australian Engineers, to assist with digging a communication trench across to the captured section of the German line.[22] The unit war diary notes not only the excellent work done by Capt Roberts but also the protection this trench provided for troops taking supplies forward and in the retirement of the brigade on the morning of 20 July.

A second account of the digging of a sap from the German second line to their third line by 55 Btn was prepared by 3204 Sgt Archibald Winter DCM. According to Winter, his party went forward at 6.30p.m., reached their intended position in the enemy lines without any difficulty and set to work on the sap. Winter volunteered to return for some sandbags and recalled the necessity of being quick 'to move when getting across the parapets'. For Winter and his mates, 'being our first actual fight… and seeing some ghastly sights made us feel peculiar for a while but it soon wore off as we stuck to our job'. After dark, 'Fritz started the flares going' and 'they even sent them up behind us' which gave a clear indication 'they were almost surrounding us'. Despite this situation Winter and his party kept digging.[23]

8

Twisted Heap of Khaki

On the left flank of the battlefield where No Man's Land was at its narrowest, some 100 yards across, members of the 8 Bde were also prepared and ready for their first contact with the Germans since arriving on the Western Front.

Barely a year earlier one member of 8 Bde, Rowley Lording, now a corporal in the signal section of 30 Btn, had persuaded his parents to consent to his enlistment. Now, in the days leading up to the battle, he was busy repairing and laying telephone lines. He knew the battle was imminent: 'It's going to be a big affair – I think Lille is the objective', he wrote afterwards. As six o'clock approached he was hit by a shell splinter: 'someone breaks open an iodine phial but he regrets it is not a Blighty wound'. There was still time for him to exchange details of next-of-kin with a friend before the troops went out into No Man's Land. As soon as the first waves departed, he grabbed his signaller's equipment and went out himself. In his account, Lording commented upon the wounded men in front of the breastworks then, as 'machine gun bullets kick up the ground around them… another twisted heap of khaki hits the ground'. This heap was Corporal Lording.[1]

This brigade had suffered a large number of casualties, some from shells falling short and others from German guns, particularly at about 5.45p.m. when a heavy barrage fell on the 8 Bde. In his post-battle report, Lt Col Toll[2] recorded that 'from 2p.m. enemy heavy straffed support and communication trenches… many casualties. Many of our shells falling short. Flares and ammunition blown-up in front dump. Telephone station carried away by a shell. Four signallers and two runners injured.'[3] One man given the unenviable task of carrying messages was 2078 Pte Thomas Keeling, 30 Btn, who had emigrated from Farmborough, Somerset, in August 1909 bound for New Zealand before moving on to New South Wales. Now he found himself back in Europe in circumstances he probably never imagined. His diary records:

I was picked for running with Jack Noble… 12 noon and at ½ past 3 I was sent back to our company with a message… I was still on duty as a runner… and as soon as it was light… an officer called out for 3 volunteers to carry up machine guns to the front line and I and two others stepped out and carried them up… I got a bullet through my rifle…[4]

From the very scant details recorded in the war diary of the 8 Australian Field Ambulance, it could be assumed that from this time onwards the medical staff were working under considerable pressure tending to the wounded but not to administrative tasks. Their diary simply reads, '6p.m. infantry attack commenced. Casualties began to come in and continued until end of action.'[5] At 4p.m. the four waves of the 31 Btn were in position despite the afternoon's setbacks and observers in the battalion reported heavy damage to the German positions, although some sections of barbed wire were intact. At 4.56p.m. a report was received that shells were again falling short, landing on the Australian parapet, and an urgent request was made to the gunners to move the barrage ahead. This did not happen; indeed the situation worsened. At 5.10p.m. a very urgent wire was sent demanding a lift of 100 yards. This situation subsequently improved but the support lines around Cellar Farm were again under an enemy barrage, their guns also searching to the north for British batteries. Lt Col Toll concluded his pre-battle notes by stating, 'just prior to us launching the attack, the enemy bombardment was hellish, and it seemed as if they accurately knew the time set'.[6] A figure of up to 400 casualties has been suggested even at this very early stage of the battle, a high proportion of the brigade's casualties that day. German observation of this side of the line under attack was also assisted by observers in a barrage balloon in Fromelles.[7]

At 5.53p.m.[8] (5.58p.m. according to the 31 Btn records[9] and 6p.m. in 32 Btn documents[10]), the first and second waves of the two assaulting battalions started their perilous journey towards the German wire, the 31 on the right and the 32 (led by Lt Col D.M.R. Coghill) as the left hand battalion of the entire battlefield. As soon as the first two waves left, the third and fourth waves moved into the front line trench and carrying parties from 30 Btn moved into the 300 yard trench.[11] In addition to the expected rifle fire from directly in front they were met by more fire from their left. This came from the Bavarians, who had no troops coming directly at them, since the British 60 Bde – brought down from Ypres – was not under orders to attack but provided a fusillade in support of the Australians to their right. A plan to release gas was not pursued as the wind direction was unfavourable. On the left of the attack, at 6p.m., a mine containing 1,200 pounds of ammonal was blown.

Sergeant Les Martin later wrote home from his hospital bed, 'I got over the parapet by throwing the machine gun as far as I could… we made for a big hole… it had been mined a few days before and then blown up for it was about fifty feet long by about the same width and twenty feet deep.'[12] Sgt Martin's gun team suffered badly. He recorded their fate: 'the chap who was carrying the tripod for the gun had it blown out of his hands and he was killed; the chap with the gun had it also put out of order and his legs blown off, he died within a few minutes.'[13]

A description of 30 Btn's activity was written in 1930 by Capt W.H. Zander. 'We began to move up Cellar Farm Avenue acting as carrying parties', he wrote. Casualties were sustained immediately and 'dead seemed everywhere – one man had got a hit from a shell and half his face was blown away. He lay across the duckboard track blocking it. A sergeant shifted him to one side where another man covered the dead man's face with a bloodstained tunic...'[14] Just getting out into No Man's Land was a perilous task, even without shelling and rifle fire directed at them, as the troops were 'caught in the wire that lay all over the place'.[15]

The records of 31 Btn state that many officers were lost as the troops charged across No Man's Land, which had been badly cut up by large craters and ditches full of water.[16] More casualties followed, among them Major J.A. Higgon (A Coy, 32 Btn), another British officer who had been attached to AIF during the expansion of the Australian divisions in Egypt in February 1916. Eventually he had to be left behind and was captured but survived the war. As the first two waves approached the German parapet the enemy was seen to 'dwindle' according to Bean,[17] thus allowing the Australians to climb over the parapet with little resistance. In his report after the battle, Brig-Gen Tivey noted that the artillery in this sector 'did very good work on the wire and the enemy's parapet, and many dead Germans were seen as a result of their bombardment'.[18] Some troops were observed running back to the rear and it is likely that others used their tunnel system to escape the oncoming soldiers and to move to other parts of the line. Pockets of resistance were dealt with one by one and the hold on the trench was consolidated by 6.15p.m. During the evening thirty-five German prisoners were held in this part of the line as no men could be spared to escort them to the rear. When they were delivered to the Australian lines the following morning they represented a sizeable proportion of all POWs taken that day, although this total was small in comparison with the quantity taken by the Bavarians.

A myth about the Germans' cruelty in chaining their machine-gunners to their guns was repeated in accounts of Fromelles. The reality was that these troops wore a harness to enable them to drag a heavy machine gun to a new position.[19] Another grisly tale in a similar vein was noted in Lt Col Cass's report: 'a man was seen chained to a post – apparently an observer – but his head was blown off. I did not see this myself...'[20]

Troops of the 8 Bde now found themselves in the long grass behind the German front line searching for the elusive second row of breastworks. Tivey's report states that 'the second trench was found to be only a ditch half full of water, 3'6" deep'.[21] The 32 Btn reached this point only thirty minutes after 'zero', and they described the 'trench' as 'practically a ditch with 1–2ft of mud and slush in the bottom'.[22] One line was visible to the left leading to Delangre Farm, a fortified position some

300 yards away which they were not required to attack, although some elements of the 32 Btn mistakenly believed that the farm was one of their objectives. This trench ran at right angles to the front line and was clearly not the second line: in fact it was a communication trench constructed from earth-filled ammunition boxes and called *Kastenweg*. As with the 53 and 54 Btns, the 8 Bde officers soon realised that the network of 'trenches' shown on their maps was no more than some of the ubiquitous drainage ditches or abandoned trenches.

How could such an error occur? The British Army had very skilful surveying companies who produced a wide range of maps but some of the detail, especially features that were man-made, was plotted on maps either by aerial observers or from photographs taken with large plate cameras fixed to the wings or fuselage of an aircraft. Even at this stage of the war photographic interpretation was in its infancy and thus errors, albeit significant ones for infantry officers in the midst of battle, were bound to arise.

The initiative was taken by Major A.R. White, who pulled back a group of men and their leader, Lt C.L. Halkyard, who had positioned themselves beyond these ditches. After consultation with Major J.J. Hughes, White and his troops made a defensive position along one of the ditches running parallel to the front line now behind them. Debate had centred on whether the battalion's orders did in fact refer to this ditch as being the German second line, even though, if it was a trench line, it was flooded and appeared to have been redundant for quite a while. Further doubt was kindled in the mind of White and Hughes when they observed part of the 31 Btn to the right and ahead of them. Visibility to their front was impaired by the Australian gunners' barrage which had moved to this extended range. When Major Hughes, second-in-command of 32 Btn, went to see for himself what lay ahead he was wounded; he went in and out of consciousness during the night. Command of the battalion rested with White.

On the right of Major Hughes's confused contingent, the 31 had done well to recover from the losses incurred early in the attack. Their losses had forced them to combine the last two waves and, once the German front line was taken, leave it in the custody of a small number of Lewis gun teams while the remainder, including Lt Col Toll, pressed on searching for the second line marked on their maps. They too could find nothing but ditches and fields scarred by shell fire. Occasional enemy troops were discovered in this waste land, some dead, some wounded (who were sent to the rear), and a few still very much alive but who appeared to be grouping in the strongpoint at Delangre Farm. In the absence of a proper trench Lt Col Toll elected to dig in where he was, just ahead of the 32 Btn – with whom Toll had no contact – and roughly level with the most advanced part of the 54 Btn to his right. A message was sent to Brigade HQ informing them of his decision. Toll then showed great bravery in pursuit of clear information to establish whether he had yet to advance further. Leaving the battalion's position in the hands of Major Eckersley, he set off through the Australian barrage with his intelligence officer, Lt G.A. Still, and Pte R. Eddie carrying a basket of carrier pigeons, and continued for 200 yards until he reached the lane that runs from Rue des Turcs to Rue Delvas. There he realised that he was now far beyond the supposed location of the second line. Sight of the German 'Grashof' strongpoint 200 yards away added further confirmation. Toll and his small band turned round and returned to his battalion's new position, having reached a point further forward than any other British or Australian troops that day, POWs excepted. Toll makes no mention of this episode in his nine-page report on the battle.[23]

Toll's men were isolated from the units on either side and the balance slowly began to turn in favour of the enemy who could be seen reforming; reinforcements brought up by the Germans were already within striking distance of the Australians and their gunners had found the range of the 8 and 14 Bdes' new positions. The more forward position occupied by 31 Btn was felt to be untenable and Lt Col Toll decided at 7.14p.m. to consolidate his men in the German front line, the only suitable defensive position he had found. This left an advance party 150 yards in front, initially commanded by Major Eckersley until he was wounded, and later by Capt C. Mills. Similarly a party of the 32 Btn was posted between the 31 Btn and Kastenweg. Although Capt Mills was able to communicate with Major White on his left and Lt Col Toll to his rear, he was not aware of the position of the nearest elements of the 14 Bde to his right, despite a small party being posted in this area by Lt Drayton who was also located in the German front line.

Visual communications were also being hampered, firstly by the haze that developed across the fields as evening wore on, and secondly by volumes of smoke from Delangre Farm and two burning ammunition dumps. This smoke also impaired the sight of German infantry but enabled machine-gunners to move across No Man's Land undetected. Communications systems had been prepared before the battle. In 8 Bde sector, for example:

Communication was established between Brigade Head Quarters [H.26.d.3.2] and 300 yard line and front line by 'phone. An emergency line was also laid down to the 300 yard line. 12 runners were stationed at each Battalion HQ [to] communicate with Brigade Head Quarters. These runners were given trial runs during the morning of the 19th. Pigeons were distributed at Battalion Head Quarters, 300 yard line and Company Head Quarters in the front line. Runners discs, pigeons and telephones were all in readiness to move forward across No Man's Land.[24]

Meanwhile, the next task facing Toll and Cass was the consolidation of the ragged line of infantry in German territory. A protective screen was put down by the artillery. There is little doubt that these brigades were in the intended position and the ditches by which they found themselves were probably trenches dug by the Germans in the summer of 1915, seven or eight months after the front line was established in this area, but which flooded that autumn and were subsequently abandoned. Even the task of filling sandbags to improve their position was made difficult by the shortage of spades and the clay that was found in this area and which stuck resolutely to tools and the men's hands and boots. The plan for carrying parties from the 30 Btn and the 55 Btn had also encountered difficulties as German artillery, machine-gunners and riflemen targeted No Man's Land resulting in material not being available to the infantry forming a defensive line. The scene was described as follows:

> The moment they cleared the top of the parapet it became hideous with machine gun fire. There was a slight slope – our line (of men) ran down it, and then went splash into the ditch up to their waists in water. It was slimy, but it gave some protection. The leading Lewis gunner… led the guns along the ditch, and then to the left along a continuation of it, which ran straight towards the German line. It was very good protection for the guns. About 40 yards along it the leader got hit in the neck by a machine gun bullet… The ditch was full of wounded and dying men – like a butcher's shop – men groaning and crying and shrieking. Ammunition was being carried up by pairs of men… one man would go down, and crash would go the box into the water. Shelling was very heavy. The engineers (14th Field Company) were digging a communication trench at this point beside the stream; the wounded were hopping over into this, and the engineers were having an awful time trying to dig the trench.[25]

At 7.14p.m. the 31 Btn made an urgent request for more ammunition, machine guns and crews.[26] Picks, shovels and sandbags were also needed to block the German trenches and strengthen their parados. Meanwhile, 8 MGC, commanded by Capt T.R. Marsden, was providing a defence against the German troops; seventeen members of this unit would be lost as a consequence of the night's fighting.

On arrival in the old German front line the men from the carrying parties were put to work bridging gaps between pockets of infantry, and as a result numbers allocated to carrying parties diminished. The officers among the carrying parties had been told that if they were urgently required in the German lines they should remain there; some willingly took advantage of this, but others continued to ferry supplies from the Australian to the German lines. One soldier, Sgt. A.W. Panton, was reported to have crossed No Man's Land under fire at least a dozen times. Similarly, Lt Col Toll recorded that 'it is worthy of mention that Private D. O'Connor of B Company willingly volunteered and took over three separate messages across No Man's Land which was continually swept by artillery and machine gun fire'.

Capt W.H. Zander reported on his company's entry to the enemy's position:

It seemed very easy and simple so far but the sharp cracking of a machine gun soon taught us that the Bosche had seen us. A couple of men fell, the rest, crouching lower, continued their way. We saw how our trench mortars and artillery had made great gaps in the German wire and through these gaps we hurried. We reached his parapet and slid down into the trench.[27]

Restraining troops from disregarding their orders and following their instinct to help their mates or conduct their own war on occasions was a difficult task, but an essential one if the infantry was to be furnished with an adequate supply of bombs and ammunition. Capt Zander observed that 30 Btn 'had been told on no account were we to help either of the battalions ahead of us as our work was carrying supplies but it was the greatest trouble to get our chaps to go back to carrying – they wanted to stop up there with their chums in 31st and 32nd and to bag a few Fritzes if possible'.[28]

At Divisional HQ, McCay had received reports throughout the evening informing him of the progress along several parts of the front. The general thrust up to 8p.m. was that the foothold in the German lines was being held, despite shells from both sides falling among these positions; reinforcements also were urgently required. No news had been received from the left flank, which was particularly exposed to enemy fire and which required special attention to the blocking of any trenches that the Germans might be able to use to assist their retaking of this territory. The critical task on this left flank, taking possession of Kastenweg, had nevertheless been achieved by a party of bombers from 32 Btn. German troops had fled from this communication trench and a number were shot down as they retreated to Delangre Farm. Having then blocked the trench, Lewis gunners of the 8 MGC held this important position, with the added security of an early warning post stationed to the front of 32 Btn's position. Additionally, a barricade was constructed to the left of Kastenweg by Lt E.H. Chinner and his bombers along with another machine gun in the charge of Lt M.A. Lillecrapp (8 MG Coy). This left flank appeared to be well prepared for any German counter-attack. Although no response was forthcoming from the Germans at this stage, Major Hughes sent back a message at 8.25p.m. reporting that the left flank near Delangre Farm was being heavy bombarded with high explosive and shrapnel. On this occasion the request for artillery support resulted in a successful response from the Australian gunners. Furthermore, at 8.50p.m. 8 Bde requested urgent reinforcements for 31 and 32 Btns and authority was granted for the remaining troops of 30 Btn to move forward; the 29 Btn was also instructed to occupy the 300 yard line and the original front line.[29]

By 10p.m. the 32 Btn, again under pressure from more German troops that had been brought to the front area via Delangre Farm, reported that they were being pushed back. As the allocation of 30 Btn troops intended to reinforce infantry units on this left flank had already been pressed into action, an urgent request was made for the reserve battalion (29) to be brought up to the old German line. This was declined, however, and they were instructed to remain no further forward than the original Australian front line. Thirty minutes later, in consultation with Major King, McCay's representative in the 8 Bde sector, it was agreed that in view of the severity of the situation one platoon of the 29 Btn could be used to transport more stores forward. Later, as the plight of the 8 Bde increased, a total of two companies of the 29 Btn were allowed to move forward. Around the same time it became clear at Divisional HQ that Delangre Farm, which had been struck off the list of locations to be seized, was not in Australian possession; McCay therefore ordered that the farm should be shelled in an attempt to disorganise the German counter-attack.

Among the machine-gunners on this flank was ex-railwayman 113 Pte John Ross, one of hundreds of troops seeing action for the very first time that day. Soon after his arrival in France, a letter to all at home showed the confidence of the troops: 'I don't know how long our turn in the trenches will be but at any rate you may depend the boys will do their bit'.[30] A previous letter dated 12 June, informed his friend Ivan Murray of Bundaberg that he was now 'about 1 ½ miles from the front line. Of course our Machine Gun Company is represented up there trying conclusions with the so called Hun. Our billet is of course under Artillery fire so a bloke has to watch himself for gas attacks, bombs etc so you are all in danger even if we are not up in the front line'.[31]

One of the many heroic feats that occurred on 19–20 July was the digging of the communication trench in 8 Bde sector by 200 men of 30 Btn and a party of 8 Field Coy. The companies of 30 Btn were detailed as follows: A Coy (Major R.H. Beardsmore) to construct a fire trench to connect the left of the original Australian line with the trench to be captured; B (Capt F. Street), and C (Major M. Purser) to carry engineering stores and ammunition respectively to the attacking battalions; C (Capt W. Cheeseman) to dig a communication trench from the old to the new line.[32]

The hazardous and difficult task of digging a new trench in the Australian front line to the German parapet, if completed, would create a section of new front line. After the battle it was said that there was never any intention to hold the German line. If this is so, why was so much effort expended linking the front line to the German breastworks, and why were carrying parties ordered to leave their emergency rations on the far side of No Man's Land to create a rations dump for those who were to hold the new line?

The method for digging the trench was to send men out at intervals across No Man's Land to dig pot-holes. As soon as they became large enough for other men to work, more would be sent out to extend the excavations until joined with neighbouring holes. On the morning of 19 July the trench-digging party from A Coy left their billets in Fleurbaix and moved to their assembly positions. Soon after 6p.m. the first trench-digging party emerged at the start of the trench, at the point where Cellar Farm Avenue joined the front line. Immediate progress was hindered as the wire had been inadequately cut, but soon the group of men sent out to mark the point where the trench was to join the German line was able to move out. This point was about fifty yards from the extreme left flank of the section of line being attacked, and so in close proximity to the part of the German line subjected only to rifle and machine gun fire from the 60 Bde. The signpost to mark the target was carried by Sgt Garland, but he was shot and killed close to the enemy wire; the tapes and pegs to mark the line were taken out by Lt J.S. Lees.

Meanwhile men started to dig in No Man's Land, joining craters to form the trench; during this work Lt Lees was killed as were two of the leading party, 1623 Pte C.F. Tisbury and 1134 Pte D.C. Rich. Behind them, troops passing through the gaps in the wire were easy targets for the German machine-gunners. The death of Lt Lees during the digging of 30 Btn's trench was described by Col Clark twenty years later in *Mufti*:

> Lieutenant Lees died like a hero; he came away as an NCO and was one of the first to get a commission. He was a splendid chap and during the fight had his men working digging this trench. He was first shot in the leg but kept on, then in the body, but still stuck to his job till a bullet through his head finished him. I trust if any members of the present 30th Battalion ever go into action they will get some inspiration from reading the account of this gallant officer.[33]

Once digging commenced, the heavy wet soil made it very hard work. Furthermore, men returning to the Australian lines used the excavations for cover even though they were by no means completed. The advent of dusk and then darkness assisted A Company who gradually made progress making the trench both deeper and longer. Ahead of them was the fighting around Kastenweg and the German frontline and all around them artillery shells continued to fall. By daybreak all but twenty yards had been completed (it was now about 175 yards long and six feet deep at the Cellar Farm Avenue end and three feet six inches deep nearest the enemy breastworks), and realising the danger this posed, the Germans increased their rate of fire on this new feature causing a considerable number of casualties. At this point the digging was abandoned, but the trench was available to assist the withdrawal of 31 and 32 Btn troops now being forced out of the German lines.

Although the 30 Btn did not suffer as badly as 31 and 32 Btns (about fifty-four and seventy-two per cent casualties respectively), their casualty rate was around thirty-five per cent of its total strength; nine officers, of whom four came from A Company, and 343 other ranks were killed, wounded or missing. Major R.H. Beardsmore, CO of A Company, won a very well-deserved DSO and around twenty other gallantry awards were conferred on officers and men of the battalion.

Taking a realistic view of the outcome of the battle, the officers of C Coy, 30 Btn, billeted in Rue de Quesnes in Fleurbaix just before the battle, decided to have a feast as a change from their usual tinned rations. The lady who ran their billet was requested to purchase a pound of steak and a pound of onions per man and to prepare for them grilled steak and fried onions. Very much later that evening, as they were on the point of abandoning hope of seeing their meal, they discovered that 'the ability of French peasantry appeared to be limited to eggs and chips, omelettes etc.'. Their six pounds of steak was served in one lump, partly boiled and partly baked, and the onions had been cooked whole. Five of the six officers sharing this meal became casualties that night. Lieutenants A. Mitchell and J. Parker were killed; Capt B.A. Wark,[34] Lt I.G. Fullerton and Lt E. Haviland were wounded.[35]

Despite the valiant work by 30 Btn,[36] the left wing of the attack was in a perilous state, and it was only a matter of time before the 8 Bde's position became untenable. Lt Col Toll made a curious comment on this stage of the battle when he wrote, 'it was apparent that the division on our left had either not launched an attack or had been unsuccessful' – it was never part of the plan that the 60 Bde would leave their trenches.[37] Their situation was not helped by the gap between the advanced party of the 31 and 32 Btns and the other part of the 31, which was dug in the German front line. There was also a gap across to their right where the 54 Btn was to be found. Lt Col Toll received a message from Brigade HQ at 10p.m. seeking information on which sectors were being held and which were not, so that a bombardment might be arranged in order to gain the whole line.[38] Similarly, attempts had been made by Capt C. Mills (31 Btn) and Lt Col Coghill (32 Btn) to locate their neighbouring troops, to no avail. In this location was a small group of Australians from the 31, led by CSM W. McLean of B Company, and another group from 31 Btn led by Sgt R.J. O'Sullivan. Otherwise it was an opening that could have been exploited by the Bavarians. It was not here, though, that they chose to attack; instead they renewed their assault on the right of the 14 Bde sector at a point where the line was held by little more than a few wounded men and a handful of bombers, who had valiantly held back the previous attempt to penetrate the old German front line to the rear of the 54 and 55 Battalions.

9

Destruction and Havoc

As the evening wore on information in the possession of Lt-Gen Haking was incomplete and confused making it difficult for him to issue clear instructions on the actions to be taken during the late evening and the night.

The worst example, reflected in war diary entries, of lack of real understanding of the status of the battle was that concerning 15 Bde. GHQ General Staff recorded, 'No news of 5th Australian Division... later reported that right hand brigade attack successful'.[1] First Army General Staff diary stated '5th Australian Division report right battalion of right Brigade has not entered German trenches' yet it also notes that Mackenzie's division had 'been instructed to hold on to enemy's trenches and Sugar Loaf and extend to left so as to join the right battalion of the 5th Australian Division'.[2]

Haking knew that on the right of the 61 Division the 182 Bde had been successful in their assault, unlike the neighbouring 183 Bde. The 184 Bde, replicating the fate of 15 Bde, had suffered terribly in front of the Sugar Loaf Salient, though it was possible that a number of soldiers on the left of the 61 Division (the group led by Capt Church) had penetrated the German defences. In the belief that this was the case, an order was issued at 7.55p.m. for these troops to bomb their way along the German line and link with the Australians. As the troops for whom this order was intended were probably already dead or wounded and not within the German breastworks, any expectation of compliance was futile.

Whatever details of the progress of the attack that may have reached the back areas, it was the large volumes of wounded that seemed to be the best indicator of success or failure. Lt J.D. Wyatt (Northamptonshire Regiment), attached to 2/4 Gloucesters at Divisional HQ in Estaires, had witnessed the smoke enveloping the front lines and had heard rumours of the capture of long stretches of the enemy line and the taking of two hundred POWs. His diary states that he preferred to rely upon 'concrete evidence... in the shape of ambulances crowded with wounded. It soon became evident that whatever the success the cost had not been small, the Australian casualties in particular being heavy…'[3]

In the same division, the part played in the action by the 2/1 Bucks was virtually over. At 1a.m. on 20 July the remnants of the battalion were withdrawn after relief by 2/4 OBLI and retired to billets near Lavantie prior to being conveyed by bus to Estaires at 10a.m. Coming in the opposite direction also by motor-buses were several companies of 2/8 Warwicks. The scene they encountered, wrote their historian, 'will be impossible to forget… destruction and havoc which was everywhere apparent in the front and support lines and communication trenches'.[4]

Meanwhile the centre British brigade (183) and the left brigade (184) were already formulating plans to enact Haking's order to renew their attacks; the 182 Bde, in contrast, was attempting to reinforce the small body of men of 2/7 Warwicks holding the enemy's support line. These proposed attacks were uncoordinated as 183 Bde planned to attack again at 8.10p.m. whilst the 184 Bde were requesting a bombardment of the Sugar Loaf Salient until 9p.m. as a precursor to their attack.

In an attempt to repeat the earlier two-pronged attack on the Sugar Loaf Salient the commander of 184 Bde, via the two divisional headquarters, enquired whether Elliott's brigade would be able to participate in a further attack at 9p.m. This message was sent at 7.52p.m. and was in Elliott's possession some 18 minutes later. Half an hour before receipt of the message at Brigade HQ both the 15 and the 8 Bdes had obtained authority to bring forward the remaining halves of their third battalions, the carrying parties, as assault troops. McCay's scheme for the two brigades' troops was designed to break the deadlock in No Man's Land and assist the consolidation of the new line. By 8.10p.m. the troops withdrawn from transporting stores in support of the earlier waves were either in or close to their own front line, mixing with the dead and wounded among the battered sandbags and earthworks of the 5 Australian Division's starting point.

Sending the 58 Btn forward to assist the 59 Btn was Elliott's response to the request for support from the 184 Bde. At 8.13p.m. he issued orders for them to move out into No Man's Land at 9p.m.; at the same time half the 57 Btn were ordered to move up to the Australian reserve line. Elliott also made a request to McCay for yet more reinforcements. At this time he was informed by Major H. Greenway, 15 Field Company, who was in charge of digging one of the communication trenches across No Man's Land to the Sugar Loaf Salient, that the enemy had the range of the 59 and 60 Btn men in No Man's Land and had inflicted heavy casualties on them as they took refuge in shell holes and ditches. McCay declined Elliott's request, with the consequence that the onus of making the 9p.m. attack fell on just two companies of 58 Btn.

The 58 Btn had been detailed to be in support of the attacking battalions. Its troops had moved up from billets in Sailly-sur-la-Lys at 2.25p.m. on 19 July, on the way losing one man killed and two wounded by shellfire at Windy Post. One platoon of A Coy, under 2/Lt Godfrey,[5] was left at Rifle Villa to police the roads and communication trenches; C Coy was to carry ammunition forward across No Man's Land and D Coy was to assist in digging a communication trench forward from the front line. The remainder of A plus B Coy moved into the 300 yard line; at 8.30p.m. they were destined to move into the fire trenches and charge in support of 59 and 60 Btns.

As the men of the 58 Btn prepared themselves for the difficult task ahead, Haking was provided with fresh information on the status of the three brigades in his 61 Division. Having evaluated these details, at 8.20p.m. he instructed that the 184 and 183 Bdes should return to or remain in their own front line and that the 9p.m. attack be abandoned. According to Mackenzie's notes on the battle, the order was repeated to the brigades in 61 Division 'at 8.30p.m. and approved by XI Corps (message GR16 8.55p.m.)'.[6] This order reached the 182 Bde just in time to stop a company of the 2/7 Warwicks going forward to attack; of their other two companies very few men returned to their own lines and German accounts indicate that about sixty of them were taken prisoner. Four Vickers machine guns were also lost. However, Mackenzie's order to his brigade was also sent to 5 Australian Division where it was received at 8.35p.m. At 9p.m. Haking confirmed his decision; so far as the Australian division was concerned, he sought confirmation of the extent of the enemy line it occupied and urged them to hold on to any ground in their possession as this would, he believed, assist the 61 Division when they made a further attack on the morning of 20 July. He also instructed McCay not to commit any more troops in the 15 Bde sector, but rather to withdraw any survivors of the initial assault. General Staff XI Corps's war diary contains an entry timed at 9.10p.m. recording 'instructions to 5th Australian Division that 61st Division is to withdraw to our front line with a view to attacking again tomorrow and for 5th Australian Division to consolidate'.[7] Only at 9.10p.m. when Haking's order was received was word passed to Elliott. This message read, '9.25p.m. 61st Division not attacking tonight. General Elliott may withdraw 59th Battalion and its reinforcements if he thinks attack is not likely to succeed.'[8]

Elliott recorded in his notes on the battle that McCay did not know that Haking had called off this attack 'until the 61st Division sent a message to him, received at 8.35p.m. too late to stop 58th going forward'. Elliott contends that 'here again it is impossible to acquit Haking and his staff of blame',[9] yet swift action by divisional staff may have halted 58 Btn's advance.

While this was going on the evening was drawing in, but in one section of the 5 Australian Division's sector there was a flurry of activity as a couple of companies of the 58 Btn under the leadership of Major A.J.S. Hutchinson, another of the talented leaders Elliott had gathered into his brigade, moved out into No Man's Land. Joined by survivors of previous waves that had been cut to pieces earlier in the evening, the 58 Btn advanced approximately 250 yards. Here they were abruptly halted by accurate German machine gun and rifle fire from the Sugar

Loaf Salient, despite four batteries having shelled the salient for ten minutes from 8.05p.m.[10] The troops took cover in any hole or ditch that was available. Hutchinson himself valiantly attempted to rally his men but was shot dead as he made his way closer to the enemy line. Few men were able to continue in support of their commander as the enemy had taken a heavy toll.

It is unlikely that any of Hutchinson's men succeeded in entering the German line during the attack. After the war the remains of many bodies were found in front of the German wire, victims not only of gunfire but also of 5 Australian Division staff officers not appreciating the significance of Mackenzie's message received at 8.35p.m. In all probability the only 15 Bde men to enter the Bavarian position adjacent to the Sugar Loaf Salient were wounded men recovered by the Germans. Just two prisoners were taken in this sector, Lt J.C. Bowden and Pte H.H.V. Hodson (59 Btn), both wounded. Bowden did not last the day, dying of wounds in German hands, and has no known grave. Hodson's return to Australia after the war was not a happy event as the wounds sustained at Fromelles wrecked his life, and he died on 22 July 1926, almost ten years to the day after the battle.

McCay's casual attitude towards this sequence of events seems quite inexcusable. An examination of the timings of messages from when the renewed attack intended for 9p.m. was proposed and then cancelled indicates a short span, but McCay and his staff were fully aware of the changes, and their tardiness in informing Elliott of cancellation of the 9p.m. attack was reckless. Thanks to the incompleteness of the remaining records it is also one of the mysteries of this whole action, and the truth about this episode will never be known.

It is not at all surprising that the relative absence of shell damage to the Sugar Loaf Salient should cause so much difficulty for the 15 Bde; a report on the defences in and around this prominent feature of the German front line stated that the 'enemy's front system forms a salient and is protected by a chain of strong points across the base of the triangle'.[11] The first of three locations (at N.14.b.4.3.) referred to in the document prepared by Capt S.B. Pope of II Anzac Corps was stated as probably containing machine guns; the second, Delaporte Farm, was reportedly 'very strong and backed by earthworks… wired and contained machine guns – vicinity much knocked about by artillery but farm itself and earthworks appeared to have escaped damage'. Delangre Farm, the third strongpoint, bore much resemblance to Delaporte Farm. Pope's notes state quite clearly that 'the whole of the Sugar Loaf Salient… is well built and well furnished with machine guns'. In keeping with the Germans' renowned ability to arrange strongpoints in such a way that they offered support to locations around them, Pope's commentary mentions 'a strong series of works about Ferme de Mouquet and the Tadpole containing machine guns, whence flanking fire could be brought to bear to south west'.[12]

While this gallant but needless sacrifice by 58 Btn was taking place, Haking was gathering more information, and this was to contribute to a further change of mind on his part. McCay informed Haking that despite Bavarian counter-attacks his 8 and 14 Bdes were holding their positions in the enemy line, though the lack of success in capturing the Sugar Loaf Salient was still presenting significant problems: machine guns located there were able to fire across No Man's Land right down towards the British 60 Bde as well as into the rear of the Australian troops dug in beyond the German front line. To complicate his appraisal of the situation, an RFC aeroplane that had been sent over the lines to ascertain the location of troops misinterpreted flares, probably let off by the Germans, as being signals indicating the positions held by attackers. Haking believed that the situation was better than it really was and decided that, rather than pull out from this apparently advantageous position, his infantry units would seek to hold the line and make a fresh attempt to capture the salient.

Contrary views of the staff work in 5 Australian Division were held by Elliott and Ellis. In his list of 'blunders' published in *The Duckboard* fourteen years later, 'Pompey' wrote of 'hurried and insufficient preparations' and was critical of the work performed by the staff. Ellis, on the other hand, suggests that they were diligent, and he recorded in the divisional history, 'every energy of the staff and all ranks was concentrated on the preparatory work'. Captain Ellis goes on to say, 'it necessitated the communication to everybody concerned of as much information regarding the operation as it was necessary for him to have in order to act to best advantage'.[13]

At 10p.m. Haking's chief-of-staff, Brig-Gen W.H.Anderson, went to meet with McCay and his chief-of-staff Lt Col Wagstaff. Anderson proposed to McCay that his battalions should hold the ground captured and that the 61 Division would make another attempt to capture the Sugar Loaf Salient before daybreak, Haking having telephoned Mackenzie at 9.55p.m. pointing out the desirability of getting into the Sugar Loaf Salient during the night to help the Australians.[14] Haking ordered 184 Bde to attack the Sugar Loaf during the night accompanied by two companies of 2/4 OBLI; every possible effort was to be made to carry out the attack.[15] Anderson also stressed to McCay the importance of not yielding ground, and that if possible he should join up with the left of Mackenzie's division as soon as that division was able to capture the Sugar Loaf Salient. McCay was also authorised to reinforce the battalions in the German line and to use more men to dig trenches across No Man's Land. At 3a.m., though, Brig-Gen Carter reported that his trenches were being heavily shelled while the communication trenches were blocked by wounded troops endeavouring to move to the rear, and that his troops would not be ready for a fresh attack for some time. As the situation became clearer, Haking cancelled the night attack, but at 12.10a.m. advised the 61 Division that they should prepare for another assault during the morning. The Australian troops were ordered to hold the line that should have been captured by the first waves, but were warned not too hold the line too thickly. A note of congratulations from the corps and divisional commanders on the splendid work done thus far was added to the order.

Although he had reasonable knowledge of the position of his 8 and 14 Bdes, McCay was still unable to give Haking details of the situation concerning his right-hand brigade with any confidence. At 10.30p.m. he sent a message to Elliott informing him of Haking's latest change of plan and enquired whether Elliott could capture and hold the Sugar Loaf Salient if he was provided with another battalion. At this stage, Elliott himself was little the wiser. He understood that his 60 Btn had secured a foothold in the German front line but was isolated and unable to join up with the 14 Bde to their left. Additionally, at this time he had not received firm reports of how the 58 Btn had fared in their assault. Elliott's conclusion was to reply to McCay that he was willing to make another attempt with a fresh battalion (57 Btn), but could not guarantee success in view of the very active enemy machine gun fire in this sector. This response was sent to McCay at 11.30p.m. An hour later he received what was possibly the first substantial and reliable message for some time that enabled him to accurately monitor his units' performance in the opening phases of the battle. It came from Major C.A. Denehy of the 58 Btn, and after adding his own couple of sentences he sent it on to Divisional HQ for McCay's consumption. It read:

Such men of the 60th as actually reached the enemy's trenches have been killed or captured. The two companies of the 58th mown down when close to enemy's trench and very few came back. Men of all battalions are coming back from No Man's Land and I expect that they will gradually drift back to the line. Many men are wounded, many are not. Very many officers are casualties, including Majors McCrae, Elliott, and Hutchinson, all of whom are reported dead, and seems impossible to organise… Report seems unanimous that not a single man of 15th Brigade has now arrived in enemy's trench, as enemy flares are coming from the whole of the from allotted to this brigade. I am now organising the defence of our original trenches… This message indicates that the attack of this brigade has completely failed.

McCay immediately comprehended the gravity of this message and passed word to the corps commander that any further contribution from the 15 Bde could be discounted. Elliott was ordered to organise the defence of his original front line and to arrange for a trench to be dug across No Man's Land to join with the 14 Bde's position; simultaneously, an artillery bombardment was ordered on the section of the German line that McCay had believed to be held by Elliott's men, so that the centre Australian brigade might be afforded some protection from an enemy counter-attack along their own front line. In terms of offensive action, the 15 Bde's infantry was now finished; however, Lt S.E. Evans of 15 Field Company began to establish a route for the new trench, and the 57 Btn adopted the role of defending their front line as well as setting about the difficult and dangerous task of searching for wounded men in No Man's Land.

Behind the lines at Divisional HQ in Estaires around 3a.m., a captain in the Worcesters arrived with orders for troops on loan from 2/4 Gloucesters to rejoin their unit. An ambulance took them via Laventie to Red House where they were informed that their battalion had now been withdrawn. Lt J.D. Wyatt noted in his diary the details of their losses: '2 officers killed and 5 wounded. Scrase[16] A Coy and James the sniping officer were killed. I spent a long time finding the company who were in new billets. They were dog tired and were all fast asleep having only got in at 4a.m.'[17] Fatigue was a major factor for all these troops, but there was a lot more action to come before the battlefield became silent once again.

10

Conspicuous Gallantry

While the 15 Bde's situation was being established the other two Australian brigades were holding onto the territory in their possession, but slowly the pendulum was beginning to swing in favour of the Bavarians. Confused reports of the predicament of the 15 Bde still abounded and it was thought that men of the 60 Btn really had entered the German line, a belief given greater credence by reports from returned wounded men. Lt Col Cass had received similar messages via the 53 Btn, which made the assumption that both his flanks were secure and thus concentrated on consolidating his position. Had Cass known the actual status in the 53 Btn's area he would not have been reassured. The 15 Bde had not occupied the German front line, and only a party of 53 Btn bombers was preventing enemy troops moving along their own front line to the rear of the majority of 53 Btn, which, like the 54, 31 and 32 Btns, was clinging to its position in the place where they thought the German second line should be located.

The 32 Btn was in the most danger, and around 8.30p.m. German troops in strength at Delangre Farm prepared for the next phase of the battle. German reserves had been placed on alert up to two days before the attack took place, and now a company of the 20 Bavarian RIR was brought forward to support the defenders around Delangre Farm, while a company of the 21 Bavarian RIR came from Beaucamps to retake Kastenweg. Additional troops had been allocated the task of counter-attacking from Les Clochers forward towards the German front line; similarly, men of 16 Bavarian RIR plus more from the 21 Bavarian RIR were ordered to attack the 14 Bde's position. There was confusion amongst the Germans as to exactly how far the Australians had penetrated. It was thought that they may have gone as far as the lower slopes of Aubers Ridge below the ruins of the village of Fromelles itself. Clearly this was not the case, but it is possible that Col Toll had been seen moving forward with his small band towards the Grashof strongpoint, thus giving rise to alarm. The history of the 21 Bavarian RIR gives a realistic summary, stating that the Australians did progress along Kastenweg and get close to Delangre Farm as well as approaching Grashof. Their historian also states that some attackers were seen in the vicinity of another strongpoint called Brandhof on the south side of Grashof some 800 yards behind the German line. If this is true, it substantiates claims from a few Australians who stated that they had reached this location before returning to the temporary line held by their infantry units.

The vulnerable Australian left flank was the first to be subjected to a German counter-attack and this occurred about dusk. Enemy gunfire inflicted heavy casualties on the Australians, though they succeeded in fighting off a section of the enemy attack that was trying to retake Kastenweg. Artillery support had been requested earlier in the evening but many shells were falling on the German breastworks, that is, behind the 8 Bde's position. The range was initially extended by some 200 yards and later by another 300 yards, though there was some confusion whether the shells falling close to this brigade's men were German or British. At 9.40p.m. the 32 Btn sent back a message which underlined the grim position in which they now found themselves. It stated that they could not hold the line unless they received many reinforcements as well as sandbags and water. Brig-Gen Tivey then sent forward part of his 30 Btn from the original Australian front line and replaced them with part of the 29 Btn. It appears that Tivey was not aware that in their enthusiasm to assist their mates, many men of the 30 Btn, engaged in carrying parties, had already become fully involved in defending the ground gained at great cost earlier that evening. At least one officer, Capt F.L. Krinks, took the initiative in this respect when, during his duties with a carrying party, he decided that the situation was so serious on the left flank that his men should remain and augment the troops already there. They initially used ammunition boxes to form a barricade in Kastenweg (this trench was made from earth-filled boxes, hence its name) but later moved even further to the left to a position from where his men could enfilade any German moving towards the 32 Btn. Later Krinks acquired a couple of Lewis guns to enable stouter resistance to be made. Gradually this heroic action by the 8 Bde defeated the first counter-attack.

Once the sun went down the whole battlefield was transformed and the opportunity for confusion and error increased. Capt W.H. Zander noted that soon 'it was pitch dark and one could only get glimpses of things by the flashes of exploding shells. The Hun sent some incendiary shells over and these set light to anything they came into contact with when they burst, their flickering flames throwing a ghostly light over the dead and debris lying about...'[2]

The 14 Bde was still clinging to hard-won ground ready for the Bavarians to reorganise and counter-attack. As with the 8 Bde to the left, additional troops were sent forward when McCay provided half of the 55 Btn. Col Cass divided these reinforcements, sending a company commanded by Capt Gibbins to take up a position to the left of his 54 Btn and another under Lt J.H. Matthews to the left of the 53 Btn. Although this brigade now held a much better line, there remained a gap between it and the 8 Bde: that is, from Gibbins's left flank to the nearest men of the 31 Btn, a situation which later in the night allowed the Germans to come between the two Australian brigades.

The 53 Btn was to be the first to come under pressure from the enemy. This initial assault occurred while digging in to a better position to the west of the farm track leading from Rouge Bancs Farm northwards to the German front line and then out into No Man's Land. Capt Arblaster was now displaying great leadership in organising resistance on the 53's right flank, leaving the task of doing likewise on the left, where the battalion adjoined the 54 Btn on the other side of a farm track, to Capt Murray. This track was felt to be a weak part of their defences, hence the need for Murray to organise his resources properly, including employing some Lewis gun teams led by Lt R.G. Downing and bombers under Lt A.C. Gunter, all of 54 Btn. Gunter continued to show initiative and bravery throughout the night, and for his actions during the battle he was awarded the MC 'for conspicuous gallantry in action. As bombing officer he repelled with his bombers the enemy bomb attacks. Later he counter-attacked them as long as his supply of bombs lasted and on receiving fresh supplies, bombed them away altogether.'[3]

A further exposed part of their position, unbeknown to them at present, was the very right-hand end of the 53 Btn's position, a situation created by the withdrawal of part of the 53 Btn when the remnants of Elliott's 60 Btn pulled back taking survivors from other units with them. German bombing parties made speedy progress behind the 54 Btn over the shell-blasted debris littering and obstructing the trenches that until a few hours before had been their front line. This incursion by the enemy was inevitable, such was their proficiency at regrouping and doing their utmost to recover lost territory. As they worked through the sandbags, timber baulks and other detritus, the Germans were alert for pockets of resistance, and it was not long before they encountered a group of thirty men under the command of Lt E.M. Farmer (55 Btn). The Germans sent a number of bombs into the midst of Farmer's party, but as they attempted to return this aggression with their own volley of bombs one of the significant failings of this battle came to light – the matter of bombs that had been sent forward without being fused. In 8 Bde sector the problem of undetonated bombs was solved by Lt John Chapman, 30 Btn., who had qualified at a grenade school whilst in Egypt. With the remnants of his platoon he took control of the problem and ensured that subsequent supplies were properly primed.[4] Lt Col McConaghy also observed a lack of proficiency with grenades and included a reference in his report, saying, 'there are many men who cannot handle bombs. I even saw men throwing Mills Grenades without withdrawing the safety pin. This was not peculiar to any one Battalion.'[5]

One root cause of unfused bombs being supplied during the battle was suggested by Capt G.H. Wilson who referred to an order 'to send the bombs down, "fused or unfused" so we loaded the truck and ran it down'.[6] However, the troops kept the enemy at bay while others prepared the bombs which were then put to effective use. Other men also came to the aid of Farmer's gallant band. In one particular piece of brave conduct, two soldiers who had come across to assist Farmer, L/Cpl P. Freirat[7] and Pte C.A. Mitchell, both of 53 Btn, took a bag of bombs each and outflanked the Germans, causing many casualties. For a short time this act of gallantry and initiative held back the enemy, who were now also sweeping the 14 Bde position with machine gun fire and illuminating the battlefield with flares. This fierce exchange went on for the best part of an hour, but as many men had been withdrawn from carrying parties the supply of bombs became exhausted, causing the Australians to fall back to the line of infantry in their temporary entrenched position in advance of the German front line.

The counter-attack on the 53 Btn's bombers soon proved successful and forced the remaining men to retire to their own lines, taking with them twenty prisoners and any 60 Btn troops who had veered to the left and joined the 53 Btn. This retirement took place at about 7p.m., and although Divisional HQ at Sailly-sur-la-Lys was informed, this most undesirable development was unknown to the advance party of the 53 Btn and to 54 Btn, who were now in peril of being attacked in their rear.

The second German counter-attack, ordered at 8p.m., was the beginning of the end for the Australian possession of the enemy's territory, and it was a combination of factors that compelled McCay's men to fall back to avoid being encircled by the determined Bavarians. On the Australian right the 12 Bavarian Bde was to attempt to make its way behind the 14 Bde in a movement similar to their previous assault; likewise, the 14 Bavarian Bde was to attack the 8 Bde from the front and from their left. This attack was planned to start at 11.40p.m.

The Australians were waiting for the Germans to make the next move. By now they were tired, many were wet from the flooded ditches, some were wounded and either did not merit being evacuated or chose to stay for the fight; they were short of ammunition and bombs and protected by whatever sandbagged defences they had been able to construct; they were in strange, inadequately mapped terrain, on a dark, smoky, misty battlefield without definite knowledge of where and when the enemy would appear in force.

At this stage the three battalions strung out along Cass's section of front, 53, 54 and 55 Btns, are estimated to have had a strength of no greater than 200 men, including men from a variety of engineer and other infantry units. As well as rifles, revolvers and a diminishing number of bombs, these men also had Lewis guns and Vickers machine guns (the latter under the control of Capt C.M. Spier, 14 Machine Gun Company, and subsequently Capt W.T. Dick after Spier was wounded).

With the regrouping of Capt Arblaster's men, this section of the right flank became completely unmanned and increased the danger threatening the remaining troops awaiting the next onslaught in the darkness. Around 1a.m. some troops in the 14 Bde sector started to retire to their own lines. Major Cowey of the 55 Btn gathered them and sent them back to the fight but to no avail as a number were overcome by the Germans and taken prisoner. Help came in the form of one of Cass's battalion commanders, Gallipoli veteran Lt Col McConaghy (55 Btn), who had brought his staff across No Man's Land where they encountered a couple of 53 Btn officers detached from their unit and who had no idea of the battalion's current position. McConaghy made his way across to the right flank of Cass's sector where he eventually found Capt Arblaster, who immediately gave him details of recent events in that frenetic part of the battlefield. Arblaster was very concerned about the ease with which the Germans had been able to make their way behind his men in the absence of any 15 Bde men between his position and the Sugar Loaf Salient. Responding to this concern, McConaghy despatched one officer and three men towards the ground that Elliott's troops had attempted to take, but no account exists of their return with information. It is likely that they were either killed by the Germans or taken prisoner. A second attempt was made by Cpl H. Anson, one of the men brought across to Arblaster's position by Lt Col McConaghy. Anson returned soon after when he was spotted by vigilant German troops, but this did not deter him from making another reconnaissance of the German front line. On this occasion he ascertained that the Germans had secured possession of their own line from a point close to the 53 Btn's position across towards the Sugar Loaf, though it was not possible to establish exactly how far, not that it mattered to the defenders he had left behind. McConaghy decided to place troops at barricades to the right of their location to prevent any further incursion by the enemy and place the defenders in a better position to fend off the next counter-attack.

At 2.40a.m. a strong attack was made on the right of 14 Bde and this was driven back. According to Col Cass's report, the 'enemy had rather advertised this attack by the great use he had made of flares from his Very pistols. By throwing these flares well towards the centre of the ground held by 14th Brigade, he caused the men to show up sharply against the well lit background'.[8] Conversely, the Australians were very short of flares and pistols, especially 53 Btn and 54 Btn. They were carried by company commanders, and so many had been killed or wounded that these pistols were not to hand when required. German flares were found and these were used along with their grenades and a machine gun.

Supplying additional ammunition, sandbags and other material to enable a robust defence to be made had become easier thanks to the resolute work of 54 Btn signallers, who succeeded in restoring a telephone line from their position back to the original Australian front line and onwards to 14 Bde HQ. At much the same time, 14 Bde engineers who were engaged in digging a new communication trench across No Man's Land joined it with the German front trench. Bombs and ammunition, as well as even more sandbags, were directed to where they were most needed. At sunrise, pigeons were used again to get messages back to Divisional HQ to request a barrage on the Germans advancing towards 14 Bde.

An example of a message, quoted by Bean,[9] is one from Capt N. Gibbins, the commander of B Company, 55 Btn:

> We hold the front line with 54th. CO 54th (Cass) in next trench in rear. 53rd on our right. 31st and 32nd on our left. Consolidating positions as fast as possible. Sending back to our rear trench by parties of ten under NCO's for ammunition and sandbags. We want Very pistols, flares and sandbags (plenty). Have 54th Lewis guns and five of our own under Sergeant Colless for counter-attack. Each of my men have three bombs, but require more. Expect a counter-attack shortly. Anyway, we can hold them easily.

Among the troops conveying forward much-needed supplies was Bert Bishop. No sooner had he completed a trip to the German front line than he turned around and, amid the noise and maelstrom of battle, met his cousin:

> On that trip back he (Solomon) met some more of his battalion machine gunners going in. Roy was among them, and Solomon saw again that look in his cousin's eyes that had so upset him before. They had no time to talk, each went his own way… he knew that something was to happen to Roy that night, and he had seen also that Roy knew it.[10]

Bishop's account continues with a description of the activity in the enemy front line:

> The rude trenches they had dug were full of their own dead and wounded, and the fighting was principally with bombs, the Germans had crept so close. He heard German orders being shouted on either hand, as a flare lit up the ghastly scene he saw what seemed to be droves of them moving up the trenches to the attack.
>
> While making his way back from that trip Solomon heard the sudden shriek of a shell followed instantaneously by an awful crash. He went several feet into the air, and couldn't move for some time. He had not been hit, but he had got the full force of the concussion, and felt as if he had been split into a thousand shreds. He remembered crawling back to the old front line in time to hear officers yelling out for everyone to man the fire steps, that the Germans were counter-attacking. Then they were ordered to go over again to the German trench. The sap the engineers were working on was now about half-way across the old No Mans Land and Solomon with others started to file along it. The

shouting and bursting of bombs in front grew more intense. An order went up for every man to get back to the old line as best he could, and the survivors from the captured trenches and those men going across all tumbled and raced back to the accompaniment of a chorus of German machine guns.[11]

With the provision of extra troops, the successful construction of the communication trench across No Man's Land and the stoic resistance displayed by Capt Arblaster's men, the 14 Bde position was made easier, though the threat clearly had not gone away. As the divisional and corps commanders now realised, 15 Bde was in no position to add to the centre brigade's security, and the situation was not so good on their left where the 8 Bde was dug in awaiting the next move from the enemy. Not only had many troops earlier in the evening gone forward as carrying parties and stayed to fight in the new front line but the entire detachment of the 30 Btn provided for this purpose had not returned thus presenting an immense problem for Major Purser the 30 Btn's officer in charge of the movement of stores who had now run out of men. Furthermore, whereas the 14 Bde's engineers had succeeded in linking the Australian and German front lines with a new communication trench, the 30 Btn had yet to start one of their two trenches in the 8 Bde's sector to provide cover for troops. The supplies of ammunition and other requirements were consequently patchy and the 8 Bde was never as well off as the 14 Bde in this respect. It was estimated that about 300 men, mainly of the 31 Btn and 32 Btns, were currently holding the left flank, blocking routes that could be exploited by counter-attacks and improving their temporary trenches. A further significant problem was flood water, owing to the flow of the Laies being obstructed by shell holes and by the interruption to German pumping systems.

In support still were men of 56 Btn; 'about midnight an increasing number of wounded began to stream back', wrote H.R. Williams. He continued:

Many were in a state of exhaustion and bleeding from wounds that had not been bandaged. They told us of the almost hopeless task of trying to form a trench line while the German bombing parties appeared from everywhere. We were not surprised when about 2a.m. our platoon officer and a sergeant came and told us that our troops were about to retire.[12]

Lt Col McConaghy reported later that around 3a.m., 'some foolish orders were circulated, something to this effect;"our own Artillery are shelling us – we have been ordered to retire"'. McConaghy estimated that he and other officers were able to check the confusion within a twenty-five-yard radius, but a number of troops beyond made their way back to their own lines. The enemy noticed this and attempted to exploit the weakness by making a bombing raid on McConaghy's flank.

The war diary of 56 Btn reveals this vulnerability, and during the retirement by the left-hand brigade, amid much confusion, most of their troops moved back to the 300 yard line. Capt Fanning noticed this and sent Capt W.R. Sheen to steady the men. Sheen displayed great leadership in stemming the disorder and making this part of the line secure against any enemy counter-attack. The battalion's casualties amounted to twelve killed, seventy-seven wounded and thirteen missing, along with 2/Lt Day and four men wounded during the recovery of troops from No Man's Land.

At 2.25a.m. confirmation of the enemy counter-attack on the Australian left reached Col Cass along with an urgent request for more bombs. Although he was now aware of the absence of Elliott's men, this knowledge was not widespread amongst the troops. Two instances demonstrating the uncertainty surrounding positions and identities of troops are recorded. In the first, figures were seen moving through the mist across open ground towards the Australians' rear in the direction of the old German front line. The troops on this right flank were ordered not to open fire as it was believed that they were probably 15 Bde troops falling back. Several men opened fire on the Germans in an attempt to repulse them. In doing so they incurred several casualties and at least one, Pte Mitchell (53 Btn), who lost the sight in one eye, was captured by the enemy. Eventually the men on the extreme right were pushed back a short distance, and it dawned upon them that not only were they being hit by rifle fire from the front, where they knew and expected return fire to come from, but also from their rear; the enemy had now managed to get behind them and there was a grave danger that they would be cut off. At this stage the Australian defenders were now in two distinct, separate groups, united only by their common need for more men, more bombs and more ammunition. It would require a phenomenal effort if the order to withdraw to the sanctuary of their own lines was to be realised, taking with them anyone who could get himself back or who could be assisted if wounded.

In the absence of this order, Capt Arblaster gathered his men and made a thrust through the Germans now to their rear, push through the old German front line and regained No Man's Land. Having reorganised his men, Arblaster gave the word to move out. They left their temporary positions and ran towards the enemy who were blocking their path to safety. Unfortunately there was little element of surprise and the Germans replied with heavy rifle fire, causing many casualties and forcing the Australians to fall back to their starting trenches. Arblaster himself was badly wounded and his gallant part in the battle came to an untimely end. He was later found by the enemy and taken to hospital in Douai where, on 24 July, this brave and well-regarded leader died.

Col Cass was fully aware of the remarkable fight shown by his battalion. Three of Cass' messages indicate the urgency of the situation now facing the men in his sector. The first, at 3a.m., stated, 'It is reported to me that the 53rd on my right has given way slightly and that the Germans are coming in about N.15.a.91/2' (this point was 350 yards west-south-west of Cass's HQ). The second message, twenty-two minutes later, further demonstrates the impending danger: 'Position is serious, as we have no grenades and enemy is preparing to attack from the vicinity of N.15.a.8.6 to N.15.b.4.6'. (This refers to two points behind the German lines; the first was a trench called Teufelsgraben and the second was Rouge Bancs.) Thirdly, at 3.45p.m., Cass wrote, 'Position very serious. 53rd are retiring. Enemy behind them and in their old front line N.9.c.6.1 and within 100 yards of my right.' This latter message concurs with reports that groups of 53 Btn troops were retiring and declining exhortations to remain in the fight.

Shortly before 4a.m., Cass was informed that there was now a danger that rapid progress by the Germans might threaten access to the new communication trench across No Man's Land close to Cass' HQ. While yet more reinforcements were sought, two attempts were made to halt the enemy. In the first instance Sgt F.T. Stringer (54 Btn) organised a few men to act as a bombing party; secondly, Col McConaghy, on Col Cass's instructions, arranged for Lt W. Denoon (55 Btn) to gather men and lead them in an assault along the old German parapet in a further attempt to beat off this attack. With their bomb supply replenished, Denoon's band made their way along the old German front line, lobbing grenades at the enemy as they went. Lt Denoon was soon wounded but his men forced the Germans to retreat seventy to eighty yards. It is unclear how much support in repulsing the enemy was given by the machine-gunners of the 15 Bde. About this time they had nine guns in the front line, six in the 300 yard line and a further four in the reserve line. Although their manpower was adequate on paper, many of those left were ammunition carriers and untrained in the operation of the guns.[13]

Pte A.T. Winter (55 Btn), engaged on digging a sap between the German lines, was clearly confused about the German counterattack at daybreak. He wrote after the war: 'God knows which way he came – we don't. He appeared to come from every direction. We were unsupported, consequently Fritz could come in on our flanks.' Snipers also took their toll, and when 'we got to close quarters with our bombs... we were only a handful and Fritz was there in his thousands'. Inevitably, in the confusion, Winter's small party became divided, 'Fred Carpenter was wounded and when he left that only made two of us'. Later,

> Through the orders of a very excited officer... Vin (Baker) and I became separated. This same officer was flourishing a revolver but I am sure he never once fired it at Fritz. Later we got the signal to retire – this must have been about 8a.m. In the retirement I found myself with the Colonel and RSM. They went along a sap and we followed. The sap was half-full of mud and nothing but dead men. The boys suffered whenever they attempted to get across the parapets.[14]

A very clear summary of the critical position now staring the 14 Bde in the face was sent by Cass to Brigade HQ at 4.20a.m.:

> Position almost desperate. Have got 55th and a few of 54th together and have temporarily checked enemy. But do get our guns to work at once, please. The 53rd have lost confidence temporarily and will not willingly stand their ground. Some appear to be breaking across No Man's Land. If they give way to my right rear, I must withdraw or be surrounded.[15]

Supplies of bombs were now being brought forward. In addition, troops of the 56 Btn engaged in digging the communication trench volunteered to join the fight and assist with finding bombs. Reinforcements arrived, part of the 56 Btn's detachment that had been instructed to remain in their own lines, and helped to repel the enemy and, like Denoon's men, win a much needed respite.

In their determination to expel the Australians the Germans also launched an attack from the south straight at the 55 Btn's positions. Here the Australians were very exposed and the skilful siting of a machine gun caused considerable difficulty for the defenders, until a quick-thinking machine-gunner of the 55 Btn found that by resting it on the shoulder of Cpl Stringfellow he could pin the enemy down and eventually force them to take cover. One particular act of courage, rewarded with a DCM, was that by 2426 Pte T.C. Rowley of A Coy, 56 Btn. Rowley stood on the enemy parapet and, in full view of the Germans, threw grenades with such an effect that the enemy was forced to withdraw, thus enabling eighty men to retire across No Man's Land.[16]

11

The Final Stages

While the 14 Bde was doing its utmost to detect Bavarian troop movements in the darkness, aided by the many flares sent up by the enemy, the left-hand brigade, 8 Bde, still had a fight on its hands.

The Germans gathered their troops around Delangre Farm before moving them into formation for each assault. Just after 2a.m. they brought heavy rifle fire to bear on the 32 Btn, which responded by immediately asking for an artillery bombardment on Delangre Farm and its environs. Shortly after, 31 Btn reported that it too was under pressure from infantry approaching from the lane running east–west towards Rouge Bancs. Col Toll at first cast some doubt on this report, preferring to suspect that the 'enemy troops' were in fact a row of trees mistakenly identified in the darkness. His opinion was shattered soon after when the noise of a bomb fight was clearly heard from the 31 Btn's sector. The advanced position of the 31 Btn was manned by Lt Drayton and a small group of his men, and they now withdrew to the original German front line leaving a gap between the two brigades' advanced lines. The 31 Btn had been ordered to hold the remainder of their advanced position and had been informed that it was intended to relieve them with men from 29 Btn. No sooner had Capt C. Mills, commanding this outpost, been informed of this plan than he was contacted by Major White of the 32 Btn, who reported that another wave of enemy troops was preparing to attack his position. His remedy was for the Australians to attack, and he wanted Mills to extend his men along the line and hold it while this counter-attack was underway. Mills went back along the line to organise his own troops. Unfortunately, while he was gone the Germans again attacked. Finding himself in an untenable position he was forced to surrender along with some of his men.[1] Others fell back to the Australian lines having decided that this was the best course of action.

Col Toll, still located in his temporary HQ, was also under threat. However, Lt Trounson[2] armed with a Lewis gun, Lt A. Flack with a Vickers machine gun and a handful of men fought off the enemy. The situation adjacent to them was deteriorating as the Germans managed to force their way behind the main part of the 32 Btn, expelling the few troops of the 29 and 32 Btns defending this sector. The other part of the 32 Btn, in the advanced position, had not been displaced, but the net result of this impetus by the Germans was that they now had the 32 Btn just about surrounded. It was unlikely that this advanced group was aware of their predicament until Capt K.M. Mortimer of 29 Btn made contact with Lt S.E.G. Mills, who commanded this outpost, and informed him of the success the enemy had achieved in getting between this outpost and their own former front line. After conferring with Mills, Mortimer made his way towards Kastenweg to check on the very left of the line, but appears to have met a party of Germans and was never seen alive again. His body was never identified and he is commemorated at VC Corner.

The time was now approaching 3.30a.m. In these desperate circumstances it was decided by the remaining officers of the 8 Bde that their best option was to move towards the German front line and force a passage through the Germans who were on the point of encircling them. Lt Mills gathered his machine guns together and informed his remaining men that they were to attempt this difficult manoeuvre but that they should await the signal from him before moving out, and in the meantime maintain fire in the direction of the enemy. This organisation took Mills until 3.38a.m.,[3] by which time he had mustered no more than 150 men. At the same time, his men were under machine gun fire from the Tadpole, Delangre Farm and De Mouque Farm, as well as from German artillery fire.[4] On the given signal they left their ditches and courageously made their way towards the enemy through the smoky night. Very soon they came face to face with the enemy, and fierce hand-to-hand fighting took place amid the wreckage of the German front line before part of this group regained No Man's Land and stumbled back to safety. Numbers were depleted along the way by rifle fire and by enfilade machine gun fire, particularly from the section of line opposite the 60 Bde. By 4.10a.m. 32 Btn survivors had regained their lines followed twenty minutes later by 31 Btn.

Inevitably a small group of men did not receive the instructions to fall back, including those who had valiantly blocked the enemy's passage along Kastenweg throughout the night; as the Germans closed in, they were either killed or taken prisoner, a poor reward for performing such a heroic task. Another group led by Capt Krinks had been located around Delangre Farm from where they could make out the enemy troop movements in the dark. Once they realised that they were cut off they formulated a plan to dash for their own lines with the agreement that if they ran into serious trouble they would stand and fight for each other. This is exactly what happened as they approached the German front line; two of them were seized by the enemy and the others rounded on them, forced them to release their companions and then fled across No Man's Land and crossed the parapet of 60 Bde's trench. Capt Krinks, Cpl A. Forbes, Pte J. Wishart and Pte T.L.

Watts were among those who made it back to the British lines, but two of their group, L/Cpl S.B. Wells and Pte E. Amps, became caught in the German wire; Wells was shot and Amps wounded. They lay out there all day, and on the evening of 20 July Krinks, Forbes, Wishart and Watts made their way from the rest area behind the lines back to No Man's Land where, after dark, they searched for their companions. They recovered Wells and Amps and turned back to their own lines. As the men approach the breastworks an Australian sentry opened fire, suspecting either that they were an enemy patrol or displaying a moment of uncontrolled fear. Whatever the reason, it did not affect his marksmanship, and he shot dead both Watts and Wishart at the very moment that their brave act was about to deliver two wounded men to safety.

The trenches to which the troops fell back were described by Sgt Les Martin (8 MGC):

Ghastly… shell holes everywhere… fires were still smouldering… dead bodies lying in all directions… some without heads, other bodies torn about minus arms or legs, or pieces cut clean out of them by shells, one chap who had been wounded was crawling to safety was killed by a shell hitting him right in the middle of the back, the shell was a dud.[5]

Spr Donnan of 14 Field Coy was more succinct: 'the front line was like a disorderly butcher's shop'.[6]

By 4a.m., not only was daybreak not far off but also the Australians were still awaiting a fresh assault by the 61 Division on the Sugar Loaf Salient. This had taken on renewed importance now that Col Cass had to fight his way back to safety and could have done without the added impediment of machine gun fire from the Salient. Fortunately, during the night McCay had ordered the salient to be bombarded on two occasions, at 2.40a.m. by the heavy guns and 3.15a.m. by the field guns. In addition, at 3.30a.m. the 15 Bde had been instructed to be prepared to maintain heavy rifle fire on the German trenches to deter movement once the sun started to rise. Further instructions were given to the field artillery at 3.45a.m. to shell the enemy positions just to the right of the location Cass was believed to occupy, and similarly the 60 Bde were to bombard the eastern side of Kastenweg to offer some protection to that flank.

At Sailly-sur-la-Lys a 5a.m. conference had been called to assess the position and decide the course of action for the coming day. Haking, Mackenzie, McCay, Monro and Barrow were in attendance to review the sorry tale of the night's events. Mackenzie informed Monro of the difficulties encountered during the night and how committing more troops to the attack would have produced little more than a longer casualty list. Maj-Gen Mackenzie also informed the conference that 'they have 3 battalions in our front trenches', a statement that showed how out of date his information was at that time.[7]

Having heard this account, the conference was on the point of debating what the 61 Division should now do to retrieve the situation when fortuitously McCay received a telephone call from Col Wagstaff at 5 Australian Division HQ. Upon making enquiries with the 8 Bde, Wagstaff had been told that the 31 and 32 Btns' troops had been compelled to withdraw from the German lines. Furthermore, Wagstaff informed Haking that he had been advised by Col Pope (14 Bde) that the few men left in the German lines, including Col Cass, were now in a very dire situation and that in order to help Cass fight off the enemy Pope had authorised the use of part of the 56 Btn. Now in receipt of situation reports from both brigades, Wagstaff sought a decision from McCay on whether to withdraw the remnants of 14 Bde or whether to commit more troops. The corps war diary records that eight messengers had been sent to 14 Bde troops to instruct them to fall back, but apparently none had reached these troops and no movement had been observed; other records suggest that this plucky eighth runner was successful. The RFC had been asked to attempt to drop a message, but was of the opinion that it was as likely to fall into enemy hands; the RFC also offered to make a close reconnaissance of the situation.[8]

McCay passed this report on to Monro and Haking, and after a short discussion they pronounced that the 14 Bde was to be pulled out of the German lines and that the attack was to be abandoned. Cass was already aware of the action taken by the 8 Bde when he received word from McCay at 6.30a.m. Col Toll, still in the German line, similarly was aware of the fighting withdrawal by his neighbours, and had had some difficulty in persuading some of his own men not to join them in their retreat. Some did leave their positions, weakening Toll's hold on his position as the Germans moved to his right, cutting him off from the 14 Bde. This enemy attack, preceded by strong bombing parties, was recorded as occurring at 5.30a.m. The supply of grenades was exhausted and so only fire from rifles and machine guns could be offered in resistance. The Germans cunningly moved behind their own parados to avoid observation by British gunners. At 5.45a.m. it was apparent that the battalion would have to retire;[9] Toll had no choice but to make his way back to the Australian lines with the remainder of his men, reaching safety by 6a.m.

The Lewis gunners played an essential part in holding the line as troops fell back under pressure from the German counter-attack. On the 8 Bde right flank an incident was witnessed that was similar to a story that would occur at Manchester Redoubt on 21 March 1918 in the German Spring Offensive:[10]

One Lewis gun crew stuck to it to the last and after all the rest had fallen back they could still be heard firing. We could see the Bosche working along the trench on both their flanks towards them but they still stuck to their posts and the gun kept firing. We saw some stick bombs thrown into their little strong-hold – then silence! Their job had been done at the expense of their lives.[11]

According to Toll, the 'enemy then swarmed in and the retirement across No Man's Land resembled a shambles, the enemy artillery and machine guns doing deadly damage. Our own lines were reached at last, but the artillery bombardment was intense and even under the shelter of our own trenches the casualties were awful'.[12]

As well as the infantry pulling back, the 14 Bde's machine gun company and trench mortar battery had just about concluded their part in the battle. The machine-gunners had lost six guns during the night. In addition to losing 2/Lt Hoddle Wrigley, who was killed, and their CO Capt Spier, wounded, fifty-one other members of the unit were listed as casualties when the first count was taken. The trench mortar battery had fared a little better; two men, Capt C.B. Hopkins and 1981 Pte J. McDowall, had been killed early on 20 July, and seven others had been wounded.[13]

In 14 Bde sector, men of 56 Btn witnessed the retirement of the troops that had gone forward during the evening and night:

We were powerless to assist them, and had to watch them being shot down at point-blank range... we stood on the fire step to assist with this race with death. It seemed an eternity of time until the lucky ones reached our parapets, to be pulled in by willing hands. No sooner was our field of fire clear than we blazed into the Germans who had lined their parapets to punish the retiring troops. Few of the rearguard escaped.[14]

In preparation for the inevitable withdrawal by the last of the 8 Bde, Capt Gibbins of the 55 Btn had taken action to protect the now exposed left flank of the 14 Bde. Lt K.R. Wyllie had been delegated the task of improving a communication trench linking the 55 Btn with the German front line and had then been sent over to the right of the brigade's position. Inevitably the Germans went both left and right when they re-entered their old front line between the 14 and 8 Bdes, but when they reached the 55 Btn another defence, a party of bombers, met them and compelled them to retreat. Gibbins incurred a head wound, however, causing him to leave this part of the line in the control of Lt P.W. Chapman. Another officer, Lt N.A. Robinson, was despatched back to the Australian lines to muster reinforcements, but managed to gather only a handful of men. Ironically, while the decision was being made to withdraw them the 14 Bde were improving their situation, but in the early morning light the sight of other troops returning to their own lines could not have been very reassuring to those still embroiled in bitter combat with the Germans. Conversely, the enemy must have realised by now that it was just a matter of time before their manoeuvring achieved its objective and the front line was once again firmly in their possession.

One of the last tasks allotted to Capt Gibbins was the formation of a rearguard to cover the withdrawal and to be the last to leave. However, the message to him from McConaghy was confused, possibly as a result of McConaghy's fatigue, and he interpreted the phrase 'Hold first Hun line until further orders' as being an instruction to move to their old front line. Lt Col Cass asserts in his report on the battle that he

> directed Col McConaghy to hold the German frontline as a rear guard and to ensure that his men covered the retirement to the rest of the force. He gave orders (I understand) to Capt Gibbins whose Coy was on my left to form this rear guard party and then left. Capt Gibbins seems to have misunderstood this and withdrawn his Company at once.

One company of 55 Btn was detailed to act as a rearguard, and the machine guns were sent back singly so that their removal might not be so obvious to the enemy. Cass was of the view that this allowed the Germans to move ahead of and behind 54 Btn, compelling his men to charge through the enemy and thereby incur many casualties. Lt Col McConaghy's report, however, states that Gibbins and his men 'fought very gallantly' and notes Gibbins's death and that '2 officers and 25 men of the party are missing'.

Despite their tenacious fight, Cass and his men must have welcomed the message received from McCay, delivered by the eighth runner who attempted to reach him, instructing them to abandon their territory and return to their own lines. Cass told his men:

> Be prepared to withdraw on the order being given. The old German front line will be held to the end. Make arrangements to dribble men in very small parties back through sap across No Man's Land to our front line. Make no move until I send the word 'withdraw'.

Time was running out for those troops on the brigade right, particularly the 53 Btn which was being isolated by the enemy moving further along their old front line. One or two more groups were captured and others fought to the last, while many wounded had no option but to await collection by the enemy. Col Cass was still waiting for the command to pull back, and he requested a box barrage around them while he collected his wounded to give them a chance to escape, but waited for the order to retire rather than make the decision himself. It was now 7.20a.m., and it is evident that Cass did not receive the order to withdraw for another thirty minutes,[15] by which time it was broad daylight. At last at around 8a.m. he sent his remaining men through the new trench across No Man's Land. Others, amid the confusion, made a dash across the open ground and yet more casualties were inflicted by the German machine-gunners, but the Australians also fought with their bayonets any Germans they encountered.

Not all of Cass' outposts had heard the order to retire, and some doubted its authenticity. Their opinion changed once they observed the Germans severing their escape route, and many more were either killed or captured as they too tried to gain No Man's Land. One party, led by Lt Lovejoy, was still in German territory after 8a.m., but they managed to return safely. Col Cass and his adjutant Capt M.J. Lowe were among the final troops to depart. After this, Capt Gibbins rallied his Lewis gunners, who had also decided it was time to leave. Collecting their weapons, spare parts and any remaining unused pans of ammunition they followed him along the new sap. At the far end Gibbins found the trench blocked by wounded men so he hopped up on to the edge of the trench, and was immediately shot through the head by a German sharpshooter.

Another who fell at the moment of reaching the Australian breastworks was 3247 Pte Vinton Baker, 55 Btn. According to a diary entry made by Sgt Archibald Winter DCM, 'Vin Baker waited his chance to hop over but unfortunately as he got to the top of the parapet he was hit in the back of the head by a machine gun bullet or a sniper. He fell back dead his haversack acting as a pillow for his head.'[16]

One of the fortunate members of 32 Btn who returned to their own lines was Pte K.A. Dunk. In keeping with Pte Dunk's actions in rescuing an officer, it is entirely fitting that one of the enduring images to come out of the events of 19–20 July is the recovery of wounded men from No Man's Land. This aspect of the battle has been recorded in the splendid sculpture by Peter Corlett entitled *Cobbers* which now stands in the Memorial Park at Fromelles. In Kenneth Dunk's case, the rescued soldier was Capt Frank Lloyd (32 Btn) who was wounded and left helpless in the German front line. His story was published in *The Register*, an Adelaide newspaper, on Wednesday, 10 January 1917. He was described by the newspaper's journalist as 'like a man who was dead and is alive again', an accurate assessment indeed.

According to the paper, 'of the battalion he led over the parapet, 250 men strong, all but 66 were either killed or wounded. Of six officers who left South Australia with him, four are dead'. It continued by saying that Capt Lloyd was hit by a bullet, though 'he never felt the hit, only a burning, stinging pain in the right breast. He dropped in a heap, unconscious, to be awakened some time later by the sharp hand of a piece of shrapnel, which caught him by the back and shook his whole body with piercing fingers'. Frank Lloyd was hit early in the attack and only became conscious again at dusk; his next recollection was when he was found by Pte H.J. Bampton, who was also wounded. Unable to move him alone, Bampton went to find a stretcher and another soldier to assist. It was a considerable time before they returned. On the way back to Lloyd, Bampton and the second soldier discovered David Low,[17] an Australian Rules football player with South Australian National Football League team West Torrens, and they took him back to a dressing station. The two soldiers then carried Capt Lloyd to safety, but by now the second rescuer had also been wounded.

In the 16 January edition of *The Register*, the second, unknown solder was identified. This man was Pte K.A. Dunk from Morgan, South Australia. Dunk had written home on a sheet torn from his notebook that had a hole through it where it had been struck by a piece of shrapnel. He also recorded that 'I am feeling OK except for the scratch I received in our charge – a bullet through my elbow'. The wound incurred by Kenneth Dunk was certainly played down, but he must have suffered badly as a consequence. He told his family that 'it (the bullet) hit like a ton of bricks, and knocked me from the top of their first line of parapets to the bottom'. He describes Lloyd as a 'poor fellow… had five bullets in him, and seemed nearly done. I have heard nothing of him since, but I suppose he had a chance of recovery'. These accounts appeared under the titles 'Stirring Story of the Thirty-Second' and 'The Other Hero'; one can only guess what effect this 'stirring story' might have had on recruitment for the AIF at this stage of the war.

The death of Gibbins and others in the final dash marked the end of the action, and once again No Man's Land parted the two adversaries. At 2p.m. it was agreed that the 5 Australian Division would pass back to the control of II Anzac Corps. In the air, 16 Squadron Royal Flying Corps made a final attempt to disrupt German movements by dropping four 112lb bombs on Fromelles and another four on Aubers.[18]

The engineers who had heroically dug the communication trench across No Man's Land now had another task to perform, though, namely to prevent the trench being of advantage to the enemy. Men of 14 Field Company – Cpl E.C. Banks, L/Cpl P.T. Griggs and Sprs T. Anderson, R.A. Shaw and F.H. Alta – went out under fire to block the trench, an act for which they were commended by Major Bachtold.

Although the British and Australians were now back in their own lines, the Germans had not totally regained possession of their territory. A few pockets of Australians held out either until they ran out of ammunition and were captured or until German troops put an end to resistance with bombs, bayonets and bullets. From the Australian lines, signals urgently requesting reinforcements could be seen, and occasionally a white flag was raised as the defenders realised that to resist further would bring certain, wasteful death. This closing-down process by the Germans was not quick, and they recorded at 9.20a.m. that 'the last Englishmen who were defending themselves have been captured'.

12

A Fearful Price

Throughout the battle the British and Australian front line areas had been a hive of activity as carrying parties transported stores to the front and beyond, the engineers made running repairs to the trenches, messengers dashed to and fro on their urgent missions and the wounded made their tormented way to dressing stations. The Australian line was in a rather different condition when the troops returned after dawn. According to Capt W.H. Zander, 'the Hun barrage had played havoc with our trenches – huge gaps yawned here and there, parapets in places were blown entirely in, fire bays completely wiped out and the whole place littered with dead and debris'.[1]

The dead lay wherever the force of bullet or shell threw them or had dropped where they stood. The chaplains, busy reassuring men before they went into action, now had the grim task of comforting the wounded and dying. One padre to come to attention was the Rev. Bennett (2/8 Warwicks), awarded the MC for his work during the battle, the first such award to the battalion on the Western Front.[2] Another was the Rev. Spencer Maxted,[3] a clergyman in New South Wales until the war came and he volunteered for service. He served at Gallipoli as a stretcher-bearer, was attached to the 14 Bde in Egypt, and participated in the ill-fated Sweetwater march. In France he declined the opportunity to remain in the rear areas, instead preferring not only to be on the front line but also to venture into No Man's Land to help bring in wounded troops. His luck ran out on the second day of the battle when he too was killed, and he now lies in Rue Petillon Military Cemetery. The death of Maxted was reported in the *Sydney Morning Herald* in September 1916:

> During the fight we unfortunately lost one of our chaplains – Capt Rev SE Maxted MA BD. Dog-tired with running for stretcher-bearers during a fierce cannonade, he turned aside for refuge and rest into a trench, and sitting down in the corner he immediately fell asleep. It was a front-line trench, and by and by a

high explosive landed on the parapet, a fragment killing him instantly. The loss is much mourned throughout the brigade.[4]

A huge effort was being made to evacuate the wounded. The 5 Australian Division Pioneer Battalion, for example, on 21 July provided forty men under Company Sergeant Major Gaylor for rescue work in No Man's Land, particularly in the 14 Bde sector. They found no wounded men but recovered two Lewis guns, a large number of rifles and various other items that were worth salvaging. In the course of this activity the battalion lost one man killed.[5]

Some troops were sent to the rear once their part in the assault had ended. Bert Bishop recorded, 'men all terribly knocked up and shaken; everybody had a peculiar ashen grey colour'.[6] Among those deeply affected by the state of the returning men was 'Pompey' Elliott. Two veterans, Tom Brain and Arthur Ebdon,[7] related stories of seeing their Brigadier-General in tears at the sight of survivors of the battle. A. W. Bazley, Bean's assistant, saw Elliott greeting his troops and wrote, 'no-one who was present will ever forget the picture of him, the tears streaming down his face, as he shook hands with the returning survivors'. Bert Bishop described his own state of exhaustion:

He felt dazed, stunned. He went into the orchard alongside the farm-house, went to a quiet corner, and threw himself down in the long soft grass. The sun shone bright and warm; birds hopped and twittered in the hawthorn hedges and among the apple and plum trees bees droned contentedly among the buttercups. But Solomon noticed none of these things. His brain felt stupid, he could not think clearly – could not realise all that had happened since yesterday. Was it only yesterday, he asked himself, that he was a happy carefree boy. A boy who had seen nothing, experienced nothing of the hard side of life, a boy who had seen nought of suffering – who had never looked on death? And was all that horror of the night real? All those dead men – those bloody mangled human creatures that lay everywhere – those broken, bleeding, living men who cursed or shrieked in their agony – was it real – or was he mad?[8]

Bishop already knew that his cousin Ray Bishop ('Roy' in his Soldier Solomon manuscript) was missing in action, and wrote of his fate in his next letter:

About daylight the word was given to retire to our own trenches again and it was then that Ray got hit. He and another chap volunteered to try to shift a party of German bombers near their gun who were giving a lot of trouble, and so give the gun a better chance of getting away. Each took a load of bombs and made for the Germans. Ray's mate was killed before he had gone three yards, Ray himself got hit but before he had got halfway. He fell and then crawled on his hands and knees a bit closer to the Germans and threw all his bombs into them. He then commenced to crawl back, but before he got far the Germans, who were now coming on in scores, cut him off. It was impossible for his mates to do anything for him, it was all they could do to get their gun back. I did not see this myself but the chaps on the same gun told me all about it afterwards. It was a splendid action and his mates reckon he deserved a V.C. for it. I suppose he'll be booked in the casualty lists as 'wounded and missing' which sounds pretty bad, but if the Germans do the right thing by him he ought to be all right.[9]

A sergeant informed Bishop that when the Germans were about to encircle them, their officer had asked for two volunteers to throw bombs and cover the withdrawal of the other men. Ray and another man stepped forward. They went forward bombing the enemy but the other man was hit and fell back; Ray continued despite being badly wounded. The sergeant helped him back into their position in the German trench but had to leave him, dying, as the enemy swarmed back to re-occupy their old position. It had been hoped that Ray was a prisoner of war but this was not the case.[10] A few days later Bert received news of his other cousin, Billy Bishop, 56 Btn, who had died of wounds in hospital in Epsom, Surrey. This was a high price for one family to pay; it was certainly not unique at Fromelles.

Cousins Chris King and Billy Outlaw had both perished in the battle, but some mixed reports regarding Pte King's fate were gathered subsequently including one submitted by 3442A Cpl W. Wallace in November 1917 in No. 4 Australian General Hospital, Randwick. He wrote:

Chris King was in my section. About the 19th July we went over at Fleurbaix. Just after we went over a shell burst and killed several men, King being one of those killed. We had to advance and I do not know where he was buried. King was a real white man, a good conscientious man, a general favourite.

Conversely, 2099 Pte Keeling (53 Btn) wrote from Ward 14/11 in the Northern War Hospital in Newcastle: 'King was slightly wounded in the head. He went back to hospital (with informant) but was only there four days. Informant thinks it very probable that he was kept back on base details, instead of being sent back to his old battalion as he was very young'. This Pte King was in fact another 'King' and not Billy Outlaw's cousin.

Outlaw's parents received the official telegram bearing the news of the loss of their son and a letter written on 11 August by Arthur Stegga from the VAD Hospital, Pinner, Middlesex. Stegga and Billy Outlaw had made a pact to write to one another's family after the battle. Stegga started: 'I must tell you about our little affair of the 19th & 20th July… No doubt you have heard from Billy by this. When we were together last we promised to write a few lines, whatever happened…' Stegga continued by telling the Outlaws that he had been transferred to the Intelligence Section at Brigade HQ but this had not prevented him seeing his chums just before the attack. He says that he 'wished them all sorts of luck… but you should imagine how I felt when they did not answer their names at the roll call'. Stegga also regretfully informed the Outlaw family:

> There was only a very few of his Battalion left, barely 50 men… I made enquiries about them and all I could get was Billy was out near the Huns lines wounded. I do not know how. Jimmy Martin had run against a machine gun. Jimmy Cavin was lying in a ditch wounded. And nothing about Chris or Jack Willis. But no doubt they are all here in England.

Arthur Stegga had himself been wounded by a shell but offered to make further enquiries on behalf of the King and Outlaw families. No record remains of subsequent correspondence and all that remains of King and Outlaw are names on the memorial at VC Corner.

After the battle many wounded men could be seen in No Man's Land, some having been out there since the very first waves went over. To recover them was bordering on suicidal and practice was that a truce with the enemy was strictly forbidden. As the final troops returned to their own lines any thought of a cease-fire to recover the wounded was inconceivable. German artillery was taking advantage of the congestion in the front area and was sending shell after shell into the crowded trenches. A counter-attack by the Bavarians was suspected but on balance was unlikely; they had expelled the British and Australians and had no need to launch their own assault. As a precaution General McCay ordered an artillery barrage to be brought down on the German frontal area. The German war correspondent W. Scheuermann of the *North German Gazette* commented in his lengthy newspaper report on the battle of this apparent waste of shells by the British. By late morning both sides had lost their appetite for killing and the battlefield fell silent.

Among the accounts of the battle, Elliott, on 20 July in a letter to his wife, was quite honest about the outcome:

> My brave boys have done all that men could do… but we paid a fearful price… We broke the German lines and captured a number of prisoners but were over-whelmed with machine gunfire and artillery. Poor Geoff McCrae is missing and reported killed… Sterling, a friend of Geordie's, was blown to pieces by a shell. He was wounded earlier in the day by a rifle bullet through his neck but had returned to lead his men… Bert Layh[11] is safe. He had a beastly experience. He dashed out and a huge shell burst and blew him into a deep 10 feet hole full of mud and water and half drowned…

H.R. Williams thought that 'the dead were saddening to look upon, but a worse sight were the wounded lying out in No Man's Land beyond our aid'. He too noted the attempt by an officer and NCO to obtain permission from a German officer to collect the wounded without being fired upon. The request was turned down,

> so we had to see our wounded lying there to suffer the torments of the damned. They called out unceasingly for help and water. The sun and flies persecuted them. Those of them who were able to crawl were sniped at by the Germans. One man almost in front of our bay crawled inch by inch towards us, drawing a badly wounded pal with him. He got within a few yards of our parapet when he was fired upon by a German sniper. The two of them took shelter in a shell-hole, and called to us for water. A bottle was filled and heaved over the parapet to them.[12]

In contrast to the Australian sector, in the line opposite the 61 Division, the Germans appear to have co-operated with the British; the 2/5 Gloucesters, one of the units given the task of clearing the dead and wounded, recorded in their history:

> The lot that fell to the Glosters was the depressing task of bringing in and burying the dead. This operation took three or four days to complete and it is notable that the Germans allowed the stretcher-bearers and others to wander about No Man's Land in broad daylight, picking up the dead and wounded, without firing a shot.[13]

Elsewhere in 61 Division's sector recovery of the wounded was also undertaken, though not without incident. Sgt Petty went out to recover Capt Ivor Stewart-Liberty of D Company, who had been so badly wounded in the leg that subsequently it was amputated, but the gallant sergeant lost his way in the dark and almost stumbled into the German lines. For his actions during the battle, Sgt Petty was awarded the Military Medal.

It was also the time for a few soldiers to attempt to recover wounded friends from No Man's Land. A number ran the risk of attracting the attention of German snipers or machine-gunners. The following day, 21 July, one of the Australians to do this was Pte W. Miles (29 Btn), who went in search of Capt Mortimer and in so doing came very close to the enemy wire. He was challenged by a German officer, who suggested that he should obtain an officer with whom he could make arrangements for collecting the wounded. On returning safety, Miles spoke to Major Murdoch (29 Btn) and a message was passed to Divisional HQ.

McCay, via Brig-Gen Tivey, heard the request from Murdoch but chose to stick rigidly to GHQ policy that 'no intercourse was to be allowed under any circumstances

nor could any flag of truce be entertained';[14] this decision was later endorsed by both
Monro and Haking. McCay's response was passed to Murdoch; he did not return to
the Germans and plans for a formal truce were abandoned. It is recorded, however,
that 'the Germans appeared to give our stretcher bearers a good chance of collecting
the wounded provided they did not expose themselves very prominently'.[15]

In correspondence between Bean and McCay in 1926, McCay is quite clear
that GHQ forbade any 'negotiations of any kind, and on any subject… with
the enemy'. He continued, 'some arrangement had been made, apparently at
first between a captain in my trenches and a German officer, for a temporary
"armistice" for picking up wounded. In view of the definiteness of GHQ orders…
orders were at once sent to put an end to the "truce", and this was done'.[16]

Murdoch wrote to Charles Bean in 1926[17] confirming that the report by Capt
Ellis, in connection with the history of 5 Australian Division, on Murdoch's
part in helping the wounded in No Man's Land was 'practically correct'. He
added, 'Private Miles and myself carried as many filled water bottles as possible,
distributing them to the wounded… which action was not resented by the
Germans'. Major Murdoch also gave details of 'the interview with German
officers which, he says, was not marked by anything of a hostile nature'. The
German officers with whom he communicated received a message from their
Divisional HQ stating that No Man's Land should be divided in two and that the
Germans and Australians would recover and evacuate the wounded from their
own half. Murdoch would be 'blindfolded and held hostage in their trenches
as a bond of good faith that the conditions stipulated would be carried out'.
He continued by saying that 5 Australian Divisional HQ 'would not agree to the
conditions laid down'. Finally, the intrepid Major Murdoch reported that he and
Pte Miles were in No Man's Land for about 20 minutes.

In subsequent correspondence, Bean asked Murdoch various other questions
about the detail of arranging this local truce. Confirmation is given that a board
bearing a red cross was waved from the Australian parapet in order to attract
the attention of the Germans, and that once this had been done Murdoch and
Miles ventured into No Man's Land distributing water bottles as they went, while
waiting for a response from the German Divisional HQ. The two Australians
did not enter the German trenches but spoke to them from the enemy wire
entanglements. Murdoch acknowledges 'how fortunate Miles and myself were
to return to our own trenches. When we were interviewing the Germans, who
fortunately were Saxons, a shot was fired from our lines. Possibly this did not have
any ill result, otherwise we would undoubtedly have had to pay the penalty'.

Opposite 8 Bde, on the German right, casualties among the Bavarians' 21 RIR
were so high that 104 Saxon Regiment was brought in to replace them. Bean
states that this occurred on 21 July,[18] and Major Murdoch, when negotiating an
informal truce on the same day, was sure that he was dealing with Saxons. The
Saxons had a reputation for being less anxious to wage war than some of their

countrymen, a trait that so nearly enabled Murdoch to obtain a truce for recovery of the wounded. Murdoch also asked Bean for his help in tracing a photograph taken by a German of himself and Miles in No Man's Land; no record remains of whether this was located.

A humanitarian response was not always the norm. On 23 July, in 15 Bde sector, a German soldier was reported to have left his trench and thrown a bomb at a wounded soldier, killing him.[19] This act may have been a mercy killing but the Australians construed it as murder and opened fire on the enemy soldier, forcing him to take cover in a shell hole for the rest of the day. Brig-Gen Elliott recorded this atrocity in a letter to his wife on 24 July:

> There was one poor fellow lying close to the German trenches. Our watchers saw a German come out and thought he was going to help this poor chap. But instead he deliberately put a bomb against him and blew him up. When they saw this our men opened a lot of fire on the German and he was unable to get back into his own parapet but hid in a shell hole until dark. I am afraid we did not get him though which is a great pity.

The lurid details of other accounts of treacherous behaviour may have matured each time the story was told. One incident recorded by Capt Zander mentions

> a Bosche officer... found wounded in the old Hun front line by a young Australian officer. The Hun made a gesture that he was wounded and unarmed and asked pitifully for water. The Australian officer unfastened his water bottle and slung it over to the Hun, keeping a little distance away from him. The Hun bent down to pick-up the water bottle which had fallen at his feet and as he did so he whipped out a revolver and fired point blank at his would-be benefactor. Luckily the shot missed but not so the Australian officer's one.

Raymond Page, 14 Field Coy, also witnessed the difficulty of evacuation of the wounded, and stated that 'the Germans showed no mercy to those attempting to recover them. The wounded lay for days where they had fallen and their cries for help and for water were pitiful to hear. Some of the wounded crawled back at night'. Sgt Page's account indicates that their experience at Fromelles changed their attitude to the Germans.[20] Many years later he told his son that the Germans were seen to shoot wounded Australians, and that some 5 Division men claimed that from then on they did not take prisoners. This absence of mercy no doubt existed on occasions and frankly is only to be expected in the heat of battle.

Even 'Pompey' Elliott wrote home about German sniping at the wounded. On 20 July he informed his wife, 'I think over 2000 of my own Brigade alone are killed, wounded or missing and very, very many of these will be killed as the Germans fired at them as they lay all night and all day...'. Elliott also commented:

> We are going to send out rescue parties tonight. It has been impossible during the day to get men out as the Germans have been shelling us badly but there is one officer we must try to get in. Poor Liddelow who came with me from the old 7th is out there badly wounded and we must get him if at all possible...

Elliott was very loyal to those officers he brought from 7 Btn, but New Zealand-born Capt Aubrey Liddelow was never recovered and is now commemorated at VC Corner.

Downing wrote about an alleged misunderstanding when the Australians were at fault:

> A noble act here lights up the murky record of the German army. Two gallant enemies carried a wounded Australian to our parapet, stood at the salute, then turned and walked away. They unfortunately neglected to secure a safe conduct, and were shot, to the sincere regret of every Australian there, by someone in the next bay, who, owing to the shape of the line and the direction they had come were in ignorance of their errand.[21]

Although no formal truce was permitted, decisions were taken, for a while at least, to stop belligerent action. The Australian centre artillery group, for example, was told on 21 July not to fire 'as everything was quiet';[22] this may have been tacit approval of the efforts to recover wounded men which, with a similar stance by the Germans, thus created an informal truce. Curiously, the writer of the Australian Commander Royal Artillery's war diary, in recording the gunners' inactivity on 21 July, thought that some deal existed between the two warring sides, as he notes, 'parties were sent out to No Man's Land to collect wounded. For this purpose a partial truce existed and our wounded were collected without molestation...' A contrary view is recorded by Capt Knyvett, 57 Btn, who noted that 'I have found the Bavarian even worse than the Prussian, and this day, and the next, and again did they sweep No Man's Land with machine guns and shrapnel, so as to kill the wounded'.[23]

3101 Sgt S. Fraser, 57 Btn, the soldier depicted carrying a wounded man in the *Cobbers* statue at the Memorial Park near VC Corner, sent a letter home describing his experience of recovery of the wounded:[24]

France
July 31st 1916

Dear Donald, Peter and all at 'Brisbane Hill', 'Airde' and 'Waroona',
    Just a sheet to you all to let you know I have been through the mill and came

out without a mark, except for scratched hands through cutting and putting up wire entanglements.

Our battalion did not hop over with the divisional stunt, fortunately for us it did not come off the day intended though we were ready.

I had been sent by Capt Cameron with a party for two nights to get the barbed wire ready. We were supporting when the charge was made… the battalions who weren't over met with too hot a reception and suffered severely; the distance was too far. When we came up… we did a 200 yard sprint across the open… for the next three days we did great work getting in the wounded from the front and I must say Fritz treated us very fairly though a few were shot at their work. Some of the wounded were as game as lions and got rather roughly handled but haste was more necessary than gentle handling and we must have brought in over 250 men by our company alone. It was not light work getting in with a heavy weight on your back especially if he had a broken leg or arm and no stretcher bearer was handy you had to lie down and get him on your back then rise and duck for your life with the chance of getting a bullet in you before you were safe. One foggy morning in particular I remember, we could hear someone, over towards the German entanglements calling for a stretcher bearer; it was an appeal no man could stand against; so some of us pushed out and had a hunt; we found a fine haul of wounded and brought them in, but it was not where I heard this fellow calling so I had another shot for it and came across a splendid specimen of humanity trying to wriggle into a trench with a big wound in his thigh; he was about 14 stone weight and I could not lift him on my back, but I managed to get him into an old trench and told him to lie quiet while I get a stretcher then another man about 30 yards out sang out 'don't forget me cobber'. I went in and got four volunteers with stretchers and we got both men to safety.

Next morning at daylight… I saw two figures in their shirts and no hats, running about halfway between our lines and the Germans: they were our Captains Cameron and Marshall (VC) hunting for more wounded. Capt Marshall got his VC on the Peninsula and if Cameron does not get his here, well he dammed well deserves it.[25]

McCay had a duty to follow the orders of his commanders but he was running the risk of being branded as uncaring for his men, and indeed this decision was to contribute to his nickname 'Butcher' McCay during and after the war. Certainly public feeling at home was going through troubled times, as the longest casualty lists since the early days of the Dardanelles campaign had been published in Australian newspapers. Had the attack been a success, a relaxation of the truce policy may have been more readily given, but under these circumstances a propaganda victory may have been claimed by the Germans in addition to their military achievement.

Nightfall did not stop the search for more stranded soldiers; under the cover of darkness large numbers of soldiers were organised with the specific purpose of continuing this work. In 15 Bde sector it was reported that about 300 wounded soldiers were brought in. Certainly this work continued for another three days and a few casualties were incurred doing this task. How long men survived in No Man's Land is difficult to say; one account refers to a soldier coming in after nine days, and the diary of Major C.A. Denehy records that on 30 July two men of 14 Bde came in having been in No Man's Land since the first day of the attack. Downing reports that 'a few crawled in three weeks later, with shattered limbs and maggoty wounds'.[26] This claim sounds exaggerated bearing in mind the risk of gangrene and the absence of an adequate water supply. His comment that 'some of the wounded were never found' is certainly true; others were eventually located after the Armistice when the Germans pulled back from Fromelles, some by the village priest M. Dahiez during his period in the area from 1919–1922.

Many men had received a coveted 'Blighty' wound, though hopefully not so serious as to be life threatening. Williams's account mentions a group of his friends who now had experienced their first and last fight on the Western Front. 'My pal Fred', wrote Williams, 'was a walking wounded case, hit in the back by shrapnel. He paused to say a few words to me… he went out, never to return to France. Shortly afterwards Alfie came, with his hand and knee bandaged… he did not stop to speak as he went past… he also went back to Australia.'[27]

Those troops returning to billets reported for a roll call. In 61 Division sector a record remains of one parade held in Estaires where the full extent of a battalion's losses became clearer. Major Christie-Miller, 2/1 Bucks, wrote:

> It was one of the saddest I have ever attended. B Coy were a fair sized Coy, C Coy had two fair sized platoons and the rest of the Battalion was represented by a handful of men and practically without NCO. Of all the officers practically all those with experience including all four Company Commanders had gone and except for B Coy those present were the new ones who had just joined.[28]

A similar situation occurred when 29 Btn relieved 30 Btn on the evening of 20 July, and 30 Btn troops moved back to the Croix Blanche crossroads where 'a roll call was taken. Some platoons were platoons in name only having but 2 or 3 men left out of the 40–50 that had started out…'[29] Likewise, Col J.W. Clark, 30 Btn, writing in *Mufti* twenty years later, stated that he 'can still visualise to-day our roll call near the road junction of Croix Blanche. The greatest shock of my life was the heartbreaking feeling I had lost so many fine men from a battalion I had watched grow from a motley mob into an efficient unit…'[30]

As far as Haking was concerned, the battle was largely concluded by 2p.m. on 20 July when the 5 Australian Division returned to the command of II Anzac Corps. An hour later, his advanced Corps HQ at Sailly closed down.

13

Casualties

As a measure of Australian commitment to the war, 416,809 men and women enlisted of whom 331,916 embarked for overseas service. They paid a high price: 60,278 were killed, 82,136 were wounded and a further 87,957 suffered sickness or other injury; 936 died before they left the shores of Australia. Among the wounded, one man was recorded as having been wounded seven times, ten men on six occasions, 105 on five, 807 sustained four wounds and 5,582 three times. A sizeable proportion these casualties resulted from the Fromelles fiasco.[1]

For the Australians, it was to be the AIF's first experience of the evacuation of wounded from a major operation in France and Flanders. The official history of the Australian medical services describes the battle of Fromelles as 'typical of the kind of warfare in vogue at this period'. It goes on to say how this relatively low-key assault became 'a most serious and tragic affair… of sufficient significance to call for a special chapter'.[2]

In II Anzac Corps, casualties from sniping, machine guns and shelling averaged just under one hundred a week, though a single incident such as the shelling by a battery of enemy 5.9-inch howitzers of 9 Btn billets near Rouge de Bout on 20 April accounted for twenty-five dead and forty-nine wounded including the battalion medical officer.[3] Total Australian casualties[4] on the Western Front up to 30 June 1916 were 2,406 battle casualties, of which the highest proportion were 'wounded in action', and 5,575 non-battle casualties of which 5,437 were classified as 'sick'. Haking's scheme for the Aubers area was destined to make these figures appear minor when the end of July position was calculated.

Overall responsibility for the care and evacuation of wounded men during the assault on the German lines in the Fromelles sector rested with the Director of Medical Services of the Second Army. On 15 July typical arrangements in hand included transferring medical materials from the stores at Hazebrouck to locations nearer the battle zone. A delivery of 12,000 first aid dressings, 3,000 shell dressings and 400 stretchers is typical of the items provided. Plans were compiled for the evacuation routes[5] and a new main dressing station had to be found. This was located at Bac St. Maur in a factory partly occupied by the artillery (at map reference G18.b.8.5). By arrangement with the gunners' CO, Col Kershaw, the machinery rooms were obtained for use by medical staff and it was estimated that accommodation was available for 2,000 patients. Finding premises was not the end of the problem; as no water was on site, water carts and 10-gallon tubs were provided. Both 14 and 15 Field Ambulance were ordered to staff the dressing station by reducing their complement at L'Estrade Le Nouveau Monde Doulieu, whilst the ADMS, New Zealand Division, took over the Advanced Dressing Station at Bois Grenier. Any sick or wounded men were sent back to No. 2 Australian CCS at Estaires. By 18 July, 544 stretchers were available at Bac St. Maur, with another two hundred in transit. Less than twenty-four hours later, at 12.30p.m. on 19 July, the first casualties arrived – one officer and eleven other ranks.

Similar arrangements were specified by the 61 Division in 'Medical Arrangements XI Corps, Operations Order No. 6',[6] dated 16 July. This included requirements for 'the Regimental Aid Post at Red House, Hougomont and Winchester House to receive supplementary supplies of dressings and the regimental bearers be reinforced by bearers from Divisional Field Ambulances, those to Red House and Hougomont by ADMS, 61st Division and those to Winchester House by ADMS 31st Division'. Evacuation from the front lines would be via tramways and the communication trenches known as Great North Road and Strand. The Advanced Dressing Station at Laventie was expanded by the pitching of tents and utilisation of the barn opposite in order to accommodate 150. The Main Dressing Stations would be No. 2/1 (S.M.) Field Ambulance and No. 2/3 (S.M.) Field Ambulance in La Gorgue, supplemented by the use of the gymnasium or recreation room there for the reception of walking and other lightly wounded cases. Evacuation from the Main Dressing Stations would be done by No. 2 Motor Ambulance Convoy and, if needed, 31 Division would hold No. 94 Field Ambulance in readiness to act as a reserve or furnish reinforcements.

The arrangements made in 61 Division sector would bring their wounded to two Main Dressing Stations at La Gorgue run by 1 Field Ambulance (at L.34. b.6.2) and by 3 FA (at L.35.b.9.9). Also located at La Gorgue was the divisional theatre, which was to be used as a holding area for sitting and walking cases and to be staffed by 3 FA. An Advanced Dressing Station was at Laventie (C.34. c.6.3) where accommodation would include a barn requisitioned for the purpose as well as the goods shed at Laventie railway station; these would be used, in particular, for walking and slightly wounded cases. Col James Young, ADMS 61 Division, also strengthened the medical arrangements by use of personnel from 31 Division which had been pulled out of the line and which would not be participating in the battle.[7]

The 8 Field Ambulance Operation Order No. 1, dated 18 July, laid down the framework for that unit's participation on the care and evacuation of the wounded. At certain points stretcher parties were maintained not only for work in the immediate vicinity but also to maintain contact with artillery units in case they too sustained casualties. Walking cases were to be sent to a single collecting point from where they would be redirected to a location further back. Signs would be placed along routes to be used to direct ambulances, stretcher bearers and the walking wounded.

This order optimistically stated that 'care will be exercised that M.O.'s, bearers and ambulance drivers are not overworked to the exhaustion point as trained men will be hard to replace'. A further judgement is called for stating 'sufficient supplies of stretchers, dressings, anti-tetanic serum, iodine, ammonia ampoules, oxygen, for all emergencies will be maintained at all posts held by the Unit'. To facilitate the decision of what is 'sufficient', this order wisely records, in paragraph 11, that 'preparation will be made for heavy casualties'.

In the Australian sector for example, Regimental Aid Posts (RAP) had been established; these were at Pinney's Avenue (58 Btn) and Cellar Farm Avenue (57 Btn). From there, casualties were sent back via Advanced Dressing Stations (ADS) at Rouge de Bout, halfway to Sailly-sur-la-Lys, and Croix Blanche, to the rear of Cellar Farm Avenue, and then on to the 8 Field Ambulance main dressing station at Fort Rompu by the Lys. During the attack the battlefield within the Australian sector was to be treated as being in two parts, Fort Rompu being the focus for the left half and an additional main dressing station at Bac St. Maur.

In the days leading up to the assault, casualties were incurred; Pte L.W. Colley-Priest MM, serving with 8 Australian Field Ambulance, later wrote, in respect of the events of 15 July, that 'a great number of patients arrived… we were just beginning to realise what war meant'.[8] During the period immediately before the attack, more casualties were treated as German shelling increased; Pte Colley-Priest described the severe shelling as 'rather a trying time'.[9] Around midnight a small batch of prisoners came through but at 2a.m. orders came for every available man in the unit to move forward to the front line. Colley-Priest later wrote:

> It was rather a long march, about five miles. The sky was lit up with flares and coloured lights and the roar of the artillery and machine guns was terrific. On arrival at the Regimental Aid Post we found a terrible congestion of wounded. The sight was ghastly… we set to work immediately to get them to a place of safety. Luckily the loading post was only ¾ mile away.[10]

The evacuation through the trenches was immensely difficult. As they fought their way through debris and bodies, often under fire,

> Dead Australians were piled up four and five deep… the sap was so narrow… that it was a hard job carrying a stretcher. At some points the stretcher had to be carried over our heads. It took two hours to carry out of the trenches and

on arriving at the Aid Post the congestion seemed to be worse in spite of all the extra men working. [11]

Dressing stations coped well during the evening of 19 July, but the war diary of 8 Australian Field Ambulance includes copies of messages that illustrate how this situation changed during the night. [12] Communications proved to be a problem during the battle, Col C.H.W. Hardy describing them as 'weak and irregular', and one of the more reliable methods for keeping appraised of the situation was for the DADMS of the 5 Australian Division to ride around from one medical post to another on a motorcycle to gather first-hand reports for Col Hardy. [13] A typical telegram from 8 Bde HQ sent just before midnight states, 'Medical Officers asking for 100 men to take away 150 wounded and all dressing stations full in addition and can you assist'.

Col Hardy noted after the battle that 'all wounds were treated, all bleeding stopped and where necessary vessels tied and amputations or operation done. All cases were injected with anti-tetanic serum and all fractures properly set. It was found quicker and more satisfactory to dress with dressings cut at the time to suit the case than to use first aid dressings'. [14]

Cover of darkness could not guarantee greater protection for the wounded. During a spell when the German guns fired incendiary shells into the melee,

One poor wretch who had his arm blown off by a shell was crawling painfully across No Man's Land when one shell splattered him with its burning contents. He was seen to be frantically trying to smother the flames eating into his flesh… his screams could be heard for a second or two – then silence. We passed his body the next morning, one side cruelly charred and burnt. [15]

Shortly after 7a.m. on 20 July it became apparent at 5 Division HQ that although those men reaching dressing stations were being processed adequately, there was another serious problem in the front line occupied by 15 Bde similar to that in 8 Bde's sector in the La Cordonnerie area. Large numbers of men were still in the front line area awaiting evacuation, and the 15 Bde were fearful of the medical arrangements matching the infantry debacle of the previous hours. The CO of 14 Field Ambulance, Col Tebbutt, had himself visited the front line area and could personally confirm that wounded soldiers were not being cleared from the front trench or the battlefield itself, due to a shortage of infantry to evacuate the wounded and the inevitable state of exhaustion of stretcher-bearers. Furthermore, communication trenches were obstructed by men, materials and enemy shell damage. Throughout the action stretcher-bearers went forward to collect casualties, but many were not seen again.

Withdrawal of the wounded from the front area continued well into the morning of 20 July, while all dugouts and other places that might contain wounded men were checked and cleared by 10a.m. The workload at the advanced dressing stations did not ease until 21 July, when a 'normal' situation again prevailed in the frontal areas.

Various graphs were drawn after the battle to illustrate the numbers of casualties, types of wound and so on, but the expectation before the assault that high casualties would occur was proven without the need for statistical tables. During the Great War the proportion of 'wounded' and 'died of wounds' to 'killed' in the AIF was about four to one; in the 15 Bde at Fromelles it was less than one and a half to one.

The table contained in Col Butler's account[16] differs somewhat from the corps diary.[17] Butler quotes the following figures for the period noon on the 19 July to 8p.m. on 21 July:

	Killed in action	Died of wounds	Prisoners of war	Wounded in action	Total
8 Inf Bde	477	51	166	1,086	1,780
14 Inf Bde	438	58	283	948	1,727
15 Inf Bde	726	98	5	904	1,733
Other units	60	9	16	208	293
Totals	1,701	216	470	3,146	5,533

A different table is provided in the war diary of the ADMS, 5 Australian Division, who noted that 'on the night of 20/21 wounded recovered from No Man's Land. Next couple of days still busy preparing returns.' On 26 July the diary provides the following details:[18]

	Officers	Other ranks	Total
Died	30	476	506
Missing	45	1,655	1,700
Wounded	102	3,224	3,326
Totals	177	5,355	5,632

Categories of wounded passing through main dressing stations also helps to give a measure of the workload handled:

	Walking	Sitting	Lying Down	Total
8 Field Ambulance	17	211	358	586
14 Field Ambulance	453	324	637	1,414
15 Field Ambulance	347	373	557	1,277
Totals	817	908	1,552	3,277

Additionally, a record of the site of wounds is also available. If a comparison with the 61 Division existed (some 934 casualties passed through the latter's dressing stations), it would be a point of interest to see their figure for head and neck injuries, bearing in mind that many of the Australians had not yet been issued with steel helmets. Butler's list, and one compiled by Lt Col Horne in respect of his 15 Field Ambulance, read:

	Butler's list	Horne's list	
	%	Numbers	%
Upper limb	31.79	424	25
Lower limb	31.00	496	30
Head and Neck	16.67	328	19
Thorax	7.93	–	–
Abdomen	4.27	48	3
Back	2.22	91	5
Shell Shock	6.12	121	7
Shoulders	–	99	6
Chest	–	70	4
Total	100.00	1,669	–

Even after the war, debate on the medical aspects of Fromelles continued. In 1919 Lt Col Charles MacLaurin wrote about the wounded: 'in early morning we noticed a change in the spirits of the incoming men. They became dull and apathetic, they would not talk; not a word could we get out of them as to how the day was going'.[19] Their fatigue and disappointment at not subduing the enemy showed, but, as MacLaurin notes, as 'most of the wounds were in the right arm or leg or back, and we could infer that our boys were being enfiladed', they had been right in the thick of the fight. This changed as 'further, so many wounds were of such a trifling nature that it was obvious that they were being tried too severely for raw troops'. Later remarks by other commentators, about 'half-trained, half-disciplined' troops, appears to be a valid comment; their valour, though, generally could not be doubted.

In his appraisal of the medical arrangements instituted for 61 Division, the ADMS made an entry that contrasts vividly with the records left of the situation that had to be managed by his Australian counterparts. The war diary records:

All the arrangements worked perfectly and without a single hitch. At no period was the accommodation strained and the evacuation from the Main Dressing Stations and the Divisional Collecting Station, where the slighter cases were dealt with, was most effectively carried out by the No. 2 Motor Ambulance Convoy and No. 13 Motor Ambulance Convoy respectively. By nine a.m. on the 20th, I was able to report that the whole of the trenches were clear of the wounded. The total number of wounded dealt with was 977 including 46 officers.

In the light of this summary, it has to be asked, in the absence of any information, whether 61 Division could have provided more assistance to the Australians in their hours of dire need.[20] Overall the Surgeon General, DMS Maj-Gen W.W. Pike CMG DSO, was satisfied with the conduct of the medical services;[21] however, despite their valiant work, for many soldiers this would be the beginning of years of physical or mental hardship.

Immense numbers of casualties were incurred by the 5 Australian Division during the battle, and rather fewer by the 61 Division, but relatively light numbers (1,500) of Bavarians were killed, wounded or taken prisoner. GHQ General Staff recorded a more optimistic outcome, noting that 'about 45 prisoners taken near Fauquissart' and then 'total prisoners taken 120–130 of which 103 unwounded. Our casualties estimated at 61st Division 57 officers, 1,300 o/r. Australians 3,500 all ranks but latter figure very rough as no reliable details yet available. So far as can be ascertained German losses must be severe.'[22]

It is difficult to come to an accurate figure for the casualties for this battle as there are a large number of tables given in various war diaries. Official figures are given as 1,404 for the 61 Division[23] and 5,533 for the Australians. Another early calculation for the 61 Division stated that 1,547 men had been lost from its fighting strength killed, wounded, missing or believed to have been captured. A table for the 5 Australian Division shows:[24]

	Officers	Other Ranks
Killed	7	144
Wounded	65	955
Missing	27	1,845
Unclassified	63	1,969
Total	162	5,363

The unclassified figures refer to the 14 Bde and had not been sorted at the time the corps diary was compiled. By mid-August the First Army revised statistics for 19–20 July showed a total of 231 officer and 6,767 other rank casualties.[25]

Many unit diaries give a summary of casualties, but these cannot be taken as definitive totals since 'missing' troops would have turned up and others confirmed as killed. The matter of men who were 'missing' complicated records of casualties; at some stage the unit had to draw a line in accounting for and recording casualties. An example of this can be found in a report on 5 Australian Division casualties from 13 to 16 July that records '72 missing'.[26] This figure subsequently dropped when twenty were established as 'killed' and a further forty-three were 'wounded'.

'Pompey' Elliott's notes on the battle contained his own version of the units' strengths before and after the attack:

	19 July			20 July			Change
	Officers	O/R	Total	Officers	O/R	Total	
15 Bde HQ	5	19	24	5	19	24	0
15 MG Coy	8	134	145	6	94	100	−45
15 ALTM	4	43	47	4	38	42	−5
57 Btn	27	861	888	26	851	877	−11
58 Btn	25	759	784	13	366	379	−405
59 Btn	28	912	940	8	120	128	−812
60 Btn	23	891	914	6	100	106	−808
Total	120	3,622	3,742	68	1,588	1,656	−2,086

However, it is the staggering 5,533 officers and men in McCay's division that had been lost (killed, wounded, missing and POW) that takes the headlines. The comment by Pte Jim Cleworth (29 Btn) – 'You are entitled to your opinion but we called him Bloody McCay and Bloody McCay he'll stay'[27] – is understandable. Inevitably, of the assaulting battalions those on the flanks incurred the most casualties, demonstrated in these early figures from war diaries:

Unit	Officers	Other ranks
29 Btn	7	209
30 Btn	9	343
31 Btn	16	528
32 Btn	17	701
53 Btn	24	601
54 Btn	19	521
55 Btn	11	330
56 Btn	2	149
57 Btn	2	33
58 Btn	11	237
59 Btn	20	675
60 Btn	16	741
Total	154	5,067

Scrutiny of CWGC records indicate the following numbers of fatal casualties (excluding 8 in the 60 Bde plus 25 New Zealand troops supporting the attack on the left of the Australians) though it is very likely that some who died of wounds have not been identified:

61 (South Midland) Division			5 Australian Division		
	Officers	Other Ranks		Officers	Other Ranks
Artillery units	4	16	Artillery units	2	12
2/6 Gloucesters	7	81	29 Btn	2	59
2/4 Royal Berks	4	38	30 Btn	3	115

2/4 OBLI	0	14	31 Btn	5	151
2/4 Gloucesters	2	34	32 Btn	7	217
2/5 Gloucesters	1	4	53 Btn	13	227
2/1 Bucks	7	131	54 Btn	6	163
2/5 R Warwicks	0	1	55 Btn	2	77
2/6 R Warwicks	6	102	56 Btn	1	39
2/7 R Warwicks	3	94	57 Btn	1	24
2/7 Worcesters	0	2	58 Btn	6	136
2/8 Worcesters	0	6	59 Btn	8	321
1/5 DCLI	1	5	60 Btn	9	380
182 MGC	0	5	Signals	0	2
183 MGC	0	4	Engineers	2	20
			MGC	4	41
			Pioneers	0	2
Total	35	537		71	1,986

In 53 Btn, Major O.M. Croshaw commented on the 'almost entire annihilation of clerical staff… and the fact that I have not even an officer to act as Adjutant'.[28] George Rankin recalled this battalion's roll call; the losses were so great that 'it was a sad time… it hit me pretty hard'.[29] As an indication of how long a wounded soldier might be away from his unit, it is noted[30] that on 3 September, when General Plumer presented medal ribbons at the 5 Division Bombing School, several officers and men wounded in the action at Fromelles were still absent through wounds.

On 22 July, Maj-Gen Mackenzie inspected 2/1 Bucks. On paper, the strength of the battalion was 19 officers and 545 other ranks; the actual muster was rather different. 'B' was a fair sized company, 'C' was represented by two platoons of medium strength, but the rest of the battalion produced 'a mere handful of men and practically no NCOs'.[31] As Major H.L.C. Barrett and Capt H.S.G. Buckmaster had just been invalided to England, the battalion had now lost the last of its four company commanders.

German losses are difficult to state with any accuracy, but did not amount to any more than 1,500. Their unit opposite the 61 Division, the 17 Reserve Infantry

Regiment, lost 269 men, and the 21 Reserve Infantry Regiment incurred 775 casualties; 468 burials can be readily identified in the Fromelles area. There were 140 prisoners taken, forty or so by the 61 Division and the remainder by the Australians. Conversely, the AIF had 400 men taken prisoner and the British a further eighty, of whom around sixty were 2/7 Warwicks. One report[32] submitted by 2/7 Warwicks evaluates German casualties. The report states that the CO estimated at least 200 Germans were killed, the remains of the German trenches were strewn with dead, a good many dug-outs were blown in and Germans were seen crawling out; the assumption was that a good number were buried. The Adjutant believed that altogether the German dead on the 2/7 Warwicks front totalled 400.

It is unclear what animal casualties were incurred in the battle; the war diary maintained by the Assistant Director Veterinary Services shows a wastage, within the 5 Australian Division, of 52 animals during week ending 20 July,[33] whilst the scant records of that Division's Mobile Veterinary Section indicate that twelve mules and horses were evacuated to hospital on 20 July and a further twenty-eight on 24 July.[34]

Soon after its arrival in France the 5 Australian Division issued routine orders concerning the matter of the burial of the dead and the marking of their graves. Order 1601 dated 30 May 1916, 'Prohibition of Permanent Memorials over Soldiers' Graves',[35] forbade the erection of permanent memorials, stone crosses and monuments during the continuance of hostilities on graves in British Military Cemeteries, communal cemeteries, churchyards or on isolated graves in France or Belgium. The presence on the Western Front of a number of these memorials, some of which were erected during the war, suggests that a common policy was not enforced rigidly by all five Armies in France and Flanders.

The Adjutant-General also issued instructions to Chaplains on the location and registration of graves:

> Bodies will be collected by the burying parties, the identification discs will be removed after the particulars have been noted on a label supplied for the purpose and this label will be securely attached to the body. The Chaplains or others conducting the funeral services will make a careful note of the names of those whom they bury in communal graves. Each grave will be marked by a piece of wood or anything suitable and on this will be written the Chaplain's initials and a number. He will thus have a tally. Details would then be passed to Graves Registration Unit No. 1 Bailleul with a list of the men buried in the said grave.

New burial grounds were prepared, and the cemeteries to be used by 5 Australian Division were to be Estaires Communal Cemetery, Sailly-sur-la-Lys, (Anzac and Canadian) Laventie, Rue du Bois, Rue Petillon, Rue David, Y Farm, Brewery

Orchard, Ration Farm, Erquinghem Communal Cemetery and Croix du Bac. The effects of the deceased and missing troops were to be sent to Messrs Cox & Co's Shipping Agency at 16 Charing Cross Road, London, whilst the property of the sick and wounded was to go to Boulogne where it would be kept for ten days and if not claimed sent to AIF Administration HQ at 130 Horseferry Road, Westminster, London.[36] The dead are buried or commemorated in at least eighty-two cemeteries or memorials in Western Europe from Berlin to Flanders and on to Scotland.

A tour today around the former German-held areas reveals many burials from 19–20 July. Not all date from the immediate aftermath of the battle. At Aubers Ridge British Cemetery, for example, a plot was created after the war for both divisions involved in the action, along with further plots for the dead recovered elsewhere on the battlefield. Other graves can be found near German hospitals, and yet more cemeteries – such as Lille Southern and a number in Germany – contain prisoners who died of wounds or other causes. The Germans created several mass graves. One at Fournes was exhumed by the Imperial War Graves Commission in June 1920 and re-interred at Cabaret Rouge. Only one, from a machine gun company, was identified and another was believed to be an officer of the Royal Warwickshire Regiment. In July 1923 a unit returned to exhume a further 176 burials which had various dates of death including one plot entitled 'large trench grave No. 1.M.4.3' which contained 51 British soldiers buried between 23–25 July 1916. Initially only five names were listed (three 2/7 Warwicks and two from a machine gun company) but subsequently a disc was found on another (3501 Pte P. Gearing 53 Btn).

Contemporary photographs also show piles of dead soldiers on German trench railway wagons. Some were transported to Fournes but the whereabouts of the remainder is a mystery. In aerial photographs, two large pits which probably contain burials have also been identified on the southern edge of Pheasant Wood some 500 yards north-east of Fromelles church.

Reinforcements who were rushed forward to strengthen the depleted battalions did not necessarily escape becoming a casualty for long. Pte George Eamens was one such example, arriving with 53 Btn on 25 July. A few days later the battalion war diary records that 'Private Eamens killed on working party in trenches'. He had been in France for thirty-seven days and with his battalion in the so-called nursery sector around Bois Grenier and Fleurbaix for ten days.

One fact above all puts the Fromelles casualties into perspective. The Australians incurred the highest casualties by any division in the Great War in one day apart from 34 Division at La Boisselle on 1 July 1916, the opening day of the Somme offensive.

14

Captivity

Whilst so many troops had trained for battle but had been killed going into action, there was another group whose service in the front line was also concluded but for whom a different battle for survival lay ahead. These men were the prisoners of war.

It is estimated that about 3,800 Australians were taken prisoner on the Western Front (during the Great War 170,000 British POWs were taken), and Fromelles accounted for 496 of whom thirty-eight died of wounds. This figure would be surpassed only by the number captured at Bullecourt (1,170) in 1917; the fighting at Pozières accounted for an estimated 500 but this was in a period from 14 July to 4 September 1916. As a proportion of those fighting, Fromelles represents about four per cent, whereas Bullecourt amounts to a staggering fifteen per cent.

In the case of POWs taken at Fromelles, the route to Germany started with a trudge up to the top of Aubers Ridge before being marched back to Fournes or another nearby town and thence to the Citadel in Lille, known to the British as Fort MacDonald. A cursory look at the numbers of POWs per battalion represents a spread of POWs by brigade to be expected from the course of this battle. The 8 Bde, on the left, lost 186 men including ninety in 32 Btn alone. In the centre, 14 Bde had 299 men taken prisoner; 54 and 55 Btns bore the brunt, losing 118 and 103 men respectively. The encircling movements by the enemy and the hazardous fight to regain the Australian front line accounted for a large proportion of these troops. In stark contrast, 15 Bde lost seven soldiers as POWs, probably all of them wounded troops recovered by the enemy. The breakdown by battalion shows the following figures:

8 Bde		14 Bde		15 Bde	
29 Btn	36	53 Btn	67	57 Btn	2
30 Btn	17	54 Btn	118	58 Btn	4

31 Btn	37	55 Btn	103	59 Btn	1
32 Btn	90	56 Btn	1	60 Btn	0
8 MGC	6	14 MGC	9		
		14 Field Coy	1		
Total	186	Total	299	Total	7

Statements by POWs taken at Fromelles[1] reveal accounts of traumatic times as they fell into enemy hands. Some accounts provide information on their part in the advance and fighting in the German trenches, and several give a summary of the construction or other features of the enemy defences. Most contain information of the critical moment of capture, but there appears to be a distinction between 'surrender' and 'capture'; in all cases, the authors of these documents are keen to make it clear that they had not allowed themselves to fall into enemy hands either without a fight or without being in a situation where surrender was the only option.

Other unpublished stories exist, including a reference to two brothers in 29 Btn who were both captured during the battle. It was during the fighting withdrawal that Walter Antrobus was overwhelmed by the Germans and was compelled to surrender along with 1321 Sgt O.S. Cole. His brother, Aubrey, was not with him but he too fell into enemy hands when he became stuck in a deep, muddy ditch. Aubrey was in hospital in Douai for a week after capture and was reunited with Walter in Lille.

Having two Antrobus brothers as prisoners caused confusion in the POW Department of the Australian Red Cross in London. There the indefatigable Miss Mary Chomley, who later worked with Capt Charles Mills to improve provision of parcels and other comforts for prisoners of war in Germany and who, like Mills, received an OBE for this work, did not realise that there were two soldiers of the same name and had been sending just one parcel; this was soon rectified. There were other brothers captured in the battle including Ptes R.V. and S.A. Purdon, Ptes A.I. and A.J. Seymour, Ptes F. and W.R. Smith, Ptes A.V. and H.D. Bolder (all 55 Btn) and Ptes G.H. and G.M. Featherstone (32 Btn).

4748 Pte Herbert Carter, 54 Btn, was another soldier who trained for nearly a year but experienced just a few hours in action until he was captured by the Germans during the early hours of 20 July. Carter was eventually sent to Friedrichsfeld camp in the Rhineland, and a group photo, which included Herbert Carter, was published in the *Sydney Mail* of 25 July 1917. Subsequently he was interned at Dulmen, Westphalia, and was repatriated to England where he arrived on 17 December 1918. His health was badly affected, and his medical report states that he was 'badly starved'[2] and that he was suffering from 'effort syndrome', presumably a euphemism for 'overworked and underfed'. Late he embarked on the *Karoa* bound for Australia and disembarked at Sydney on 10 May 1919.

The circumstances of capture varied considerably from those who were wounded and collected by the enemy to others who fought until their situation became quite hopeless. In some cases, an officer would order his men to cease fighting. Pte Mitchell, 53 Btn, reported in 1918:

> I was told whilst a prisoner of war in Germany, by Corporal Kiss and Corporal Bert [names changed by Mitchell][3] that it was Lieutenant Bowman who ordered the men to surrender. They declared that Lieutenant Bowman himself surrendered to the Germans. Two German soldiers were escorting the officer away when our fellows shot both of them. They also threatened to shoot Lieutenant Bowman.[4]

4518 Cpl B.E. Horne also reported this incident: 'Lt Bowman appeared on our right in the custody of two Germans. We promptly shot the latter and Lt Bowman came over to us. He told us that he had orders from Capt Murray to surrender and ordered us to do so. We did so and thus became prisoners'. This version is corroborated by 4812 Pte K.W. Keirnan, who stated that 'Capt Murray… came along and advised us our only course of action was to surrender which we did at about midday by which time our numbers were reduced to 28, including the two sergeants'. The details of this event differ slightly in the account by 3311 Pte F.G. Harrison, who wrote that 'about daybreak the enemy worked round on our flanks and Capt Murray gave the order to surrender; about 60 gave themselves up'. In another case, three privates in 32 Btn recorded: 'we were digging in beyond the German third line. Somebody hoisted a white flag in the trench to our rear. Lieutenant Agars promptly fired on the flag with the machine gun and ordered the men to open fire on it with their rifles.'[5]

In 8 Bde the records claim that no unwounded men were captured. From photographic evidence this is patently untrue. An account by 856 Sgt A.E. Luly who was one of those who attempted to make a dash back to safety descirbed the moments leading up to a dramatic attempt to avoid capture:

> Later in the morning Lieut Mills of D Company, who had been wounded twice walked along the line and told us that we would have to charge through the German front lines back to our own but we had to wait for orders… after firing for some time we noticed on our left that our men were making a charge for it. I could see that it was useless remaining where we were so those who were near me also charged.[6]

Among those who were captured was 3577 Pte R. McKenzie of 55 Btn. He was wounded 'by a bullet through the eye… I fainted… and in coming round I tried to stand up but could not do so. I then crawled across No Man's Land and fell into a trench. I do not know whose trench it was… I do not remember any thing more for a fortnight when I found myself a prisoner of war in hospital at Valenciennes'. 3419 Pte A. Richards, also of 55 Btn, had been badly wounded by grenades, and remained in the German lines until 21 July before being evacuated. His right leg was amputated by German medical staff.

Lt G.D. Folkard, 55 Btn, reported that he was not captured until 10a.m. In the company of 2/Lt Lovejoy of 54 Btn and eleven others of 14 Bde he saw the 'Germans come over in swarms. They were all round us, and we were completely cut off and unable to put up a fight'. In the same battalion, 4828 Pte J.H. Hammond stated that his position had been 'surrounded at about 2a.m. on 20 July when we were forcing our way back to our own lines I was wounded in the stomach by a bullet and lay in a shell hole until about 5a.m. when I was taken prisoner'. Another casualty of the attempt to breakout of the German lines – 3436 Cpl G.H.T. Stringfellow, 55 Btn – reported that Lt Agassiz had:

> informed us that we were to try and fight our way back. It looked a very stiff job but nevertheless we were determined to try it. Partly walking, running and crawling we had crossed about 40 or 50 yards when I noticed Lt Folkard and Lt Cummins… I also noticed that we were entirely cut off and surrounded. I lost sight of Lt Agassiz… I believe he was severely wounded… we took cover… as the Germans were almost upon us now and they were bombing us as we advanced (we could not retaliate as we had no ammunition). We waited a while then suddenly the Germans were upon us and we were taken prisoners at about 9.45a.m.

Major J.J. Hughes (32 Btn) had crossed No Man's Land in the third wave but had subsequently been wounded by a shrapnel bullet that paralysed his left side. He noted:

> Sgt Luly… and a private came over to see me… but he and 1618 Pte Elmer refused to leave me. As I could not walk they attempted to drag me but as the ground was badly broken by shell holes it was impossible to get away. I then made certain that any papers in our possession were destroyed and had just completed this when we were captured.

1611 Pte J. Butler had made the return trip as far as the edge of No Man's Land but was 'hit about 8 times the worst wound being in the stomach. I lay in No Man's Land for about 24 hours… the Germans came out and picked me up the evening after our attack'. 351 Pte J.M. Good was unwounded but marooned 'in a shell hole unable to get back on account of machine gun fire' and was taken prisoner.

It was not only men in No Man's Land who waited days to be recovered. 1284 Pte J.A. Henry had been wounded in both thighs and crawled to a third line trench, where he remained for two nights and two days before being taken away. 222 Sgt P.C. Donovan, 29 Btn, was 'picked up next morning by the Germans from off their own parapet' having been wounded and having built a sandbag barricade around himself and 80 Pte Sam Farlow. 3859 Pte B.P. Neil, 32 Btn, on the other hand, claimed that he and several other men 'got back to within 30 yards of our original line… here the enemy rushed us and we were forced to surrender'. There is no evidence that the enemy advanced more than a few yards beyond their own parapet in the course of expelling the Australians from their lines.

One of the POWs who showed remarkable devotion to duty was 4301 Pte Russell Burton (54 Btn). Burton recalled that within moments of leaving the Australian lines when he was:

hit in the head by a shrapnel pellet or splinter. I had not gone 10 yards, just clear of our own wire entanglements when I was rendered temporarily blind but recovered in a couple of minutes and went on… I had my damaged eye roughly bandaged with some rifle rag and my handkerchief. I could see fairly well with my right eye.

Pte Burton continued towards what he believed was the German third line where he assisted in the construction of a defensive position. He remained in the enemy lines until dawn when a soldier with him, 4316A Pte A. Singleton:

was shot through the head and a machine gun fired furiously from the old German line in rear. Lt Gunter ordered… to crawl back along the trench then everything became a blank. When I woke up I was in a German hospital in Wavrin. I had been wounded in the right side of the abdomen and was suffering from severe shell concussion all the way up the right side. From end to end my right side was bruised black and blue.

A further wounded soldier who was unable to resist capture was 5385 Cpl A.B. Mason serving in 14 Field Coy, Australian Engineers. Mason 'was wounded with shrapnel between my eyes and left cheek. Lt Merkell advised me to get back to our own lines… I was unable to see and was put in a dugout with a number of other wounded and told to remain there. At about 4a.m. the Germans dragged us out as prisoners'. Not all those who were prepared to surrender were treated with mercy. Two soldiers in B Coy, 32 Btn were badly wounded and were lying close to 587 Pte A.T. Nelligan who, upon his return after the war, reported that one of these men left his 'more badly wounded mate in as restful a position as he could devise, went forward towards the German line to give himself up and get assistance for his mate. A German whom he approached – I took him to be a German Red Cross man and an officer – shot him through the head with a revolver'.

A forlorn situation was noted by Lt H.R. Lovejoy, 54 Btn, who informed the army after the war:

> I found myself and about 8 or 10 NCOs and men absolutely surrounded and cut off. Having no bombs and practically no ammunition left and what few rifles we had (probably 6) all full of mud and water, it was impossible either to fight our way through, get away, or make any attempt at resistance, as we were hopelessly outnumbered.

During interrogation by their captors, Lt Lovejoy was informed by a German staff officer 'that they knew all about the attack, including all the details, and even showed us a copy of General Haking's secret orders (re making the feint of attacking at 5.40p.m. showing dummies, bayonets etc) which had been communicated to officers only whilst in Bac St. Maur'. Inevitably this and other ruses used by the Germans at a time when their prisoners felt very vulnerable helped to fuel rumours that the Germans knew all about the forthcoming attack, but a glimpse back down the ridge towards Laventie would confirm that observers had a clear view of the British front line in this sector. Lt Folkard confirms Lovejoy's story: 'I was taken to a German Divisional HQ and interrogated. To my surprise the German officer showed me a copy of the Divisional orders which had been issued to us'. A further account was left by Capt R.A. Keay, 32 Btn, who wrote:

> When at Lille after capture, a German staff officer who interrogated us told us that if we would not answer questions because we were giving away anything we were mistaken, that all he wanted was verification and there upon drew from a satchel a typewritten copy of Gen Haking's order for the attack; this was actually signed by the General himself and was certainly the same order that we received the day of the attack.

Initially, it appears that the Germans treated their prisoners reasonably well. Cpl Stringfellow experienced 'a few butts to make me take off my equipment but they did not treat us at all brutally'. 855 Sgt R. Collett, 32 Btn, was

> escorted down the communication trench to the Btn HQ and there searched. We were then marched to what I believed to be a Divisional HQ and there met a large party of prisoners from 8th and 14th Bde and Warwickshire Regiment making a total of about 250 men. From here we marched to Lille and were interned in the fortress until 22nd July and from there transferred to Germany.

This march to Lille was mentioned by 836 Sgt A.E. Luly also of 32 Btn, who wrote that 'during the march to Lille the French people were good to us, the German sentries and police kept them a fair distance off. A couple of Uhlans made a particular point of riding in amongst civilians and scattering them in all directions'. A number of photos remain of the march to Lille and the Uhlans can be clearly identified.

The wounded also had mixed fortunes. Many spoke highly of the care they received from German medical staff but others had a harrowing experience. Pte Hammond was in hospital in Douai for one month where his wounds were dressed only three times. He then spent three months in hospital in Stuttgart but survived and returned to Australia after the war. 2081 Pte R.S. Mayston, 29 Btn, had his right arm shattered by a grenade, and in St. Clothilde Hospital in Douai 'was operated upon and my arm amputated, my consent being obtained. The treatment was as well as could be expected'. Major J.J. Hughes, 32 Btn, commented on treatment in Germany that 'the surgical treatment of officers was very good. The Chief Surgeon was opposed to amputation and saved several limbs which at first appeared to be hopeless'. The journey to Germany, though, had been less impressive, causing Major Hughes to note that he 'travelled in cattle trucks on filthy straw mattresses'.

In the Great War there were 165 camps in Germany for British POWs. Many of these prisoners were used as labour in German factories, farms and mines. A total of two and a half million Allied POWs were used in this way. By 1917, twenty per cent of adult male labour in Germany was provided by POWs. Replies to Red Cross inquiries about missing soldiers reveal that POWs were located in a number of camps. For example, Lt H.R. Lovejoy was in Gutersloh, 2390 Pte V.J. Dwyer and 3286 Pte Albert Eather at Sennelager, 1304 Pte E.W. Bell and Capt F.R. Ransom at Minden, 2835 Cpl R.S. Kiss at Munster, and 432 Pte F.E. Moir and 4813 Pte S.N. Key at Dulmen. Not all remained in Germany until 1918; Pte J. Butler, for example, spent four months in hospital and then worked in a sawmill prior to being sent to Switzerland, arriving on 28 November 1917. He remained there for nearly a year, eventually disembarking at Southampton on 7 December 1918.

Malnutrition was a serious problem, because POWs were a very low priority for food supplies. Red Cross parcels were essential for survival, but parcels could be sent to an individual soldier only when it was known that he was in enemy hands. Pneumonia, tuberculosis and dysentery all plagued the prisoners, not to mention the cruelty of their guards. One in eight British prisoners died in captivity; the outlook for those captured at Fromelles looked very bleak.

A more detailed account entitled *Life in Germany* was prepared by 3305 Sgt G. Shirley, 55 Btn, who described the overall experience as 'Hell'. It took several months for names to reach the authorities in England and it was October before the first Red Cross parcels were received by troops captured at Fromelles. These parcels, along with those provided by a variety of comforts funds, were a lifesaver for those in captivity. Sgt Shirley spent six weeks at Dulmen where 'for quarters, well, I have housed pigs better'. From Dulmen he was sent to Minden where 'the quarters were worse'. After a 12 month spell he was transferred to Soltau:

> Here we had no fires, no food and rotten bedding; full of vermin, for about 7 days. Then we were sent by train to the famed Bohmte. The first night we had to leave everything out in the wet. We had no blankets and no food for 24 hours and were bundled in like sheep. We slept on the floor until morning.

According to Sgt Shirley this treatment was typical of their existence until released and sent home via Holland.

3327 Pte G.W. Smith was another participant in the battle with less than one year's service, having enlisted on 10 August 1915. Pte Smith, like so many veterans, was reluctant to speak about the war but did relate the story of his nocturnal escape from a farm close to the Austrian border. He was recaptured a few days later and sent to a camp in Prussia, where his punishment was to be stripped naked and made to stand in the snow until he collapsed. After being revived, the punishment was repeated. This ordeal severely damaged his health and he was confined to hospital in England for some weeks after repatriation at the end of the war. He gratefully acknowledged the Red Cross parcels as an essential survival aid for the prisoners. It seems likely that years of suffering from neuritis, originating from his punishment in the snow, and hardships as a POW contributed to his death in 1968 aged 77.[7]

Cpl M.J.D. Austin also recalled terrible conditions:

> Rethemer Moor Camp was easily the worst quarters of any of the other camps I have been in; the barrack was infested with fleas and the place was run over with rats. There were two tiers of beds around the walls and three tiers up the centre of the barracks. The height of the bottom tier off the floor was 4 inches and the dirt couldn't be swept from underneath. As regards food, it was well known that even when the Germans did have it, they starved the prisoners. In Rethemer Moor where I spent 15 months of my 2 years captivity the usual diet was coffee at 6a.m., stinking fish soup generally for dinner and a yellow meal soup for tea. A small ration of bread was issued every evening and a small issue of jam every month.

Families of POWs were perhaps more fortunate than relatives of the dead as they received word from Germany[8] within a few weeks. For many others no unequivocal information would ever be received of the fate of a father, brother or son, and many mothers spent anxious hours on quaysides speaking to returning troops but never succeeding in obtaining the information they sought.

15

First View of Heaven

The wounded placed a heavy burden on the army in respect of medical attention and evacuation. One detailed account of such a soldier wounded at Fromelles was by Sgt Ridley,[1] 53 Btn, and was documented in hundreds of letters sent home during the war. Ridley had moved out into No Man's Land at the start of the attack, and had made good progress towards a second German line when he was hit:

> I must have raised my head slightly when 'crash, bang' it was a terrible smack…
> it felt like receiving a terrible smack from a cricket ball but ten times worse. It
> stunned me with the force and for a moment I hardly knew how I had been hit.
> Then the blood rushed out of my mouth and down my face in torrents… I was
> in agony nearly choking every minute.

Ridley was attended to by L/Cpl MacDonald and a soldier called Elliott, who tried to use his field dressing while holding him out of the water in the ditch into which their sergeant had tumbled. Ridley felt he was dying and 'wondered what my first view of heaven would be like then I thought of Mother and all at home and I wondered what they would say when they saw my name under "KIA"'. Sgt Ridley recalled later that 'the dirty, muddy ditch was tinged with scarlet round my body' and pleaded not to be left, but on hearing that the Australians were being pushed back he realised that he 'had no right to keep two of my section back from their work with the guns'.[2]

After lying in the water for ninety minutes or so, Ridley was helped back towards No Man's Land where he was assisted by Alf Goodwin and George Magson, until Magson was wounded in both wrists by shrapnel. A gas alert was called, and Ridley found a gas helmet and put it on; fortunately the scare was over after a few minutes, allowing him to breathe more freely. By now the sun was setting. 'By the help of Goodwin and Elliott I walked a little further down the ditch towards a trench which was being dug towards us by some engineers for the passing of ammunition.'[3]

Ridley, assisted by three soldiers, regained the Australian front line where he was directed to a dressing station. He recalled:

> I staggered on… the sides of the trench had been blown in and here and there figures lay dead in all directions – blood was everywhere… at last we saw a stretcher coming… I fell on it and they took a haversack from a pile of equipment… and put it under my head. The stretcher-bearers took up the stretcher and walked on – they were pretty tired poor fellows and they put me down every now and then… At last we turned down the little aid trench… and they put the stretcher down.[4]

Two AMC men checked the wound – it turned out that Ridley had been shot through the neck – one looked at his identity disc and wrote down his details then tied a label to his tunic while another removed his revolver belt and ammunition. In due course a doctor gave the wound some rudimentary treatment and instructed two stretcher-bearers to take Ridley to 15 Field Ambulance.

No further treatment was given on reaching 15 Field Ambulance and Ridley continued his journey to the rear 'across a field I was taken through an archway and laid in a barn'. He joined many other wounded men in this farmyard but was soon put on a wheeled stretcher and taken to another dressing station. Here 'the room was lit with a few dim lanterns and crowded with wounded. A tired looking doctor came to me and he had a look at my neck'. Again the doctor declined to operate and Ridley was put in an ambulance. The AMC man in charge was very kind: 'never mind old chap you will be in England in 12 hours time'.[5]

On arrival at Sailly-sur-la-Lys Sgt Ridley was met by Fr. Thomas King, a Roman Catholic Chaplain attached to 15 Bde, who 'gave me a blessing'. After a long wait his details were again taken and 'a doctor examined my neck, said something about a narrow escape then dressed my wound and covered my head with bandages; another doctor gave an anti-tetanus injection'. According to Ridley's estimate, around three o'clock he was put into dry pyjamas and placed on a dry stretcher where 'the air whistled through my throat as I dozed a little'. His 'blood red day of battle' was over and a long period of recovery lay ahead. Ridley served until the war's end and in his 632nd letter home in November 1918, he declared: 'news has come through that Germany has accepted our terms and hostilities have ceased along the whole front. Fancy having lived through 1133 days on active service – God be praised why was I not taken in my first battle in July 1916?'[6]

The precise nature of his wound was disclosed in a letter he wrote on 24 July from George East Ward, Edmonton Military Hospital in London. He told his family he had been shot through the neck, the bullet going in right side and out left: 'the bullet somehow threw my tongue out of gear and I can't chew or swallow much at all and my speech is slightly affected.'[7]

Like Sgt Ridley, 81 Cpl R.E. Lording (Signal Section, 30 Btn), after being badly wounded, was also one of many men now facing a difficult journey to the rear areas, evacuation to Britain and eventual repatriation. In Lording's case, 'survival' did not mean swift recovery and a return to the front but months of surgery, over fifty operations in fact, and living with the effect of the wounds for the rest of his life. In addition, he was the founder of the 30 Btn AIF Association and wrote his memoirs of the war in a book entitled *There and Back* under the pen-name 'A. Tiveychoc', the name recalling the reputation of Brig-Gen Tivey, who took so much care of his men in Egypt that they were known as 'Tivey's Chocolate Soldiers'. His experience is related through the eyes of a third person, Ted, and vividly describes the ordeal of being wounded in action and all that followed. His narrative perpetuates a testimony to the wounded troops of Fromelles.

Lording was first taken to a dugout full of wounded men. His recollections continued:

> There was some dubiety whether he is alive or dead but some scissors and a jack-knife tear his uniform apart to gain access to his arm and to the tourniquet; the plug in his side is not touched as the wound is too severe to be examined in these crude conditions. The stretcher on which he lay is taken outside, placed on a set of wheels and then sent to a waiting motor ambulance. On arrival at a field ambulance he is placed on the ground, in the open, with many, many others, awaiting their turn to be examined. Eventually he is taken to the doctor, given an anti-tetanus injection in the stomach, a shot of morphia, has his wounds re-dressed and slips into a state of unconsciousness.

From the field ambulance Lording was taken to a casualty clearing station. Not all the wounded brought there survived; Lording 'saw a blanket being pulled over the head of a chap on the next stretcher'. The next stage of his journey was by ambulance train to Boulogne, where he was transferred to No. 13 General Hospital (Le Casino) and put in 'an oval room with decorated walls and ceiling and large windows overlooking the English Channel'. Not long after his arrival he was taken to theatre for the first detailed examination of his wounds, which were listed as follows:

> g.s.w. [gunshot wound] in left chest, consisting of a small hole just below the neck and a large cavity four inches in diameter on the left side (caused by a machine gun), as a result of which the lung has been shattered and the small piece left is totally collapsed, while his heart has moved and can be seen through the hole. The right arm is smashed through the elbow (another machine gun bullet), and a small piece of shrapnel lies embedded in the back of the hand; in his back are four small shrapnel wounds (one having partially paralysed the spine – the lower organs of the body function unknowingly). In addition, there

are two old, open wounds on the side of his right foot (legacies from Egypt). He cannot move his left arm, which lays twisted and contracted on his chest. The left leg has been tied down. He is helpless.

This operation was successful and Lording was sent back to his ward. The irony of his accommodation was noted in his memoirs: 'built for the pleasures of the rich, but now filled with the wrecks of human folly'. Over the next ten days he survived an attack of tetanus and ten days of racking pain: 'spasms shooting from the toes through the body… throat cords taught… the jaws locked fast'. More visits to the operating theatre followed, and his chest cavity had to be drained of pus daily. Lording's fit, young body was clearly able to endure the terrible injuries, but others expected him to die at any time. The hospital chaplain visited him to say a few last words; 'Ted agreed with all he said, but did not understand he was supposed to be dying'.

After forty-five days at Boulogne a nurse made an entry in his diary on his behalf recording that on 2 September he was to be sent to England, a month and a half after sustaining his 'Blighty' wound. From the hospital he was taken by ambulance to the harbour and immediately loaded onto a Belgian mail liner converted to a hospital ship. The diary continues:

> Before long the stretcher cases are unloaded and lined up on the quayside at Dover ready for loading on a train for the short journey to Fort Pitt Military Hospital at Chatham. The journey was an uncomfortable experience for him as was the reception at Fort Pitt as he was transferred to a bed; this was to be his home until February 1917. His new-found mates, including a few Australians and a soldier he saw at Cellar Farm Avenue after both had been wounded, looked after him, protecting him from intrusive visitors and keeping him supplied with biscuits and other titbits from the canteen. Many still doubted his ability to survive but their care for him did not diminish.

Lording recorded 'many other friends – doctors, sisters, V.A. nurses, wardsmaids, orderlies, and convalescent patients – gave untiring service, sympathetic treatment, and cheer. Their kindly words of encouragement, their jocular remarks, their little acts of kindness smoothed the roughness of the way'. Various gifts, mainly from unnamed individuals, came his way: 'fresh cream daily by post from Devonshire, oysters from Whitstable, champagne, turtle soup, cases of stout, fruit, and other nourishing luxuries; and once there arrived a box of grapes as big as plums with a card inscribed: To Cpl Rowland from Her Majesty the Queen.'

On 13 October, just over a month after his arrival at Fort Pitt, Lording underwent another major operation. He described it thus 'it was a lengthy operation. The left wall of the chest was incised and drawn back, portions of six ribs being removed… the piece of lung treated and inflated. Rubber tubes were inserted... the chest wall was brought back and sewn up.' He regained consciousness sixteen hours after the operation started; the tubes in his body were, he noted, like 'a Murrumbidgee irrigation farm'. His ribs were put in a bottle of spirit and placed on a shelf by his bed prompting a number of comments from visitors. After many weeks, he was moved to a quieter room known as the 'Dying Room' by the patients, a room, he suggested, 'to this day probably haunted by the yells of pain as well as the ghosts of those who went west within its wall'. At Christmas he was able to make a greetings card for his family back home; it depicted him in bed with the caption 'smile damn you smile' and it took him a half day to create such was the limited mobility he had regained in one arm.

Exactly six months to the day after being wounded, Lording was lifted out of bed and took his first steps; with his mates, he celebrated with ginger beer before being returned to bed. Not long after came the first suggestion of returning to Australia, an offer that he willingly accepted once he had been reassured that the medical care back home would be every bit as good as he was receiving at Chatham. The next move for Lording to endure was a transfer to Harefield Hospital in Middlesex. This took place on 6 February 1917 once the question of who – the sending or the receiving hospital – was to provide the stretcher for his journey. This, he recorded, was the first experience of bad management since being wounded. It was followed by several more episodes, a hair-raising ambulance journey in the snow to Harefield, a lack of care and attention on arrival, missing papers and a long wait on an open veranda, tempered only by discovering that he was on the same ward as a friend he had first met at Liverpool Camp in 1915. A further surprise came from a VAD who jocularly informed him that her father wanted him back in France; she turned out to be the daughter of General Birdwood.

At the end of February 1917, Rowley Lording began the journey home. A year in training, a few hours in battle and now a lifetime of suffering ahead of him. It is easy to understand why 'Fromelles' meant so much to so many members of the AIF.

Another soldier, in 59 Btn, to leave a personal account was Thomas Clair Whiteside from Leongatha, Victoria, one of many young Australians to enlist in the months immediately after the Gallipoli landings.[8] He had served for a short time in 57 Btn before being transferred to his present unit and Fromelles was to be his first action on the Western Front.

On 19 July he was engaged in fatigues as his division prepared for the coming assault; a gas alarm was found to be 'a furphy as many of them do'. The hazard of German shells and other ordnance certainly proved not to be 'a furphy' for Whiteside as he was badly wounded in the head and evacuated to England arriving at 3 Southern General Hospital, Oxford. By 28 July he was well enough to write home and his letter gave plenty of detail that would have warned families in Australia that long casualty lists could be expected. Clair Whiteside informed his mother that a 'good number were wounded before the charge but a short distance into No Man's Land the grass was thick with them'. Whiteside recalled that a German machine gun was firing into the grass on his left but it was a sniper that caught him. He wrote that he 'got a nasty one on the head... thought I was done for'.

Instinctively Whiteside turned towards the Australian lines to seek medical attention. He zigzagged back through the grass so that he would not create a clear path for a machine-gunner. Part way across No Man's Land a dry ditch was found providing a refuge until darkness fell. Later in the evening in the company of Bill Skinner, he crawled further back, waded a ditch, forced a passage through the barbed wire and 'dropped down in a trench full of friends'. From there, Whiteside made his way to a dressing station. As the Germans had the range of the communication trenches, the wounded were being held for several hours at the dressing station before moving back later in the morning to Sailly. On the morning of 21 July he was sent by hospital train to Boulogne, arriving that evening, and then the following day crossed to England on the hospital ship *Dieppe*.

At the time of writing Whiteside had not heard of the fate of others he had seen wounded or at the dressing station. Two he mentions – 'have not heard how Will O'Sullivan or Alan Russell fared' – died of wounds; O'Sullivan is buried in Anzac Cemetery, Sailly, and Russell at Bailleul.[9] He also met in Oxford a few other 5 Australian Division wounded, who related stories similar to his own experience. One, though, stated that 'some of their wounded had to lie helpless to the horrors of a gas attack'. Presumably this soldier was confused by the smoke on the battlefield as no gas was used in this engagement.

Whiteside's wound took a few weeks to heal, and soon he was able to inform his family that 'I am rapidly getting strong again... consider I was jolly lucky'. As further evidence of his recovery, he noted that 'the lady ticket collectors on the double-decker motor buses are a source of interest'! Whiteside recovered from his wounds, and despite being wounded at Bullecourt he returned to Australia after the war.

Another typical case of evacuation of a wounded soldier to England would be Bill Mair.[10] By July 1916 he was a sergeant in 54 Btn but suffered 'gunshot wounds to the abdomen' and was evacuated to No. 1 CCS, then by ambulance train to 13 General Hospital in Boulogne. On 22 July Sgt Mair was transported across the Channel on the hospital ship *St. Denis* and the following day admitted to the County of London War Hospital in Epsom. By 27 September Mair was out of hospital and sent to Tidworth; by 12 April 1917 he was back in Australia.[11] Others were not so fortunate; a walk around the Great War plot in Epsom, which, like Lodge Hill in Birmingham, has numbered plot markers laid in the grass, reveals, among many others, the grave of Bert Bishop's cousin, 3473 Pte WH Bishop, 54 Btn.

1 Maj-Gen the Hon Sir J.W. McCay, GOC 5th Australian Division.

2 Brig-Gen Harold Elliott, OC 15 Australian Infantry Brigade.

3 The chief members of the Armistice Commission in Spa, Belgium, November 1918. The third man from right in uniform is Lt-Gen Sir Richard Haking, GOC XI Corps.

4 Aerial view of the Sugar Loaf Salient, 19 July 1916.

5 Australian prisoners of war with German soldiers at Fromelles, 20 July 1916.

6 Officers of 2/1 Bucks Battalion at Parkhouse Camp, May 1916.

7 Gen Sir Alexander Godley, GOC II Anzac Corps.

8 Maj-Gen Sir Colin Mackenzie, GOC 61 Division, at the unveiling of the 61 Division memorial at Laventie, 21 April 1935.

9 Brig-Gen E. Tivey, OC 8 Brigade.

10 Col Harold Pope CB, OC 14 Brigade.

11 Col Pope in 1920, at the family residence (known as Pope's Hill) in the Perth suburb of Belmont. The children are, left to right: Harold, Don, Charles, Phylis and Vivienne. Behind are Col Pope and his wife Susan (née Slater).

12 Col Pope at an Anzac Day parade after the war.

13 Lt-Col W.E.H. Cass, OC 54 Battalion.

14 Major Geoff McCrae, 60 Btn, who was killed leading his men into action on 19 July 1916.

15 Grave of Major McCrae.

16 Capt Will Harris, 54 Btn. Harris was awarded the Military Cross for gallantry at Fromelles.

17 Capt Clive Hopkins, who left a staff post to lead the 14 Light Trench Mortar Battery. Killed in action on 19 July 1916.

Left and opposite above: 18 & 19 Pte Billy Outlaw and his cousin Pte Chris King. Both members of 53 Btn were killed at Fromelles and are commemorated at VC Corner.

Above, left and right: 20 & 21 Pte Aubrey Antrobus and his brother Pte Walter Antrobus, both of 29 Btn. The twins were taken prisoner at Fromelles.

Above: 22 Father Louis Dahiez, parish priest at Fromelles from 1919–22, pictured in 1919 with the remains of a soldier killed at Fromelles.

Left: 23 Pte Kenneth Dunk, 32 Btn. Dunk performed the gallant act of rescuing a wounded officer from the German front line.

24 Wedding of Jim (29 Btn) and Ethel Cleworth on 13 December 1916, with
Charlie Peters MM and Rose. Cleworth joined up just twelve months before the
battle, married an English girl and took her back to Australia.

25 Eaglehawk Boys (C Company 29 Btn) at Seymour Camp on 25 July 1915 less
than twelve months before the attack at Fromelles. From left to right, back row: Bill
Hanly, Joe Hocking, Jim Cleworth, F. Moyle, T. Madden, J. Martin. Front row: -?-, W.
Tibbett, -?-, C. Peters, J. McConnell. All survived Fromelles and the war.

26 Villagers in front of Fromelles church before the First World War.

27 The main street of Fromelles before the war.

Right: 28 Men of 53 Btn
immediately prior to the
attack on 19 July 1916.

Below: 29 German trench
railway in the damaged
village of Fromelles, 1916.

Left: 30 The *Cobbers* statue in Fromelles Memorial Park.

Below: 31 British and Australian prisoners taken in the battle marching through Haubourdin on 20 July 1916.

Gefangene Engländer nach den Angriffen bei Frommelles 19.7.16.

32 Australian dead lying in the German front line, 20 July 1916.

33 VC Corner at Fromelles, the burial ground of over 400 unidentified soldiers from the battle.

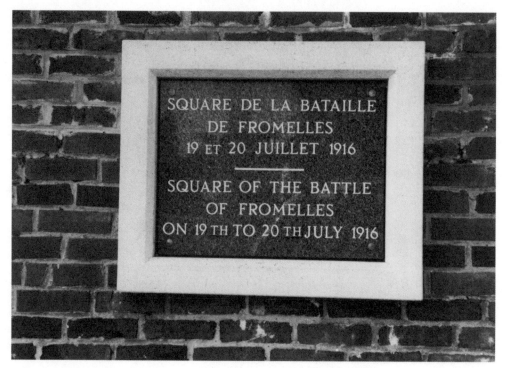

34 Commemorative plaque, Fromelles village.

IN EINEM GEMEINSAMEN GRABE
RUHEN HIER
91 DEUTSCHE SOLDATEN
DREI BLIEBEN UNBEKANNT

FRIEDRICH LOY ERSATZ-RESERVIST † 20.7.1916
JOHANN HOFBECK ERSATZ-RESERVIST † 19.7.1916
JOHANN SÖLLNER LANDSTURMMANN † 19.7.1916
HEINRICH WEISS KRIEGSFREIWILLIGER † 20.7.1916
WILHELM BEISEL PIONIER † 19.7.1916
KARL LOY ERSATZ-RESERVIST † 19.7.1916
GEORG SCHRAML INFANTERIST † 19.7.1916
LEONHARD RÖSCHLEIN INFANTERIST † 19.7.1916
OTTO SCHIRMER LANDSTURMMANN † 20.7.1916
JOSEF OSTERMEYER PIONIER † 19.7.1916
ANDREAS NAGEL ERSATZ-RESERVIST † 20.7.1916

Above and opposite: 35 & 36 German mass grave from 19–20 July 1916 in Beaucamps German cemetery.

... JOSAL... ERSATZ-RESERVIST † ... 7.19...
GEO... ...PFER INFANT... ...ST † 20.7. ...16
JOSEF B...ND... LANDSTURMMANN † 20.7.1916
FRIEDRICH OCHS GEFREITER † 19.7.1916
JOSEF MAILER ERSATZ-RESE... ...ST † 19.7.1916
JOHANN THOMA ERSATZ-RESERVIST † 20.7.1916
JOHANN STÖSSEL UNTEROFFIZIER † 20.7.1916
MICHAEL HÄNFLING INFANTERIST † 19.7.1916
JOHANN VOLKERT INFANTERIST † 20.7.1916
JOHANN FRÖSCHL ERSATZ-RESERVIST † 19.7.1916
FRANZ EIBNER INFANTERIST † 19.7.1916
JOHANN CHRISTOPH GEFREITER † 19.7.1916
LUDWIG SCHÜBEL ERSATZ-RESERVIST † 19.7.1916
PAUL HEMM ERSATZ-RESERVIST † 19.7.1916
WOLFGANG KRAFT INFANTERIST † 19.7.1916
FRIEDRICH WALLMÜLLER INFANTERIST † 19.7.1916
MICHAEL DIRSCHERL WEHRMANN † 19.7.1916
AUGUST PEETZ UNTEROFFIZIER † 19.7.1916
JOHANN PFÄNDNER GEFREITER † 19.7.1916
FRITZ POPP INFANTERIST † 19.7.1916
ANDREAS KRAMMER ERSATZ-RESERVIST † 19.7.1916
JOHANN ZITZLSPERGER ERSATZ-RESERVIST † 19.7.1916
ADOLF SCHÖFBERGER LANDSTURMMANN † 19.7.1916
JOHANN MAIER ERSATZ-RESERVIST † 19.7.1916
MICHAEL SÖLTEL INFANTERIST † 20.7.1916
ALOIS MAGER INFANTERIST † 20.7.1916

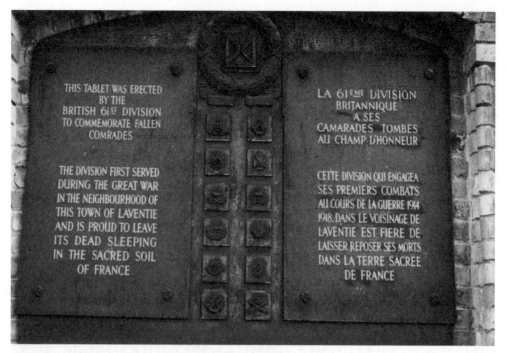

37 Memorial to 61 Division at Laventie.

38 Australian POWs in Fromelles, 20 July 1916. Capt C. Mills, 32 Btn, is the officer with his arm in a sling.

39 A contemporary sketch of Winchester Trench in 61 Division sector.

40 A German observation post at Aubers, as seen today.

Above left: 41 Pte W.C. Ecclestone, 59 Btn.

Above right: 42 Pte H. Carter, 54 Btn.

Left: 43 Sgt Maurice Burke, 29 Btn.

For some of the wounded an early return to Australia would not be their fate, but nevertheless it would be a long time before they returned to France. Twenty-year-old 331 Sgt Frederick Field,[12] from Merewether, New South Wales, was badly wounded while serving with 30 Btn. After a few agonising days he had been transported to Netley Hospital on Southampton Water in Hampshire. Netley had been built for the Crimean War, and the Great War would not be the final time that its wards would be full of wounded troops delivered either to its own jetty or by train along a short branch line that left the Southampton–Portsmouth line near Netley station. Frederick Field recovered from his wounds and eventually returned to Australia, where he married in 1921 and produced eight children!

Similarly, another badly wounded soldier in 8 Bde's sector was 966 Pte James Leonard Forrest Inglis,[13] born in Dalesford, Victoria but living near Perth, Western Australia, when he enlisted on 6 July 1915. His short training period ended at Helena Vale Racecourse before leaving as a reinforcement bound for Egypt, where he arrived on 16 December. With his battalion he was soon in France and in the thick of the fighting on 8 Bde's left flank, but he sustained shell shock and a wound described on his papers as 'rifle bullet through right thumb, palm of hand necessitating amputation of right little finger and fifth metacarpal bone removed'. As late as 1953 an X-ray revealed that a metal fragment was still lodged in his right hand. Long after the battle Pte Inglis recalled that 'he had been kneeling with his gun in his hand and just stood as a bullet hit his right hand'. If he had not stood at that precise moment he believed that his wound might have been far more serious.

From 8 Stationary Hospital at Wimereux Forrest Inglis was sent to 2 Western General Hospital in Manchester. For a time his diet was 'full stout, egg and milk' to complement 'painting with iodine and massage for third finger and hand'. Later he was moved south to No. 1 Australian Auxiliary Hospital at Harefield, Middlesex, and then to Weymouth where he was declared 'permanently unfit for general service and temporarily unfit for home service for six months'. On 12 November he boarded the *Wiltshire* and returned to Australia, arriving in Fremantle in time for Christmas. He had eight sisters and two brothers, most of whom were at the jetty to greet him. Forrest Inglis was discharged from the AIF on 12 March 1917 and lived until 24 August 1987, reaching the grand age of 92.

Sgt Les Martin was wounded with 8 MGC and on 31 July 1916 wrote home from St. Luke's War Hospital in Halifax, Yorkshire. He had written to his mother about 'a few of the milder happenings' and now wrote 'about a few of the other happenings':

I was in the real fighting for more than ten hours before I got hit... it was just slaughter... just like hell let loose in its worst form... the chap sitting next to me got a piece of shell in his elbow... and a chap on the other side got a piece in the leg and I got a small portion in the left arm which still troubles me a bit, and a piece in the tongue which stung a good deal at the time. I saw a shell lob about twelve yards away and it caught the two that I saw. It lifted them clean up in the air for about 6 feet and they simply dropped back dead killed instantly; a shell (shrapnel) burst… and I saw it take a portion of a chap's arm off, as clean as a whistle.[14]

Details of casualties were also noted in personal diaries. Major E. Lister[15] wrote: 'I am sorry to say I had my first casualty yesterday, Bdr Chippendale one of my specialists being hit by shrapnel in both arms and just under the heart. I think he will get over it though and I hope so as he is a very fine lad who had done good works'. Lister continues: 'Prior (51 Bty) had 7 specialists killed yesterday by a 5.9 falling in their telephone dugout. Also Capt Thomson [sic] of the 48th Bty was killed'. Capt Thompson is buried in Y Farm Military Cemetery at Bois Grenier but eight rather than seven casualties from 13 Bde AFA can be found in the area, six at Rue David, one in Rue Petillon and another at Anzac Cemetery, Sailly-sur-la-Lys.[16]

A different cause of artillery casualties is found in a manuscript entitled *A Soldier Looks Back*[17] by 2148 Bdr A.J. Williams, who served in 53 Bty at Fromelles. In a reference to an unspecified battery he recalled:

The artillery were short of shells and we were only allowed to fire a certain number each day. The ammunition shortage was a very serious question. We were using American shells and had a bad explosion in one gun – it blew the breach back out of the 18pdr killing two or three of the gunners and wounding a couple more.

One place which suffered an extraordinary number of casualties on 19–20 July was Bairnsdale in Victoria. At least thirteen men, serving in 59 and 60 Btns, were killed at Fromelles. One of the 59 Btn men who survived was Pte F.C. (Sam) Yeates, who later became a prominent member of the Bairnsdale sub-branch of the RSL, serving two terms as President in 1922–28 and 1938 and becoming the club's first life member.

Sam Yeates was the son of James Yeates, proprietor of the *Bairnsdale Advertiser*, and an article, based upon his letter, about his experience at Fromelles was published in 1916. Like so many men, he found that he had time to spend writing home after the battle on account of being wounded; in Sam Yeates's case he wrote from the Ontario Military Hospital in Orpington, Kent. His condition does not appear to have been that good: 'my right hand is temporarily disabled and I have to maintain a more or less prone position in bed. I have, too, just come out of a fever and have to think for a while on the experiences of the past fortnight to distinguish between those which were real and those which were mere figments and dreams'.[18]

Yeates reassured his family that 'I had to retire from the fray... but was in it longer than some of the others'. Nevertheless, he had 'two punctures and an injury to the right arm and hand'. He provided his family with a detailed description of the hospital: 'it has not been open very long... it contains over 1000 beds... there are miles of linoleum on the floors and it is said to curtain the hundreds of windows cost 1,500 pounds... the hospital has its own power house... the kitchen has 44 bread ovens... and immense soup boilers'. He describes the staff of '30 or 40 medical men... all of them of the best universities in Canada, and there are specialists in every department – eye, ear, throat, dental, mental – in addition to physicians and surgeons'. No doubt this provided reassurance that he was receiving the best medical care and attention. His welfare in other areas was also being looked after by 'an Australian Red Cross representative who brought us writing paper, razors, hair brushes, combs and other requisites which we neglected to bring when we were hurried off the battlefield before we had time to pick up our traps'.

Eventually Sam Yeates describes the attack: 'our company went into the fray with great determination and spirit with an absolute contempt for the dangers and risks it had to face'. His stirring tale of disregard for machine gun fire, shrapnel and high explosive, he claimed, 'would have made your blood tingle', though no doubt it had other effects upon those reading his letter at home. Finally, Sam mentions his being wounded: 'I saw some drop out before it came to my turn to stop – some, alas, never to rise again and others badly hurt'. Pte Yeates was fortunate that day and eventually returned to his home in Victoria.

While in hospital the wounded played another role in the processing of casualties, by providing details of men reported to be missing in action for voluntary workers engaged in gathering information to assist with the response to enquiries from the next of kin of casualties. Dozens of these reports exist, and the value of the information contained within them varies from being most helpful to well intentioned but no doubt worthless. Typical of these reports is one in respect of 3367 Pte Billy Outlaw:[19]

A.I.F. 53   OUTLAW, W.S. 3367

W & M. July 19th 1916

I knew him very well. He was a pal of mine. Came from the same place, River Street, Forest Hill, Canterbury, Sydney, N.S.W. He was at Fleurbaix. Pte O'Connor was wounded in that action, and I saw him immediately after. He said that Outlaw was wounded and left in the German lines, and he must be a prisoner. Pte Shark[20] was with Outlaw. Shark's people have had a letter from him saying that he was a prisoner of war in Germany, but as far as I know he did not mention whether Outlaw was with him.

Informant: Pte M. Ashard. 2123.

No. 2 Can. Stat. Outreau

BOULOGNE. 15.3.1917

This search for information was not confined to hospitals in France and Belgium, nor Britain. Similar exercises were undertaken in Australia, where the next of kin, such as the family of Lt C.T. Collier, 53 Btn,[21] could visit the soldiers themselves:

> Statement by 2811 AO. CRASSINGHAM D Coy 53rd Btn reported, 'I saw him wounded in the foot between our support and the front line trenches. I do not know what subsequently became of him. Unless he moved from the position, where I last saw him, he could not be a prisoner. His father and sister have been to see me here and I have told them all I know. The bombardment was terrific, and it was easily possible for him to be blown to bits after he was wounded.'

@ No 4 AGH Randwick

NOTE – A careful reliable witness. 20/2/17

These wounded soldiers would bear the physical signs of their experience for the remainder of their lives, and many children they produced would tell tales of the holes in their father's body, the limp he had or ongoing treatment for a condition developed as a result of his war service. Many others too would re-live the battlefield experience at night or make a spontaneous comment such as 'a good night for a raid'[22] when out walking after dusk with a child; others could only speak about the war on Remembrance Day or Anzac Day when in the company of their mates who had shared the hardships they had endured. The photographs of later Anzac Day parades show the faces of men now aging but wearing their medals with pride. Their memories have now gone to the grave with them, and many of those memories were probably too awful to relate to anyone who had not been there.

Casualty lists, a steady feature of many papers during the war, soon contained the details of Fromelles casualties. In an article entitled 'The Annals of Bendigo', the 'reappearance of casualty lists in the Press indicates that the Australians were once more taking an active part in the war'. As far as Bendigo was concerned at least 30 local men lost their lives at Fleurbaix, as the action was then known. The list headed 'Bendigo's Honoured Dead 1916' contains names such as:

Anglin M. Bendigo 20/7/16

Arbon R.E. Bendigo 19/7/16[23]

Bone R.H. Eaglehawk 19/7/16

Barger W.G. Bendigo 19/7/16

Buchan W.F. Bendigo 22/7/16
Crammond J.H. Cpl Bendigo 19/7/16

These few casualties from 57 and 60 Btns were mixed with some from Pozières and other contacts with the enemy on the Western Front. Their dates of death really do confirm the newspaper's view that, after a lull following the evacuation from Gallipoli, the AIF was back in business.[24]

16

Bitter Legacy

After the battle a number of messages of consolation and congratulation were sent to be read to the troops. It was claimed that the divisions had prevented the Germans moving resources to the Somme and by implication the battle must therefore have been a success. Analysis of the events leading up to the battle and its conduct were the cause of debate and acrimony for years to come, culminating in 'Pompey' Elliott's pamphlet published in 1931 in which he detailed his views on the whole affair. Charles Bean, in volume 3 of the *Official History of Australia in the War 1914–18*, provides two chapters brimming with information on the battle from the Australian point of view. His description and appraisal is both full and objective, but despite recognising the task also faced by the 61 Division and the constraints upon it, he ends the second chapter with a vicious sting in the tail by writing, 'the Australian soldiers tended to accept the judgement – often unjust, but already deeply impressed by the occurrences at the Suvla Bay landing – that the "Tommies" could not be relied upon to uphold a flank in a stiff fight'.

Letters sent home by the troops informed their families of the awful experience of the battle. The influx of correspondence, plus the telegrams and lengthy casualty lists in the newspapers, ended the lull in such horror stories on a grand scale that had existed, for the Australians at least, since the end of the Gallipoli campaign. Very soon after, a similar tide of reports would follow as a consequence of the fighting around Pozières. Bert Bishop's letter dated 1 August illustrates the feelings of a typical soldier:

Dear All,

I suppose by the time this reaches you, you will know about Ray and Billy… You will have read in the papers of the charge made by the Australians, near Armentieres on July 19th, and so have a pretty good idea of how things were. So far I do not know for certain what happened to Billy. I saw a couple of chaps in the same company as him… thought he had been killed in the charge. I was

not in the charge, being one of a party told off to carry ammunition, water, etc,
from our own trenches to the captured German trenches. The first and second
German trenches were carried about 5.45p.m. and a start was at once made in
fixing them up for ourselves. The machine gun Ray was on went across to the
second captured trench about 6p.m. I was speaking to Ray for a few minutes
there and saw him again for the last time about midnight, when I was over with
a load of ammunition… Our boys stuck gamely to the position, the losses on
both sides were horrible. I'll never forget those early hours on Thursday morning. The shells were bursting everywhere… while machine gun and rifle bullets
were whistling round us all the time. About daylight the word was given to
retire to our trenches again and it was then that Ray got hit… I didn't receive
a single scratch all through… The Germans also suffered heavy casualties. They
had some of their dead thrown up on top of their parapet to act as additional
protection where sandbags had been blown away… I'll never forget some of
the awful sights we met with… I couldn't help noticing the look on the faces
of the men as they came out. They all had an ashen grey pallor and looked years
older than when they went in… The old Gallipoli men among us all agree that
there was nothing on the Peninsular to equal it, not even the landing… A parcel
arrived for Ray the other day… hoping you are all well.[1]

The Germans were not deterred from redeploying troops to their Somme front;
even the British Official History states, 'there was no reason to suppose that any
German reinforcements had been drawn to the front of attack'.[2] The papers of XI
Corps note that on 19–20 July raids on the enemy's trenches had been carried out
by the 31 and 39 Divisions in accordance with XI Corps Order No. 58.[3] Three
raiding parties entered the German trenches and had brought back prisoners by
which means identification was obtained proving that no withdrawals of German
troops had taken place from opposite the fronts held by these two divisions.

Three short newspaper cuttings from London papers in Bert Bishop's exercise
books, in which he wrote his account of the battle three and a half years later in
Australia, were sufficient to remind him of the futility of the battle. One is the
infamous synopsis of Haig's report, 'we carried out some important raids on a
front of two miles in which Australian troops took part'. A second, a Reuter's
report headed 'German Official – Amsterdam', records that the British penetrated
the German lines but were repelled. The third supports the Gallipoli veterans'
view of the awfulness of the battle in its headlines, which read, 'Anzacs find France
worse than Gallipoli – Hot work in great night raid near Armentières'.

On the German side of the line Falkenhayn telephoned the HQ of the Sixth
Army for an update on the fighting on 19 July; he had believed that an attack
would be made in this Army's area and now it was happening. The response he
received assured him that the situation was not critical. He made contact again
on the following day and was informed that a captured XI Corps operation

order had revealed the extent of the attack and that it had been contained. Such were the reassurances that Falkenhayn had little difficulty in deciding to transfer resources from the Lille sector to the Somme.[4]

The British press published virtually nothing about the events of 19–20 July, but not so the Germans. The paucity of the newspaper account was noted by Sgt Ridley, 53 Btn, in his 147th letter home: 'enclosed two cuttings from English papers of our little affair. It doesn't sound much but had they been there they might have put a bigger heading'.[5]

On 3 August the *North German Gazette* carried a long article from their war correspondent W. Scheuermann in which he gives a useful description of events from the German side and opinions on Haking's attack, opening with observations on the build-up:

> After the English artillery had been fairly active in the sector west of Lille during the whole of July the possibility had to be reckoned with that they intended to get busy when heavy fire which started on 16th July grew in intensity making it clear to us that the enemy had amassed a considerable amount of artillery including many batteries that had not previously been located by us.

Scheuermann then reports the fighting itself. It is difficult to know how much of his material came from first-hand observation, or whether, like Charles Bean (particularly in the case of Fromelles), he relied on reports and personal accounts related after the battle:

> The trenches had suffered severely under the heavy bombardment and the wire entanglements had been completely swept away. The first line was completely wrecked and our losses were, naturally, not light but the garrison was not cowed for a moment. The sentries continued their look-out and when one fell another immediately volunteered to take his place.
>
> At five o'clock in the evening the enemy lifted his fire on to the rear lines and showed himself apparently ready to leave his trenches. In order to disquieten the Germans he had stuck bayonets over the edge of his front line but this was only a ruse which the English are very fond of playing in order to entice our men into the trenches. Very shortly afterwards he again laid his artillery onto the fire trenches; once again the bombardment became as intense as it possibly could and continued till 5.45p.m.
>
> Then, on a front of 3km the English advanced out of their trenches. They appeared everywhere in close order apparently with the intention of forming a line of skirmishes and carried with them portable bridges, machine guns and hand grenades.
>
> Their whole attitude showed that they had over-estimated the success of their heavy bombardment. In a few seconds the whole of the remainder of the

garrison were out of their dugouts and ready to defend the line. Machine guns were hoisted out of their hiding places and put into position in the open. At the same time our artillery was informed and a few minutes later the carnage began which in the English history of the war will for ever be associated with the name – Fromelles.

Ironically 'Fromelles' has become the name associated with this battle, and was chosen by the battle nomenclature committee after the war. Fromelles was never captured, and the British referred to the fighting here as 'Laventie', the main town behind the 61 Division, while the Australians called it 'Fleurbaix', similarly a principal billeting town behind their sector. The newspaper continued:

> The course of the battle may be divided into two parts, the greater, that in which the hostile attack, partly in front of and partly actually inside our former wire entanglement was repulsed, and secondly where the English temporarily gained a footing in our lines. At one place in front of a place called Obstgarten [the Orchard] out of which the enemy came in masses, about 800 dead lay in front of our trenches on a breadth of 250 metres. In the Orchard itself our patrols counted 250 more. At this location, in addition to rifle and machine gun fire, our artillery did splendid work against the advancing and retreating masses of the enemy.

Mopping up is briefly reported in the *Gazette* though the account implies that the repulse was dependent upon the voluntary, rather than directed, response by German troops:

> Each group looked upon it as its duty to turn the enemy out of its own section of trench and help came from all sides. Anyone who was free in the neighbouring trenches came forward voluntarily to attack the English. Night in the meantime had fallen.
>
> Slowly but irresistibly the storming troops threw themselves against the front and flanks of the enemy. Comrades from the neighbouring sectors where the enemy had already been beaten came up of their own free will and did their full share of the work with great bravery. As dawn of 20th July broke, our troops advancing with irresistible force also managed to clear the first line of the rest of the English.
>
> At 9 o'clock in the morning the Staff sent out the following message – 'Our positions are firmly held by our Division'.

The account recognises that a large part of the opposing force was Australian, probably one of the first reports in the German press concerning German units encountering the AIF in France and Flanders:

The English troops who took part in this action were Australians. For the most part they are war volunteers and amongst them were many well-to-do farmers, strong, youthful men who undoubtedly attacked with great bravery and proved themselves clever and tenacious in close fighting.

The final section of Scheuermann's report more or less accurately appraises the failure of the assault.

The English enterprise against Fromelles has caused headshaking everywhere amongst ourselves as well as in neutral countries and perhaps even amongst the French and English themselves, for no-one could imagine what the intentions of the English really were.

Had it merely been a demonstration against the enormously strong German defences of Lille it would appear to have been undertaken with either too large or too small a force so that the whole affair would have remained a mystery had we not captured the English Operation Order. From this it appears that the English were of the opinion that we were taking troops from this part of the front for employment on the Somme. They wanted to prevent this and to bind down our forces and, if possible, cause us to drain our reserves on the Somme.

This plan absolutely came to nothing, for the Bavarian Division which was attacked, gained from the ascendancy by themselves, without bringing up a single gun from any other position, and without needing, even for a moment, the reserves which were naturally ready to come up from the neighbouring sectors.

Not a single extra man or gun was used in addition to the number which had been provided from the first for the defence of this sector.

The English used enormous quantities of ammunition of American origin especially from the Bethlehem Steel Co. whose pious name can be read on many duds. The quality of these American shells fortunately varies.

Owing to the severity of the attack and the great superiority in artillery which the enemy had assembled, the losses of the Division were naturally not small. Our troops were not, however, dismayed as they could see for themselves, that the English lost in dead alone four times as many as they did, only counting the bodies lying in No Man's Land and not taking into account the number who died later of wounds. The spirit of the troops, the vast majority of whom have been fighting since the beginning of the war, and have fought in a number of bloody battles, was very much raised by this splendid success.

The *West Australian* newspaper carried a number of reports about the battle, the first being Haig's statement that contained the lines, 'yesterday evening, south of Armentieres, we carried out some important raids on a front of two miles in which Australian troops took part.' In the following day's edition the following first hand report was published:

One officer was splendid when things were at their worst. He took over the command when the senior officer was killed and kept the men in good heart so that they organised the defence against the German counter attacks; they were surrounded by German grenadiers, and suffered heavily from artillery, machine gun and sniping fire… all the bombs had gone and there were not many rounds of ammunition left. The officer rallied six good men and ordered the others to retreat with the wounded, and take their chance across No Man's Land, while he put up a last fight. He stuck to the barricade until all but two were killed. He was the last to leave and by a miracle came back unwounded except for a few scratches. His courage saved many lives.

Gradually the Londoners [sic] withdrew straggling across no man's land under a great shell fire. All the ground was strewn with our wounded. Here an officer said 'I must pay tribute to the enemy' there were a lot of white men against us. They let us collect our wounded unhindered when the fight was over. It was difficult enough to get them and many stayed out on the field suffering great anguish for days and nights.

The German view published in the *Berliner* appeared on 24 July:

The situation should fill Germany with the greatest confidence as the pressure on Verdun has lured the British from their trenches and weakened them appreciably. Britain bleeds from thousands of wounds as never before during the empire's existence. When the small results and enormous losses become known the British cries of victory will soon be silenced and a bad awakening will follow.

Friday evening's German communiqué stated Yesterday's English attack in the Fromelles region by two strong divisions were repulsed. We took 481 prisoners and counted 2000 bodies in front of our lines. The enemy's strong attacks… on both banks of the Somme failed. The enemy captured only two miles of our front line southward of Hardecourt.

The same edition also carried a story from neutral Holland which does not quite reflect what appeared to be German understanding of the purpose of the 19 July assault. The Central News Amsterdam correspondent stated:

German War correspondents are puzzled by the British attacks at Fromelles and south of Armentieres, on Wednesday evening in which two strong divisions were engaged. Some consider that this introduces a new offensive. Some that there is a serious attempt to advance towards Lille being initiated, and others that the attacks were merely a demonstration to prevent the Germans sending troops to their menaced sectors near Hooge.

On 28 July the *Sydney Morning Herald* published Bean's report. Under the heading 'Australians – Attack Trenches – Temporary Success – Take 200 Prisoners', he gives a brief appraisal based upon information he gathered after his arrival on the Fleurbaix sector on 20 July. In his final paragraph, Bean told the people at home that 'our troops… had to face shell fire which was heavier and more continuous than was ever known in Gallipoli'. This sentiment was to be echoed by the veterans of the fight and prepared the public for war on a greater scale than the AIF had experienced hitherto. His final line, 'the losses amongst our troops engaged were severe',[6] warned Australians of the carnage; casualty lists in the coming weeks would substantiate Bean's warning beyond any doubt.

Another summary of the battle appeared in the *Argus* newspaper on 10 April 1920, possibly the first detailed post-war account. Entitled 'Fromelles 1916! – A Glorious Failure – What Really Happened', it claims that 'for a long time the secrecy of war kept a veil drawn over the details of this sad page in the history of the Australian Imperial Force'. This newspaper article does not reveal any new information, especially bearing in mind that Ellis had already published *The Story of the Fifth Australian Division*. However, an interesting comment that does not appear to be recorded in any war diaries is the observation by night-time patrols that the German wire was minimal, but that this was deemed to be insignificant as the artillery had yet to finish pounding the entanglements. The subsequent absence of any reports of substantial delay caused by the enemy's barbed wire paints a rather better picture of the wire-cutting work done by the artillery than might be construed from the overall performance of the Australian batteries.

The report does claim that 'the enemy trenches [were] entered by elements of 60th. They appear to have had some temporary success for they sent back a few prisoners.' This is not backed up by any other reports and appears to be quite erroneous; there is no evidence that any penetration of the German strongpoint was achieved on either side of the immediate Sugar Loaf area. A fair assessment of 14 Bde is given, including the quandary in which they found themselves when the support trenches shown on their maps could not be found. Recognition is also given to 8 Bde's success and the retreat to their own lines long after sunrise.

Not surprisingly, of all newspaper reports it is the phrase about the 'important raids… in which Australian troops took part' that has left one of the most bitter legacies of the battle.

17

Better Than I Expected

Four days after the battle Haking sent a single-page synopsis of the operation[1] to First Army HQ, accompanied by a report from the 61 Division (The Australian report was not yet to hand). It contains a number of inaccuracies and shows precious little support or encouragement for his own battalions. Haking wrote that it was absolutely necessary to use the two new divisions because it would not have been practicable to move any other divisions into the position in the time available, and that the lessons to be learnt from the attack applied more to the divisions who took part in it that to ordinary trained divisions. He claimed that 'the artillery preparation was adequate, there were sufficient guns and sufficient ammunition'.

Haking's evaluation of his two divisions was concise and disingenuous: 'the Australian Infantry attacked in the most gallant manner and gained the enemy's position, but they were not sufficiently trained to consolidate the ground gained', while 'the 61 Division were not sufficiently imbued with the offensive spirit.' Had trained troops been available, 'the position would have been a gift after the artillery bombardment'.

By 26 July Haking had received McCay's report and was more forthcoming in his recognition of the Australian efforts. This imbalance no doubt reflects an immediate appraisal of the relative success of the two divisions, but also demonstrates Haking's poor regard for Territorial units, though he conveniently overlooked the numerical weakness of Mackenzie's battalions. His covering note to Plumer stated:

I think the attack of the Australian Division… was carried out in an exceptionally gallant manner. There is no doubt that the men advanced with the greatest
determination. Their difficulties on the right flank were caused by the failure
of the 61 Division to carry the Sugar Loaf. On their left flank the Australian
Division were unable to consolidate sufficiently during the night and conse-

quently when that flank gave way the remainder of the line was compelled to withdraw. The artillery work turned out even better than I expected though many of the Batteries had very little experience.[2]

An error was made placing the divisional boundary midway across a prominent, well-defended battlefield feature such as the Sugar Loaf Salient. As for secrecy, it was difficult to conceal preparations and details of the forthcoming attack were well known. George Rankin, 53 Btn, recalled that 'everyone in town knew the attack was coming',[3] and Bert Bishop wrote that 'rumour was everywhere about a stunt we were booked for'.[4]

McCay had ordered that the Stokes mortars and Vickers machine guns should be brought forward only when it was evident that the Australians held the German line. Similarly, the Lewis guns were to follow the infantry waves. The absence of firepower affected the troops' ability to take and hold the enemy line. Intelligence provided for the attacking troops was unreliable. Some of the enemy's support 'trenches' were ditches, while some were indeed trenches but had long been abandoned. Haking has also been criticised for holding a battalion in each brigade in reserve (though some men were used as carrying parties). Had these troops been sent forward the casualty lists would have been even longer and the net result of the attack would have been no different.

Communications were problematic. Many of the officers who were killed carried the flares that were to be used to signal to aircraft so that they could identify the position of troops. The use of red screens laid on the ground to mark the troops' position was inappropriate for an attack launched in the early evening in murky weather.

The performance of the artillery units varied. There were plenty of guns available and the artillery commander did not doubt that they could do the job given to them. Provision of extra guns strengthened his confidence in success. Communications were difficult for the gunners too. Cables to the rear from battery positions were buried, in theory, to a depth of six feet, but cables running forward to a forward observation officer were exposed to shell fire and accidental damage by troops. This was confirmed by the OC 61 Division Signal Company who recorded that 'lines from Ops to FOOs were continually cut'.[5] Observation was handicapped by the weather delaying registration, and then by smoke from burning ammunition dumps and the evening haze which covered the battlefield. Runners were an alternative, albeit with obvious risks.

The haste with which the operation was instigated further affected the performance of the artillery. The 5 Divisional Artillery had at best seven days to prepare but those batteries of 4 Australian Division employed at Fromelles did not move into position until the nights of 14/15 and 15/16 July. Movement of ammunition from the Divisional Ammunition Sub Park to battery positions, where it then had to be unboxed and positioned beside each gun, was a further onerous task. The sheer effort by inexperienced gunners to be in the line ready for the battle was overlooked by Haking, and compounded the error of his assurances to his Army Commander.

The 61 Division CRA reported that his gunners performed well during the preparations for the attack and during the action itself. The unit war diary notes that the enemy wire was extensively damaged, as were the trenches, and mentions that 'a very strong machine gun emplacement has been uncovered by our fire at N.19.a.4.7 built of concrete. This emplacement is about 5' high by 12' long and has 3 large fire holes about halfway down.'[6] Despite this good work, the GOC 61 Division acknowledged in its report that 'other portions of the line did not suffer so much, particularly the Sugar Loaf and the Wick. The enemy machine guns were not destroyed by the bombardment.'[7] However, he commented that the artillery may have done too well: 'as regards the enemy's parapet, the portion captured later by the 7 Warwicks on the right was so knocked about that it afforded them no cover when they got into it'.[8]

The accuracy of the Australian gunners' shooting was not as good as the infantry may have liked, due to inadequacies in the training and preparation of gunners of 5 and 4 Australian Divisions. Moreover, the dusty conditions of Tel-el-Kebir were far from ideal preparation for a major operation against a skilful German division in well-constructed positions on the Western Front. Other factors also contributed to their performance at Fromelles, including the loss of momentum in training brought about by their reorganisation in Egypt and then again after arrival in France, and the low proportion of personnel with any artillery experience, which was inevitable when the AIF was a completely new army that dwarfed the pre-war Citizen Forces. Furthermore, No Man's Land, particularly on the left flank opposite 8 Bde, was only about 100 yards across; registration had been impeded by the weather; smoke and mist from the battlefield hindered visibility, and communications were relatively primitive and thus made rapid response to changing circumstances difficult. The accuracy of the Australian guns was poor, thus preventing close support of the infantry and leaving them exposed to rifle, machine gun and mortar fire.

Pte Jim Cleworth reminded a 5 Division gunner of their shortcomings in 1972 when he moved to Sydney. His son, Bob, was friendly with the son of this gunner and introduced them as they had both been 'in the first show'. On being informed that his new mate was a gunner, Jim reminded him that 'your blokes dropped short on us at Fromelles', to which the response came, 'Yeah, but we made up for it at Polygon Wood!' The two veterans then spent the afternoon deep in conversation.[9]

However, the 'Report on Operations carried out by 8 Infantry Bde' notes that the artillery 'did very good work on the wire and the enemy's parapet, and many dead Germans were seen as a result of their bombardment'; it also notes that the 'Artillery Group Commander responded promptly to every request sent him for increased rate, lifts etc'. Miscellaneous signals comment differently on the work of the Australian batteries. For example, the FOO of 57 Bty (left group) noted that 'our fire seems v.g. and well on parapet also in wire'; the OC A171 Bty noted that 'parapets also consistently damaged'. One FOO in the Australian right group reported at 8.50p.m. on 19 July shells were 'falling short between our front line and enemy's front line'.[10] At 7.35p.m. the FOO of 114 Bty reported 'great volumes of pure white smoke… left of Les Clochers; smoke drifting in thick clouds'. A third FOO (54 Bty) about the same time sent back a message saying, 'huge fire on left… smoke going back over enemy lines making an ideal screen'. At 7.23 the following morning a further report noted, 'smoky air makes observation impossible'.[11] It is evident too that there was a difference of opinion among infantry officers; Lt Col Toll, in his report on the events of 19–20 July, commented that on the first day many shells fell short. He was very critical of this aspect of the attack, but Brig-Gen Tivey recorded that the artillery work in his sector was well done.[12]

In some sectors the wire was certainly cut to such an extent that the infantry could make rapid progress towards the German parapet. These breastworks too had been badly damaged in a number of places and was confirmed in post-battle reports. However, no satisfactory explanation has been uncovered for the failure to inflict greater damage on the Sugar Loaf Salient itself; of all the features of the section of line under assault, this was the most critical point, and had to be damaged in a way that would minimise the ability of its defenders to withstand the attack by both the divisions.

Although the infantry may have had justification for their criticism of the Australian gunners to direct fire accurately, it was not for want of attention to detail in this aspect of planning by the artillery. The 14 Australian Field Artillery Bde issued orders to some of their batteries to make arrangements for forward observation officers to advance into the captured sector during the night and obtain places from where they could direct the fire of their batteries. They were to be positioned in the German lines such that observers in observation posts could see them and maintain visual signalling. One particular order stressed that 'it is of the utmost importance that tactical information should be got back during the night to the Group'.[13]

The Australian CRA, General Christian, made little study of how well his gunners, and those on loan to him, performed. In the war diary he notes that communications were good, but comments that they were fortunate that the German gunners were ineffective in their attempts to break communications within the artillery lines. In respect of his own guns he records, 'the enemy wire does not appear to have been an obstacle to our infantry and from reports received seems to have been well cut'. This is a fair appraisal of wire cutting. In respect of the German trenches he states, 'the front parapet was also heavily damaged. Our first false barrage apparently had no effect as the forward officer in the trenches reported that the enemy did not appear to man his parapet during the "lift".' No mention is made of the inadequacy of the bombardment on the Sugar Loaf Salient despite requests for additional shelling. Furthermore, no comment is made on the serious issue, for the 8 Bde in particular, of shells falling short. Finally, the war diary records that 'the action of the TM battery was good and their tasks were carried out in a thoroughly capable and praiseworthy manner'.[14]

Considering the difficulties that the 5 Australian Division's artillery experienced during its formation, these batteries performed as well as could be expected. Fromelles was a grossly unfortunate baptism of gunfire, but it does not appear to have tainted their reputation as the war on the Western Front progressed towards ultimate victory in 1918.

A number of other factors indicate the vulnerability of the two divisions at Fromelles. Understrength 61 Division battalions consisted of troops not fully trained and lacking experience in trench warfare. The infantry did not go into battle fresh and rested and this impediment was commented upon in the history of the 2/1 Bucks Btn, which says, 'the formation of dumps of SAA, rations, water, engineer stores, etc, necessitated having fatigue parties work for days beforehand, and even the troops detailed for the attack were not exempt up to the last moment'.

The gallantry and determination of individual troops was remarkable. Although 2/6 Warwicks had been badly mauled by shell fire and then by machine gun and rifle fire, and some troops had reached the enemy parapet, their war diary records that 'the conduct of all ranks throughout the action was most excellent, orders being cheerfully carried out without the slightest hesitation under the most trying conditions'.[15] However, the cost was huge. Major Christie-Miller estimated that 'about 300 men must have gone over… less than 100 got back. Of the officers all three of A and of C Coy were killed, of D Coy all three were wounded. The only company officer of the three assaulting Coys left was Capt H.S.G. Buckmaster who collapsed under the strain.'[16] These casualties in 2/1 Bucks included many key people. Capt Church and Lts Hudson, Phipps, Brewin, Parker and Atkinson were all killed; Lt Chadwick died of wounds; Capts Stewart-Liberty and Ranger, 2/Lts Drakes, Oliver, Relf, Rutherford, Baddeley and Pitcher were all wounded. Lt Atkinson and 2/Lt Hudson were both missing, later to be confirmed as killed.[17] The loss of two CSMs, brothers Arthur Brown and Ralph Brown,[18] and some of the other experienced NCOs, rendered three of the four companies virtually useless as a fighting force. Their battalion history noted, 'the attack therefore, though successful in preventing the withdrawal of German Infantry or guns to reinforce in withstanding the offensive on the Somme, failed to gain the local objective'.[19]

The inability of the infantry of both 184 and 15 Bdes to secure the Sugar Loaf Salient was attributable to poor shooting by the gunners, the enemy still active in this key location, and the width of No Man's Land. What appreciation did the artillery have of the plight of the infantry? Major E. Lister recorded in his diary that the gunners 'heavily bombarded the German positions from 11a.m. until about 6p.m. when our infantry went over the parapet and captured three lines of trenches', and that 'the infantry are reported to have captured about 300 Germans and 30 machine guns but their jubilation was cut short early this morning when the Germans counter attacked and kicked them out of the trenches altogether'.[20]

The loss of officers, especially early on, and the difference it made to the command and control of troops in the assault, was also recorded in McCay's division. Taking 53 and 54 Btns we find:

Lt Col Norris, 53 Btn, was killed not long after making the hazardous crossing of No Man's Land.

Major Sampson, Norris's senior company commander, was also killed in the early stages of the occupation of the German front-line.

Capt Arblaster then took on a significant leadership role but he too was badly wounded in the early hours of the morning of 20 July and subsequently died in German hands on 24 July.

In 53 Btn, Capt H. Paulin was killed, F.R. Ranson and D. Thomson were both wounded, and Lts G.E. Allan, C.T. Collier, H.L. Moffitt, C.E. Mudge, B.J. Nelson, W.E. Noble and T.N. Rickard were all killed during the fight.

Eight lieutenants (T. Francis, A.E. Jackson, C.A. Johnson, J. Lang, N.B. Lovett, H.C.W. Pain, W.E. Smith and A.O. Thompson) were wounded.

As early as 17 July, Lt J. Alpuget (54 Btn) was killed whilst wire cutting in front of the German line.

Major Roy Harrison, second-in-command of 54 Btn, was killed in No Man's Land.

Capt H. Taylor, Lts T. Ahern, C. Boone, H. Hall and J. Strangman (all 54 Btn) were killed in action.

Major R. Holman, Capts J. Hansen, B. Jack and C. Lecky were wounded, as were Lts R. Downing, A. Hirst, A. Morris, E. Sadler, C. Shaw, H. Sudbury, O. Tedder and H. Young.

Col Cass's appraisal of 54 Btn's participation, in his report 'The Raid at Armentieres', records the losses sustained before his men even left their own front line as a consequence of very accurate shelling. The barrage, combined with machine gun and rifle fire, accounted for yet more casualties in No Man's Land, but Cass stated that the German trenches 'were easily captured and two m.g.s in addition. Our men followed the fleeing enemy for about 600 yards.' He stated that 53 Btn were in contact with 15 Bde to their right. However, as the night continued the situation, as reported by Cass to Divisional HQ, became very confused, and the 53 Btn moved into the section of the line held by his battalion.

Reference is made to the surrender of groups of men and to the story of 'at least 6 Germans in Australian uniform' who crossed to German held positions as an inducement for others to follow, though Cass acknowledges that 'in the half light there may be some mistake about this'. Troops from 53 Btn were also falling back to their own lines, which added to Cass' difficulties. At 4a.m. he located Lt Col McConaghy, the CO 55 Btn, and tried to organise a bayonet attack. A small party did do this and drove the Germans back fifty yards, but not long afterwards 8 Bde retired leaving 14 Bde's flank exposed. The remainder of Cass's report concerns the further breakdown in communications and the ragged withdrawal to the Australian lines.

Col Pope's 14 Bde generally had been successful in its part in the battle. It had suffered the loss of Lt Col Norris, CO 53 Btn, early in the assault and its right flank was exposed as a result of 15 Bde being unable to advance. Another early setback was the destruction of telephone wires between the brigade and the battalion; communication was lost for 'a considerable time'[21] at the start of the attack.

As early as 7.36p.m. the 54 Btn had asked for reinforcements in the belief that the 8 Bde to their left had withdrawn. The brigade succeeded in pushing more troops forward to assist Lt Col McConaghy, and in conjunction with a successful delivery of sandbags and the capture of German machine guns the brigade was in a relatively strong position by midnight. This situation was maintained until 14 Bde was left with both flanks unsupported, making withdrawal inevitable. Overall this brigade performed well, the infantry and engineers particularly so; it was the remarkable achievement of the 5 Division Pioneers in digging a four-foot-deep communication trench across No Man's Land which enabled 54 and 55 battalions to retire in some degree of safety. However, the strain of the battle was too much for 54 Btn's CO, Col Cass, who returned to Australia, according to Elliott, 'broken-hearted at the loss of his battalion'.[22]

Brig-Gen Tivey appraised each of his units in his report following the battle.[23] He states:

> 29 Btn… carried out their orders promptly and all ranks worked well.
> 30 Btn – throughout the fight worked vigorously and kept the supply of stores, bombs etc going under heavy artillery and machine gun fire, and later rein-forced the 31 and 32 Btns in the captured trenches. Great keenness was displayed by all ranks.

Col Clark, 30 Btn, was very proud of his men, and recognising that twenty years had passed when he came to write a piece in *Mufti* in 1937, he referred to a letter he wrote to his family. In that letter he stated: 'never in my wildest imagination did I dream my officers and men would behave and fight as they did, not one failed me; every officer was cool and courageous, and the NCOs and men obey immediately and without question every order given them, even though it was generally under a most hellish fire'.[24] Tivey was generous in his praise of 30 Btn, whose digging feat was a remarkable story of determination and courage under fire. He continues with plaudits well-earned by units of the 8 Bde:

> 31 Btn – advanced from our right flank and took three lines of the enemy's trenches, notwithstanding heavy casualties. This battalion held on to their positions until the last, and only retired after units on their right and left had fallen back.
>
> 32 Btn – advanced and captured three lines of the enemy's trenches under a hail of artillery and machine gun fire. They hung on to their position until the counter attack of the enemy rolled up their left flank.
>
> Brigade Machine Gun Coy – was a tower of strength and all ranks did everything that was possible for men to do… the gunners held on till the last to help the infantry.

On the left of the battlefield where Tivey's 31 Btn fought, even a cursory read of Bean's account or of war diaries provides a good appraisal of how well these troops performed. In addition, Lt Col F.W. Toll, CO 31 Btn, wrote detailed notes. He estimated that 500 Germans were killed and 120 captured in his battalion's sector.[25] This figure represents a sizeable proportion of the estimated 1,500 German casualties. His battalion's creditable work started with careful scouting of the front line area that the battalion would occupy during the battle. On 19 July, even before the attack was launched, Toll's troops suffered heavy casualties from enemy shelling (and Australian shells falling short), causing carefully organised formations to be broken up. Six of the eight runners were killed before 31 Btn had left the support lines. So great were the casualties that Toll referred to 'the first wave or what was left of it'.[26] To the battalion's advantage they found that the artillery had wrecked the German positions and killed many defenders. Toll himself acted decisively in searching for the German second line, and his Battalion HQ party had themselves cleared many Germans 'hiding in underweeds, in trees and ditches'. Lt Col Toll established communication with Major Eckersley on his right and sought to establish a robust flank, gathering pockets of troops throughout the night so that an organised resistance might be made.

In Toll's report the number of officers and men he commended by name indicates his regard for diligent troops, a number of whom received honours after the battle. Others, including the private 'who carried the pigeon basket through a hail of shell fire', were rewarded with promotions. The attack, hold on the German line and withdrawal were as successful as could be expected, largely due to Toll's leadership set against the background of a tally of over 500 casualties.

Some Australian casualties were unnecessarily incurred. Among the wounded, some sixteen per cent had head wounds; the absence of steel helmets was a critical shortcoming for many. Going into action in a felt hat may have been perpetuating a hallmark of the AIF, but shrapnel balls and shards of iron travelling at high velocity do not respect outward displays of *esprit de corps*.

The 15 Bde suffered extraordinary casualties for no gain. Even after the battle, Elliott continued to believe that his brigade had achieved far greater success than was actually the case, and he noted that McCrae's 60 Btn 'reached the German second line trenches but were eventually all killed or captured'. In his pencilled notes for 19–20 July, however, he had no doubts about the outcome of the battle: 'we made the attack yesterday as ordered but it was a bitter failure except for the courage of the Boys'. Furthermore, it was Elliott's view that 'the 5 Division was crippled by the fight at Fromelles and not until the end of the summer when it raided the German trenches frequently and successfully did it regain its full self-confidence'.[27]

The inexperience of the troops left them exposed. Troops who were delegated the task of carrying stores forward joined in the fighting, many of whom were not proficient in the use of the Mills grenade; some instruction was given in the midst of battle but many bombs were distributed without detonators. Other tasks would have challenged the most tested troops, such as filling sandbags with wet clay-mud which proved impractical and inhibited the construction of defensive barriers. Lt Col MacLaurin, in his *Sydney Morning Herald* article in 1919, acknowledged that the 'infantry showed amazing courage, but their lack of training was their undoing'.

One success story was the work of 5 Australian Division Signal Company, which reported that 'communications to HQ of all Brigades and to all points behind the lines worked without interruption during the whole of the engagement. The telephone exchange and sounder lines were kept busily engaged... and gave entire satisfaction.' The diary goes on to state that surface line inevitably suffered considerably, 'but the Brigade sections performed excellent work and kept in touch with their battalions by telephone almost continuously'. A pigeon service 'was used satisfactorily for delivery of several messages which in some cases originated in captured enemy trenches. The average time of flight from the trenches to the lofts was 17 minutes.'[28] The timing of the battle had limited the use of birds as they could only be employed with any real chance of success in daylight.

The signallers' transport had mixed fortunes during the battle. Their lorry and motor car were said to be useful in conveying material to replace damaged equipment or to lay new line. Motorcycles were used extensively to the point that they 'almost broke down on account of the large number of priority dispatches'.[29] The distribution of the unit's fifteen motorcycles had been two with the Divisional Artillery, one with each infantry brigade and the remaining ten at Divisional HQ. This number was subsequently stated to be adequate at ordinary times but insufficient during an attack.

All three Field Companies of the Australian Engineers prepared well for the battle and served with distinction. Their casualties varied quite considerably, with the 8 Field Coy[30] on the left flank suffering the highest number. Their losses amounted to five killed, thirty-three wounded and four men missing. The centre company, 14 Field Coy,[31] had one officer wounded, three other ranks killed, a further eighteen wounded and three missing. Nearest the Sugar Loaf Salient where the 15 Field Company were located, one officer was wounded, two other ranks were killed, twenty-one were wounded of whom one subsequently died of wounds, and five men were listed as missing, though one was soon established to have been killed and another rejoined his section. One of the missing men was Cpl Forbes, who 'turned up much bruised and shaken after lying in the German wire for 30 hours in a shell hole'.[32] Their work in digging trenches across No Man's Land was remarkable.

The Germans performed well. They incurred some casualties in the bombardment, but as their front line was held lightly and they had the benefit of good dugouts for shelter during the bombardment they were able to rely on the response by numerous, well-trained machine gun teams. The Germans were not misled by the appearances of imminent attack, and may have benefited from warnings from all the spies that supposedly resided near the British front areas! Col Clark, 30 Btn, was another who noted the knowledge the enemy had of the forthcoming attack. Writing in *Mufti* in July 1937 he said that 'no secret was made of the fact that we were to attack. I am confident the enemy knew the date and the hour'.[33]

Once the Australians had broken through the Germans they displayed their proficiency to re-group and recover in a relatively narrow front but they paid quite a high cost. According to an 8 Bde report:

> Many Germans were found dead in their front trench and lying about between there and their rear trenches. Many others were killed by bombs and bayonet, including several officers. The estimated number of enemy dead seen was about 600. Several machine guns and trench mortars were destroyed; piles of bombs were thrown into the ditches. Twelve Germans were killed in one dugout by one of our men who threw in two bombs.[34]

Fromelles was destined to occupy many column inches in newspapers and journals over the next fifty or more years. H.R. Williams, writing in *The Gallant Company*, makes a popular appraisal, commenting that 'The 5 Australian Division', and for that matter 61 Division as well, 'was sacrificed on the altar of incompetence. But at least by their gallantry and tenacity they proved in those bloody hours that they were fit to rate with the best fighting divisions on the Western Front.' Williams concurs with Bert Bishop in his concluding sentence on this attack: 'men who had fought on Gallipoli from the Landing to the Evacuation, admitted freely that Fromelles was the severest test they had seen'.[35]

Honours and awards were conferred upon over 200 men. A complete list is impossible to determine, but remaining records indicate the following:

Award	61 Division	5 Australian Division
DSO	2	11
MC	12	46
OBE	1	–
DCM	3	35
MM	20	50
MiD	1	36
Foreign awards	–	15

Among the papers in the AWM concerning 58 Btn is a recommendation, dated 3 August 1916, for the Victoria Cross made in respect of Major A.J.S. Hutchinson:

At Petillon on the night 19th/20th July, 1916, Major Hutchinson displayed conspicuous and gallant leadership. On the evening of the 19th/20th July, 1916, a message came from 5th Division that the 61st Division on our right would renew the attack at 9p.m. on the SUGAR LOAF Salient and notwithstanding that the previous attack by a battalion had manifestly failed, Major Hutchinson led the two companies of the 58th Battalion under his command in the most gallant manner under an appalling fire until he fell riddled with machine gun bullets close under the German parapet. His life and the lives of his men were gallantly given in the hope of aiding the attack of the 61st Division, which unfortunately was not made.

The recommendation by Elliott is countersigned by McCay and supported by statements by Lt H.R. Boyd and 2/Lt H. Dardier. The document is endorsed 'no trace of award'. There is no record of why the award was not made, but it has been suggested that it was declined as the attack was a costly failure, or perhaps because the (probably) unintentional slur on 61 Division did not endear Elliott and McCay to the British officers who would have processed the recommendations.

In 1930, on the fourteenth anniversary of the battle, Elliott was invited by the Canberra branch of the RSSILA to address members on the subject of the attack at Fromelles. His speech was printed in *The Duckboard* and later as a separate pamphlet. His two opening remarks, firstly the statistics of casualties and, secondly, an observation that the 'official historian, who is generally most lenient towards official blundering, found himself forced to condemn it in mild but no uncertain terms', set the tone for the event.

Harold Elliott had visited the German lines below Aubers Ridge after the Armistice, a long-awaited wish for him; rather than easing his mind, though, it hardened his opinion of the futility of the attack. He argued that the plan was flawed and that Haking had exaggerated the amount of artillery that would be available. He also referred to the lack of secrecy or surprise in the operation. In the course of his speech he makes little comment on McCay and, if anything, is sympathetic. He claims that 'McCay was not consulted throughout, and has so far been merely informed (on the 12 July) that his division was being handed over to Haking for an attack'. At the end, he refers to Bean's assertion that McCay had been unjustly blamed for the losses and states that his 'whole afterlife was embittered by these unjust reproaches'.

As the presentation develops it is clear that chunks of Bean's text have been summarised, but the talk is structured around 'blunders'. He makes the point, as blunder No. 4, that the Sugar Loaf Salient should have been allocated solely to one brigade. It is doubtful that this would have made any difference to the outcome of the attack in 15 Bde sector. Moreover, as it was partly Elliott's sector, his angst is even more understandable.

The visit of Major Howard to 15 Bde sector is inevitably seized upon by Harold Elliott, who acknowledges that Howard reported their fears of a 'bloody holocaust' to Haig. Although this was understood by Haig, he made his notorious annotation on the operations plan concerning the use of infantry only if 'an adequate supply of guns and ammunition' was available. By being emphatic that resources were satisfactory, Haking again attracts criticism from Elliott. Haking convinced Monro and together they persuaded Butler that the assault would benefit the Somme offensive. Sir Richard Haking, according to Elliott, also believed that his troops were keen to engage the enemy; Elliott takes the opposite view, and suggests that Haking was seeking to be seen in a good light by his superior officers.

Elliott moves on to another opportunity which Haking had to delay the assault. When the rain started, Butler reminded Haking that the Army Commander could postpone or cancel the operation; Haking also knew the limitations of the artillery at his disposal. According to Elliott, Haking sheltered 'behind the weakness displayed by Monro, by Butler and even by Haig himself at this critical juncture' and decided not to grab this opportunity. Later in the speech he is scornful of Haking's report after the battle, which claimed that the artillery preparation was adequate. Elliot does not miss the chance to refer to the infamous comment that the 'Australian infantry… were not sufficiently trained to consolidate the ground gained', and that the '61 Division was not sufficiently imbued with the offensive spirit'.

In summing up, Elliott lists his ten 'blunders'. Eight appear valid, but no. 6 was clearly in Elliott's mind from the innovation used at Le Hamel in July 1918, and there is no evidence that gas cylinders (no. 7) caused any significant problems. His list of ten is:

1. Failure of the first duty of a commander – personal reconnaissance – resulting in selection of unsuitable ground commanded everywhere by the enemy observation and fire, and which gave no position upon which to consolidate.
2. No Man's Land in front of centre of attack was too wide. (This also was due to the first.)
3. Insufficient artillery preparation, resulting in the wire being uncut and enemy front line and batteries not silenced.
4. Faulty division of front, the junction of units being opposite enemy's strongest point.
5. No arrangement for liaison between these divisions or to co-ordinate the advance itself or methods to be employed.
6. No sufficient arrangements for ammunition supply by aeroplanes or the like.
7. Gas cylinders kept in our line when it was certain that line would be bombarded.
8. Hurried and insufficient preparations resulting in mistakes by inexperienced junior staff officers e.g., in sending up undetonated bombs. As this was the first engagement of these young officers, this danger might have been provided against by Haking.
9. Sending battalion staffs forward with the last wave before any lodgement had been gained in enemy's line, thus sacrificing valuable officers uselessly.
10. No reserves provided. Had this been done it might have been possible to push a company or two across into the space that had been gained, and by attack outwards, to have cleared the front of the 15 Bde.

The newspaper *The Age* reported Elliott's address under the heading 'British Inefficiency at Fleurbaix' in their 18 July 1930 edition. 'Pompey' believed that it was an attempt to discredit him. He responded by sending the text of his speech to *The Duckboard* so a wide and informed readership would be achieved. Many readers would realise that 'blunders' 5, 8, 9 and 10 might rest with McCay rather than Haking. Some of Elliott's reaction to the newspaper report was compounded by the periods of depression he suffered plus difficulties he faced in his business life. Elliott had only another seven months to live.

In Elliott's own notes on the battle he records certain other aspects which are not obviously carried forward into his list of 'blunders'. For example, 'the reasons for this failure seem to have been loose thinking and somewhat reckless decision on the part of the Higher Staff'. He also refers to Haking being 'emphatic that he was quite satisfied with the resources at his disposal', and, escalating responsibility up the chain of command, 'Monro after consultation… gave the assurance that he was satisfied'.

Elliott also blames Mackenzie's 184 Bde for the annihilation of his brigade: 'because the British failed to take the Sugar Loaf this caused the slaughter of the 15 Brigade next to them'. He overlooks the plan which intended both brigades to advance simultaneously; could Mackenzie therefore claim that the failure of 15 Bde had caused the decimation of his own battalions? A more conciliatory note appears later in Elliott's papers, when he writes that 'the British Tommies were blamed most unfairly' for 58 Btn's misfortune. Harold Elliott's views are repeated in a letter to Charles Bean in August 1926, in which he reiterates his views on the width of No Man's Land and the visit of 'a major from General Haig's staff (I cannot recall his name at this time)'.[36]

Appraisal of the battle places responsibility for the debacle with Haking rather than with his divisional commanders. This was supported in a letter from Philip Landon (a Fellow of Trinity College, Oxford) to Brig-Gen Sir J.E. Edmonds CB CMG, dated 2 April 1937, in which he wrote:

Staff Capt to Brig-Gen Alistair Gordon,182 Inf Brigade – There is no doubt that he (Brig-Gen Gordon) held Gen Haking responsible for the Fromelles battle… it was a heart-breaking thing to him to see this valuable material wasted on what, at most, could have been a mere holding attack, a mere demonstration… it was as good an illustration as there was of the reckless extravagance in expenditure of life which ruled the minds of some of the subordinate commanders, like Gen Haking, at this stage of the war. A fine new Division, especially selected, as the 61 Division had been, for early active service, lost 50% of its attacking troops upon an objective which from the start was of an extremely limited character, and which could not possibly have been held against a counter-attack… they lost faith in their more remote commanders as a result. Haking was always 'Butcher Haking' after this battle. To my mind it is unforgivable in Gen Haking that he sought to excuse himself for this needless 'butchery' by questioning the 'ardour' of the troops, who went to their impossible task with immense courage and devotion. I visited the attacking units with Gen Gordon in the afternoon of the 19th July, and I vividly recall their cheerful and eager spirit and their keen anxiety to win credit for their battalions and their Brigade.

In reviewing 19–20 July 1916 it is clear that Haking appeared not to have learned from his previous setback on the same sector. This was compounded by other factors mentioned. Should McCay have been more assertive in pressing for an alternative plan? At the time it was not usual to challenge the corps commander, and the Australians were so new to Flanders that they had not had the opportunity to settle into the style of warfare on this front.

Furthermore, were the Diggers at Fromelles better troops than their British counterparts? This question is typical of the rather tedious Britain vs Australia debate on certain aspects of the Great War that crops up from time to time nowadays. Many members of the AIF had parents born in the British Isles; many others came from a variety of European countries as well as Scandinavia and America. What these volunteers in the two armies often did have in common was an impulse to join up. Some may have seen it as an adventure, never suspecting the horrors that lay ahead; others, particularly from the colonies, saw it as a way of supporting the mother country in her time of need, and others saw it as a means of getting income, clothing and a meal each day. Soon the novelty of war wore off and survival took over as the matter of greatest priority. The 'gung-ho' glory seekers were few and far between, whilst others had fame thrust upon them. The emergence of self-help organisations such as the Royal British Legion and RSL[37] perpetuated the *esprit de corps* felt by so many men who were ultimately grateful that, quite simply, they lived to tell the tale.

Condemnation of the 61 Division by the Australian troops has been over-stated in post-war writing and by some veterans in their later years. One unusual way in which it came to light was reported in *The Annals of Bendigo* in 1920. Rev Fr J.J. Kennedy, who won the DSO at Fromelles, wrote a play entitled *Advance Australia* which was produced at the Royal Princess Theatre on 3 July 1920. The play provoked a storm of criticism 'owing to the disloyal sentiments contained in it. Certain artists... declined to appear in the play. The Town Hall was packed on July 9 when an indignant meeting was held.' At this gathering a resolution was put forward 'that this meeting of loyal Bendigo citizens expresses its detestation and abhorrence of the disloyal sentiments uttered in the play... its emphatic disapproval of the mendacious and dastardly reflection on the English soldiers who fought side by side with the Australians in the war, and declares its profound admiration for Great Britain'.

No less a person than Elliott argued against this, saying that at Fromelles 'there had been no cowardice on the part of the Tommies. They had done their utmost.' A similar view was held by Capt V.C.R. Hood, 29 Btn, who expressed the view the 'Tommies in my opinion are great men'.[38] To add weight to the arguments against Kennedy's view a telegram from Billy Hughes, the Prime Minister, was read out in which he supported the British troops. A second resolution asked the authorities to stop further performances of the play. The meeting ended with rousing singing of the National Anthem and *Rule, Britannia!*

Outside the Town Hall a counter-demonstration was held in support of Kennedy and Dr Mannix, the Catholic archbishop who had fervently opposed conscription on the grounds that it lent support to the British and their war in Europe. Another meeting, this time inside the Town Hall, was arranged for 19 July, at which Kennedy spoke in defence of his play and stated that he had no intention of retracting even one word. This meeting overwhelmingly approved of Kennedy's stance; the Irish influence on Victorian society was still quite strong.

Among the many reports evaluating the events of 19–20 July submitted in the days after this catastrophe, a couple of phrases in Haking's report which accompanied Mackenzie's paper to First Army HQ have stuck in the minds of veterans and historians. The first refers to 61 Division, which in Haking's view was 'not sufficiently imbued with the offensive spirit to go in like one man at the appointed time'. The second remark concerns McCay's division, which, according to Haking, 'attacked in the most gallant manner and gained the enemy's position'. This could not be denied. However, his next phase caused considerable angst in the Australian press and was quoted by Bean in the Official History; Haking considered that the Australians 'were not sufficiently trained to consolidate the ground gained'.

Haking seeks to defend his own enthusiasm for the attack, and repeats his assertion that 'there were sufficient guns and sufficient ammunition'; moreover, 'the wire was properly cut and the assaulting Battalions had a clear run into the enemy's trenches'. He omits to mention that on 17 July he had reported that some gunners had never fired on the Western Front.[39]

The corps commander also suggests that trained battalions would have succeeded, and believes that 'the lessons to be learnt from the attack apply more to the Divisions who took part in it than to ordinary trained Divisions'. Later in the report he writes, 'with two trained Divisions the position would have been a gift after the artillery bombardment; with these two new Divisions there was a good chance of success but they did not quite attain it'. Haking had a good division[40] on the occasion of the May 1915 attack on Aubers Ridge but still could not breach and hold the German line. He continues his report by making the bizarre claim that 'the attack… has done both Divisions a great deal of good', as well as stating that the Germans were unlikely to move troops away from the sector for some time. He concludes by listing the chronology of dates for the attack and the reasons for postponements, making it clear that he was 'directed to attack':[41] in other words, the responsibility for the outcome was not his.

In a First Army document dated 14 August a comment is made that identification of German units made in raids along the front which was attacked, and on the front opposite 31 and 39 Divisions, 'proved that no withdrawals of German troops on the front in question had taken place'.[42] For the second time in fourteen months, Haking's plan for operations on Aubers Ridge had been a dismal failure.

18

The Dismissal of Harold Pope

In the weeks following the unsatisfactory outcome of the attack on the German line below Aubers Ridge, the finger of blame was pointed at those who had not performed well. For Col Harold Pope, commanding 14 Bde, removal from his command, not necessarily for this particular reason, came very rapidly and unexpectedly, and was the most significant example of the dismissal of an officer.

Other 'casualties' of the battle were some of the remaining Territorial officers in 61 Division, part of a clearout that had started several months earlier. Major Christie-Miller referred to them as 'victims' and had mixed feelings, considering that corps had dictated events and 'no opportunity was given to any subordinate commander to initiate any operation of his own'.[1] Commenting upon 184 Bde, he continued:

> The victims included the GSO who subsequently obtained a reprieve, the Brigadier (Carter), Col H.M. Williams of the Bucks and Col W.H. Ames of 2/4 Ox and Bucks. (The CRE Col Williams survived these two by about a month.) Of the Brigadier one can only say that great sympathy was felt for him in being sent home for the failure of a plan in which he had no share but the Brigade were heartily glad to be rid of a Commander in whom they had no confidence, who daily demonstrated his ignorance of the requirements of war, and who as far as I know made no friend in the Brigade in the 3 months of his command and left no-one regretting his departure.

It is very questionable whether Pope's dismissal was a consequence of the performance of his battalions; it was more likely that he was the victim of some professional grudge or jealousy or, more likely, the casualty of a cover-up to protect McCay. Whichever was the case, it radically affected Harold Pope's wartime career and reflected badly on his superior officers and certain subordinate officers.

Harold Pope was a 'citizen soldier', commissioned as a Second Lieutenant on 1 July 1900 and promoted to Lieutenant five months later. A Captain by September 1903 and a Major by July 1906, he achieved promotion to Lieutenant Colonel in March 1908.[2] At the outbreak of the war he held the appointment of CO 89 Btn Senior Cadets but relinquished this on 8 October 1914 when he joined the AIF, a completely new formation, at Blackboy Hill, Western Australia, where, a few days later, he took over command of 16 Btn from Lt Col H.Viales CB.

Sailing on HMAT *Ceramic*, Pope crossed to Alexandria in December 1914 and was among the troops to land at Anzac on 25 April 1915. He saw action against the Turks on a number of occasions including at Pope's Hill, Dead Man's Ridge in May, Quinn's Post and then Sari Bair in August. On 17 October he underwent surgery at the Second Stationary Hospital, Mudros and was sent to England to convalesce. In January 1916 Harold Pope was back in Egypt where, in due course, he was appointed to the temporary command of 14 Infantry Bde and by June was in France.

On 19 July, with the 15 Bde being unable to enter the German front line, Pope's men were left badly exposed. Despite this disadvantage the battalions attacking in the centre of the Australian sector succeeded in entering the German front line and held the line until they retired early in the morning of 20 July. Indeed, it was men of this centre brigade who were the last to break away and regain their own breastworks.

The 14 Bde performed well given not only the hurried preparations for the attack but also the proficiency of the Germans holding the opposite line. At 5.30a.m. on 20 July, Pope received orders for his brigade to retire. The troops remaining in the enemy line therefore had to cross No Man's Land in the early morning sunlight, but it was not until 3p.m. that Pope went to bed in order to recover from the rigours of the past days; his previous opportunity to sleep had been on the night of 17 July, when he noted in his diary, 'slept very heavily through night – including a gas alarm – had gone too long without'.[3]

So what happened to cause Pope to lose his command?

Col Pope had slept from 3p.m. on 20 July until 11p.m. that evening when Capt S.B. Pope arrived at Brigade HQ; Capt Pope (acting Brigade Major of Tivey's 8 Bde) was on loan to 14 Bde and covered while Major N.K. Charteris, Pope's Brigade Major, was himself asleep.[4] Harold Pope subsequently returned to his bed and slept until 8a.m. on 21 July, when he prepared his report on the operations of the last two days.[5] At 11.10a.m. he received a memo from McCay relieving him of command, alleging that when McCay had visited 14 Bde HQ at 4.30p.m. on 20 July, Pope had been incapable of duty. After completing a few handover tasks, Harold Pope went to Sailly and submitted a request to see McCay; this was arranged for 9a.m. the following day. At the interview with McCay the allegation of drunkenness was stated as being the reason for removal from command. Pope, while going about his business, subsequently met other battalion commanders in 5 Australian Division, all of whom expressed the view, according to Pope, that McCay had made a serious error. 14 Bde's report was not completed by Col Pope; the final page of the completed report, timed at 1.15p.m. on 24 July, is signed by the author on behalf of 'Col commanding 14 AIF Bde'.[6] The signature is that of Major Charteris.

Pope's own version records that soon after 3p.m. on 20 July, 'and following a week of mental and physical stress ending with thirty four hours continuous and sleepless activity during which I had successfully brought my Brigade through a very severe engagement, I lay down and slept',[7] in the belief that no German counter-attack would materialise and having organised adequate defence of his section of the line. An hour later Godley arrived, but on being told that Pope was asleep instructed that he should not be disturbed and went on his way. Thirty minutes later McCay turned up in his motor car, but unlike Godley he insisted that Pope be woken up. Major Charteris[8] apparently tried to do this but failed. McCay also tried, but he too was unable to waken his Brigadier. Pope said that he had no recollection of either attempt to wake him, and claims of McCay, 'being unable to discriminate between the effect of intense fatigue and the effect of excessive liquor, he put the worst construction on my condition and came to the false and groundless conclusion that I was drunk.'[9] McCay also wrote to Godley stating, 'It is impossible to continue him in command where there is the least liability of his suddenly making himself unable to command.'[10] Although McCay does not state expressly that liquor was the cause, the suggestion is there.

Later McCay met Godley and reported that Pope 'had behaved with skill, courage and energy during the whole operation of 19/20 July'.[11] However, McCay must have made contradictory comments to Godley, since he wrote to Plumer stating that 'after investigation of Pope's conduct and bearing in the fighting of the last two days,... had arrived at the conclusion that... was not competent to command a brigade'.[12] Plumer endorsed this report before passing it to Haig and recommending the appointment of Lt Col C.J. Hobkirk of 11 Btn Essex Regt as Pope's successor.[13]

Pope felt that reasoning with McCay was useless, but sought an appointment with the corps commander. This was declined on 23 July as, according to Haking, it would serve no useful purpose. Pope's response was to request a court martial, and this prompted an interview firstly with McCay on 25 July and then with General Birdwood. At the same time he met Col Griffiths (Adjutant–General) and Col C.B.B. White, both of whom appeared sympathetic to Pope. Birdwood, however, would not grant a court martial as he feared that a scandal might break out, possibly exacerbating what was already a significant setback so soon after the arrival of the AIF in France.

Birdwood advised Pope to gather evidence to support his case and submit his case to the Commonwealth Government. From Birdwood's point of view, this partly appeased Pope, as it removed the inquest from the AIF on the Western

Front and placed it firmly in the hands of officials 12,000 miles away, complete with the delays that communicating over that distance would bring. Pope's diary does not record any disappointment with this outcome.

On the morning of his interview with McCay, Pope describes a fortuitous meeting with Lt Col W.C.N. Waite. He related his circumstance 'quite bluntly and baldly to him with the object of seeing genuinely and without disguise whether he considered such a thing to be possible'. Pope elicited the response he sought: 'I found from his manner that he was simply astounded – for he proceeded to convince me that I had been perfectly sober!!'.[14] Waite, according to Pope, was quite angry on hearing this news and even produced his notebook in which he had recorded verbatim Pope's orders to him that fateful evening. A similar experience was encountered when Pope spoke to the brigade's French interpreter M. Dronquet. On meeting his Staff Captain, Capt Street, Street offered to act as his counsel at any court martial, having been a barrister at the Supreme Court of New South Wales. Pope also approached Lt Col A.H. Tebbutt, OC 14 Field Ambulance, who, after considering Pope's story, concluded that a layman such as McCay or Charteris would not be able to form a sound opinion on whether it was drink or fatigue that was the cause. On Tebbutt's advice, Pope sought a second opinion from Lt Col A. Horne, OC 15 Field Ambulance. Horne 'had made a special study of the psychology of sleep'[15] and indicated that Pope's state of exhaustion would inevitably have resulted in the condition in which he had been found.

Pope also wrote to Capt S.B. Pope and to Charles Bean, whom he had met on Thursday afternoon just before he went to bed.[16] This meeting informs us that Charles Bean was already at the scene of this disastrous attack by the AIF; Bean's recollection should substantiate Col Pope's state at that time. Unfortunately, the Official History records the 'official' reason for Pope's departure from France; Charles Bean wrote at the end of Chapter 13 of Vol. III that 'a number of changes occurred in the Australian Commands… Colonel Pope on disciplinary grounds not affecting the control of his brigade during the action'.[17]

One other aspect of Pope's dismissal that needs to be taken into account is the ability of McCay to get on with his senior officers. His personal bravery and intellectual qualities seem not to be in doubt, but as a Divisional Commander McCay may have been promoted beyond his capabilities. Birdwood, for example, would not support any bid to promote McCay after the summer of 1916.

McCay also seems to have become an increasing liability. Birdwood wrote to Senator G. Pearce,[18] Minister for Defence, in June 1917, commenting that McCay 'has a tendency very often to rub people up the wrong way'.[19] In March 1918 Birdwood again commented that 'by his unfortunate manner, he does not seem to be in sympathy with anyone, and I can hear of no senior officers in the force who have a good word for him'.[20] Birdwood even states that he thinks McCay would be glad to see him leave the AIF. Moreover, General Birdwood wrote that he could not possibly recommend him for promotion, 'nor indeed, would I be prepared now to recommend McCay for the command of a division… I could not conscientiously recommend him for it'.[21]

Furthermore, in evaluating the performance of McCay's three brigades at Fromelles Pope's 14 Bde was hardly the least impressive. If this was believed to be the case, by removing Pope so swiftly at the conclusion of the attack, McCay could avoid a key witness to any shortcomings in his command of the division remaining at the scene and the opportunity could be taken to enact the removal even before any reports on the battle could be compiled by his Brigadiers. Whether or not this was McCay's plan, he achieved both by acting as he did on 21 July, and in doing so, in some measure, he protected his own reputation.

Following Birdwood's suggestion, Pope wasted no time in preparing his submission and his list of 'officers whom it is desired should give evidence as to the condition of Colonel H. Pope CB on 20 July 1916'.[22] Listed in addition to Mitchell, Manley, Waite, Tebbutt and Horne are McConaghy, Capt Woods, Capt W.D. Harris,[23] Cass, Lowe, Capt Street and M. Dronquet of the French Mission. Pope spent all day on 26 July writing his case and presented it to Lt Col McGlinn (AA&QMG) at 4.30p.m. The following day he sent copies to Cass, McConaghy and Tebbutt. At this stage General Godley also met Pope and suggested that McCay had not intended any serious slur on his character or behaviour. This acted as a red rag to Pope, who, despite noting that Godley was 'very nice' to him,[24] pointed out the precise words said by McCay and stated that he would not alter his own position nor statement in the slightest. Subsequently, on 27 July McGlinn called by to see him and to ask if he was prepared to compromise. Pope gave him short shrift, saying that any initiative must come from McCay by withdrawal of his allegation.

Among the statements refuting the allegation against Pope are two from 2/Lt J.A.S. Mitchell and Lt S. Manley of 14 Bde. Mitchell stated:

> I saw Colonel Pope on the morning of 20 July… he was then quite sober. At about 3p.m. Colonel Pope left us to have a rest. He seemed thoroughly worn out after the continual strain of the past three days and nights. The following day I learnt that Colonel Pope had been accused on the previous afternoon of being drunk and incapable of carrying out orders. I was naturally very surprised as he was perfectly sober when he left us at the Mess Hut at about 3p.m.
>
> I have been Orderly Officer to Colonel Pope since 2 June 1916, and… never have I known him to take too much liquor, or make himself incapable of carrying out his duty.[25]

Lt Manley reiterates some of 2/Lt Mitchell's observations and concludes his testimony, 'I noticed nothing unusual in his manner'.[26]

Charteris' comment to McCay is the most likely source of the allegation of drunkenness. A clue is found in Pope's notes, which record the following events immediately after the battle when Pope conducted a debrief with some of his officers:

> I asked Colonel McConaghy and Captain Woods to have some refreshment, and they each had a little whisky – which finished all the supply in the mess. With a view to my report on the action I went carefully through the events and places of which these officers had knowledge. This was between 1 and 2p.m. Later Colonel Cass, 54 Battalion, with his Adjutant, Captain Lowe, came to Brigade HQ, he had been the senior officer of the Brigade in the German trenches, and was obviously strained by what had occurred… I asked him to have some whisky – and as we (Colonel Cass, Major Charteris, my Brigade Major and myself), were going into the Mess, I, realizing that there was no whisky left, told my batman, (Curnow), to get a bottle – the only one I had – from my hut… At lunch I took coffee. Besides officers of the Brigade Staff, Colonel Waite, 24 F.A. Brigade, and Captain Bean came into the Mess Hut.[27]

Pope records that due to his extreme fatigue he was advised to go to bed. No enemy action was expected until nightfall at the earliest, and indeed Pope slept until 11p.m. On waking he went to his office to find Capt S.B. Pope, of 2 Anzac, 'who told me that General Godley had sent him to enable Major Charteris to get a sleep'.[28]

Col D.M. McConaghy's word ought to have carried more weight than Mitchell or Manley, and in his witness statement he clearly states, 'as to his sobriety I should say he was absolutely sober'.[29] Lt Harris of 54 Btn was also unequivocal in his opinion: 'I had an extended conversation with Col Pope – he was perfectly sober and showed positively no signs of drink'.[30] The other witness statements concur with these opinions, whereas the statement submitted by Charteris differs.

The four-page document in Charteris's untidy writing is dated 28 July and lists a sequence of events that provide ample evidence to help justify McCay's action. Charteris starts with an instance around midnight on 13 July, when he went to Pope's sleeping quarters to show him an important message. He records, 'I had great difficulty in waking him, I eventually got him to take the message in his hand but I do not think he was capable of grasping its contents. I considered at the time that his condition was peculiar, he was like a man in a deep stupor.'[31] Charteris alleges that when he informed Pope of this incident the following morning, Pope had no recollection of it whatsoever.

His report then refers to a second incident, 'I think it was on the night of July 17/18 about midnight'.[32] There was a gas alarm and he went to wake Col Pope, again finding it very difficult to rouse him. Charteris claims that Pope followed him into the office where he was telephoning the battalion HQs, but Pope 'subsided in the doorway... and again went into a condition of being half awake and half asleep'.[33] A short time later, after speaking to Col Norris, Pope allegedly could not find his way back to bed. Charteris also noted that the battalion clerks had been chattering and mentioned that their CO talked in his sleep. Again, the following morning Charteris challenged Pope about the midnight events and Pope recalled nothing. The Brigade-Major then reminded Pope about the previous incident at Fleurbaix on 13 July, and it was at this point that Charteris claims he warned his brigade commander that he felt duty-bound to report any further occurrences.

Charteris' statement then moves on to 2p.m. on 20 July, when Divisional HQ ordered one battalion to be held in reserve at Croix Les Cornex. The remnants of 53, 54 and 55 Btns were collected on Charteris's orders, and he then sought further instructions from Pope but to no avail. Charteris then called Capt Street to accompany him to see Pope, to witness the response he received when he repeated his request for fresh orders. In his report, Charteris states that Pope replied, 'Let the dammed Germans have a chance';[34] Street confirms this in his statement, but adds that Pope was 'perfectly sober'.[35]

McCay's visit to Brigade HQ is the next occurrence in this statement. Charteris writes that he had to shake Pope, shout in his ear and lift him to a sitting position to try to get him to wake up in order to meet McCay. Charteris left him after succeeding in his endeavours, but on checking several minutes later found Pope 'standing leaning against the wall of his shelter with his head between his hands and a basin on the floor into which I think he had been sick'.[36] Charteris went back out to McCay and informed him that Pope was unwell. On checking again, Charteris 'saw him stagger and he reeled back on to his bed'.[37] In a seemingly singular act of disloyalty to his immediate senior officer, Charteris then 'told General McCay that Colonel Pope was drunk'. He adds that 'I was absolutely certain of this'. McCay then went in to speak to Pope but, according to Charteris, he received no reply.

McCay's own statement concurs with salient parts of other officers' reports, though he adds detail on his own efforts to awaken Harold Pope. Significantly, he states, 'I bent over him... his breath smelt strongly of spirits... he said something incoherent... I then looked to where he had been standing, and saw a vessel with fresh vomit in it... I formed the conviction that he was drunk.'[38] In his summary of events that followed his removal of Pope from his command, McCay acknowledges, 'he had without doubt had heavy work and strain and became very fatigued'.[39] McCay also 'regretted the matter' of Pope's dismissal, 'the more because he had done so well in the operation'. Pope later wrote that his batman had been close by during the period in which he slept and when Godley and McCay visited; he notes, 'if by any chance I had been sick, he must necessarily have been aware of it'.

Capt S.B. Pope's statement, written on 27 July, does not add very much of value. Indeed, at first he requested not to provide one as he anticipated being called to give evidence on oath at a court of enquiry or at a court martial. He indicates that Col Pope appeared confused. Pope apparently told him, at 11p.m. on 20 July, that he had just slept for eighteen and a half hours. This could not have occurred, and Capt Pope notes that he was not certain of the exact timing of this comment by Col Pope. The acting Brigade-Major also stated that Col Pope would attend to some papers as soon as he had had a wash and a shave; Capt Pope records that 'he had most evidently washed and most certainly shaved'.[40] The next occasion on which Capt Pope saw Col Pope was at 8.20a.m. the following day, when they chattered for 10 minutes while Capt Pope was awaiting a motor car to take him to Corps HQ. This time he noted that Col Pope 'was quite normal'.

Capt Street wrote to Pope on 26 July, not only expressing his dismay at what had happened but also referring him to the Manual of Military Law and Sections 42 and 43 of the Army Act. Speaking with the benefit of his legal training he continued, 'I can't see how anything can go against you. You have an overwhelming case.'[41] In another note to Pope, Capt Street seeks Pope's agreement to the withdrawal of his promise to represent him at a court martial. He gives his reason thus: 'I have received word – from a source that must remain unknown – that, if I do act as Counsel, it will practically settle my chances in this Division'. Street had aspirations to join the British Army after the war and acknowledged that his motives for withdrawing from his undertaking were selfish. Pope, in an act that reflects well on his character, understood Street's plight and reassured him that he appreciated the position he was in. Denial of a court martial rendered Street's offer superfluous.

It was not until 12 October 1916 that all the statements were gathered and copied to Pope by Col T.H. Dodds, Military Secretary at the Department of Defence. Harold Pope wrote to Dodds from the Grand Hotel, Melbourne, reiterating his view that 'I have been prejudiced by certain of the statements made by Major Charteris'.[42] He outlined his belief that there were factual errors in the case against him and that Charteris had deliberately misled McCay, Godley and Birdwood. Capt Pope also came in for similar criticism. It was on the basis of these points that Pope appealed to Dodds to arrange a meeting with Senator Pearce to press his case.

In a report on matters separate from the Pope affair, on 28 July 1916 Godley wrote to Senator George Pearce advising him that the three Brigadiers in the 5 Australian Division had performed well at Fromelles, 'especially Tivey and Elliott, but Pope unfortunately broke down completely before the end of the battle'.[43] Left at this, it would have left Pope out on a limb when seeking help from Pearce. However, fortunately for Pope, Godley added, 'he is a gallant officer, and did extremely good work… on the Peninsula and, till this happened, has done extremely well here too, so I hope that his having failed now, under great strain, will not be counted against him for any work he can do in Australia'. Only a year earlier, Godley, in another letter to Pearce, had stated, 'Colonel Burnage... Courtney... Cannan... and Pope... have all proved excellent leaders'.[44]

Having saved McCay's reputation and avoided any scandal, the generals had allowed Pope to recover some of his esteem once he returned to Australia. The same day, 28 July, Pope travelled from Steenvorde station to Boulogne and then crossed to Folkestone, arriving in London at 4.40p.m. on 29 July. While in London, Pope corresponded with John Monash, who at this time was with the 3 Australian Division at Larkhill on Salisbury Plain. Writing from the Royal Automobile Club, Pall Mall, on 2 August, Pope bemoaned his fate at McCay's hands, an act which he considered 'utterly unjustified',[45] making the point that his brigade performed better than any other and informing Monash that he had gone for thirty-four hours without rest before sleeping on the afternoon of 20 July. He continues, describing McCay's visit, the decision to relieve him of his command and the denial of a court martial.

On a more positive note, Pope recorded that he is 'thankful for the chance of getting home again alive and unhurt', even though it 'is a rotten home going in many ways'. Harold Pope was 'thankful to get away from the command of Genl McCay almost under any circumstances',[46] an indication of a long, simmering mistrust. Pope was not the only high level change in the division after the battle; Lt Cols Coghill (32 Btn) and Jackson (58 Btn) departed in such a manner 'that I have companions in my distress'.[47]

The following day Monash replied expressing surprise at Pope's dismissal, especially with his good record. He added, 'it shatters one's confidence very much'. The wily Monash explored Pope's comment that 'everyone was so good except my Brigade Major', asking Pope, 'I should like to know more, as it might be my fate to meet this gentleman some day'. He even concludes that McCay 'must have changed greatly for the worse'.[48]

On 5 August Pope, clearly heartened by Monash's response, replied from the Abbotsford Hotel, espousing his belief that Birdwood and Godley's reliance on McCay's word and the denial of an inquiry was a greater scandal than simply holding an inquiry into his dismissal alone. Again Charteris becomes the target of his vitriol: 'he did not and could not understand the Australian spirit – and he was not a man of any imagination or any great powers of intellect'.[49] Pope may well have been correct in his first point; the British had not yet come to understand the Diggers and it would take a while yet before they would!

Harold Pope left Waterloo station for Weymouth on 7 August and joined the transport ship *Marathon* for the long trip home. He arrived in Fremantle at 9a.m. on 17 September, well away from the battlefields but ready for a different battle.

Meanwhile, further correspondence passed between Europe and Australia and formal advice to the Minister for Defence in Melbourne of Pope's dismissal came from Lt-Gen Birdwood, in a brief note dated 19 August which concludes:

The very decisive statements of Major-General McCay and Major Charteris [Colonel Pope's Brigade-Major] make it clear that it was quite impossible to continue Colonel Pope in his command.[50]

One other factor for consideration was a recommendation by Birdwood, dated 6 July, that Pope be granted the temporary rank of Brigadier-General while in command of 14 Bde backdated to 1 May. Birdwood's message to Pearce in Melbourne informing him of Pope's dismissal came just 44 days later. Although Col Pope's promotion was approved in Melbourne on 15 July, on 23 July a cablegram was sent from First Anzac, London, stating that the order from Melbourne would not now be promulgated and that a successor to Pope was now being sought. Pearce responded by agreeing to London's action, but added that he 'trusts that a suitable Australian officer in your command will be available to succeed him'.[51]

During the voyage Harold Pope prepared a twelve-page memorandum detailing his circumstances, opening with a claim that what happened to him set a 'precedent of condemnation without trial or enquiry… which, if confirmed by the Commonwealth Government, will have the far reaching effect in opening the door to the abuse of power and in undermining the confidence of officers and other ranks'.[52] Pope was exaggerating in this instance as 'Stellenbosching' or 'degumming' of officers had happened on plenty of occasions. The document then summarises the events from 20 July until leaving England, with a three-fold purpose: firstly, to ensure that a record remained to state Pope's side of the story; secondly, to persuade the Commonwealth Government that in restoring him to a suitable job he would be vindicated; and thirdly, that the practice of promoting British officers in preference to Australians might be discredited. Would Pope now get a fair deal from the politicians at home?

From Perth, Pope travelled to Melbourne. On 9 October he wrote to Pearce enclosing various papers relating to his dismissal, inviting the Minister for Defence to give certain paragraphs, which Pope had marked in red, his special attention. In addition, he informs Pearce of the intimidation of Capt Street and the vexed question of the appointment of Hobkirk. Pope's reception in Perth was marked by 'countless scandalous rumours… in common vogue there about me – my friends were looking askance at me'.[53] A further point he made concerning his reputation was that 'my good name as a citizen – the reputation as a soldier… are blasted by the action… you… will realise the bitterness of my present position; and the bitterness of the position of my wife and children'. Indeed, in the memo detailing his situation written on board ship whilst returning to Australia Pope has annotated the margin, stating that on arrival in Western Australia 'nearly everybody assumed that I had done something discreditable'. Pope even countenances going abroad, saying, 'in any case I cannot continue to live in Australia'. In ending his plea to Pearce, Pope seeks a meeting, 'if the papers are not sufficient to convince you that an infamous injustice has been done to me'.

It is not clear whether it was Pope's letter of 9 October 1916 that prompted a swift response, but certainly by 13 October Col Dodds had made a careful scrutiny of what he called 'this unfortunate affair'[54] and had submitted a minute paper to Pearce. Again though, Pope is frustrated. Dodds states, 'in my opinion the evidence whether Colonel Pope was or was not drunk... is wholly inconclusive'.[55] He then shuts the doors on Pope's aspirations for an immediate return to France and Flanders by writing, 'whether he was or was not, it would be impossible to reinstate him again under General Birdwood'.

Dodds remained impartial, not being prepared 'to state that General McCay and Major Charteris have not made the most deplorable mistake and that Col Pope has not suffered any injustice thereby'.[56] As a token gesture, Col Dodds did agree to recommend Pope to command troops on a transport for the voyage only. He also recognised Pope's 'valuable and gallant service' as a battalion commander and acquiesced to Pope's request to pursue a fresh appointment with Birdwood and Monash once he was back in England. Pearce refused to see him but would support him in finding work in Australia. Pope looked to the Australian Government to clear his name and wrote that the 'only way to restore my name and honour is to return me to the fighting line... I cannot live in Australia under a cloud – what have I done? – have given good service.' The targets for his vitriolic diary notes are clear: 'C has lied about me. McC has used intimidation.'[57]

During October 1916 Pope's canvassing clearly paid off; by 17 October he received word that he was to join a troopship bound for England and that he was to see Birdwood when the opportunity arose. In the late evening of 11 November Pope left his home in Perth to join the *Zealandic* in Fremantle. From Western Australia he sailed round to Melbourne where he joined another ship, the *Hororata*. Soon after midnight on 23 November the ship left New Pier, Port Melbourne, bound for Europe.

On arrival in England Harold Pope was not swept off to France and Flanders, as might have been expected when an experienced senior officer became available for active service once again. On 16 February at Horseferry Road, London, he was shown a note from Birdwood, endorsed by McCay, containing the offer of command of an infantry battalion; however, it was not until 20 March 1917 that he was on the Somme, where he reported to Brigadier-General Glasgow. Glasgow, commanding 13 Bde, 4 Division, confirmed that Pope was to take over command from Lt Col D.A. Lane of 52 Btn. In late May 52 Btn was transferred to Bailleul on the France-Belgium border in readiness for the meticulously planned Messines Ridge offensive. Ironically, soon after 2p.m. on 7 June, Pope was hit in the right thigh by a bullet which broke his femur. As a consequence of this wound Pope eventually returned to Australia, and this time there was no question that his active service days were over, the effect of the enemy round being rather more decisive than the duplicity of McCay and Charteris.

On leaving for Australia after being wounded, Pope received letters expressing not only sympathy but also commendations for his good service from distinguished commanders including Glasgow, Monash, Godley, Birdwood and Brand, thus representing quite a change of sentiment from his previous departure. Despite his wound Pope made it known that he hoped to return to France yet again upon recovery. This time, aside from the fact that he was declared medically unfit for further service, Birdwood stated as early as 23 August 1918 that the probable imminent withdrawal of battalions from the front made it impossible to absorb a surplus of lieutenant colonels.

For his actions in France and Belgium Pope received a mention in despatches, to add to the Companion (Military Division) of the Order of the Bath dated 15 October 1915 and another MiD by General Sir Ian Hamilton on 12 June 1915. Lt-Gen Sir Talbot Hobbs also wrote to him commending his conduct at the front and offering his sympathy on his unfortunate treatment after Fromelles. These plaudits are further evidence of Pope's integrity. Pope returned to civilian life as Commissioner of Western Australia Government Railways, a post he held until he retired in October 1928. Ten years of retirement were to follow, ending with his death on 13 May 1938.

So was Pope the victim of a conspiracy by McCay and others or did he bring his downfall upon himself? Col Dodds's memorandum uses the word 'inconclusive', and to some extent that seems to be a fair assessment. However, Pope appears to have been victimised by his divisional commander, who was himself out of his depth, and by his own Brigade-Major who, like so many British officers, did not appear willing to endeavour to accept and understand the citizen soldiers of Australia. Pope was a successful soldier in the Gallipoli campaign[58] and on the Western Front, and his strenuous efforts to restore his reputation must be acknowledged so that in some part the record is corrected. Furthermore, he was held in high regard among his men and his peers, and that is a valid test of an officer's worth. Conversely, McCay was despised by many '19 July men', and that too is a reasonable gauge of his leadership.

19

Remembering

Fromelles remained in German hands until the end of the Great War. Once the Armistice had been signed the Germans had fifteen days to leave the occupied parts of France. At Fromelles they moved out immediately; Australian photographers took a number of pictures of the battlefield that day and there is no evidence of German army personnel. They had no reason to stay in the vicinity; Lille offered some security in numbers and there was still some opportunity to reach Germany rather than be interned as POWs. Moreover, they were, after all, the invader, and were not encouraged to stay a day longer than necessary.

The civilians displaced from the *régions devastées* that stretched across ten *départements* were in many instances keen to return. In some sectors civilians had continued to work their land in close proximity to the front, occasionally within range of the artillery. Elsewhere civilians had been able to return earlier in the war as the front line advanced, though some were displaced for a second time when the Germans advanced once again.[1]

At Fromelles the line had been static since October 1914 so no such attempt to make a start had been possible. This battlefield was a very small part of a strip of devastation, some three hundred miles long and five to fifteen miles wide, which was unmatched by any previous European conflict. It ran from the Belgian coast across Flanders and Picardy, via the plateaux and valleys of the Champagne region and Lorraine, through the Vosges mountains, and ended by the Swiss border just inside Germany.

Many parts of the Western Front were in a far greater state of destruction than the region around Fromelles, but the task of restoring the buildings and fields should not be underestimated; the wounds of four years of warfare could not be erased overnight. Fromelles escaped fairly lightly by comparison with some other parts, but many buildings had been severely damaged including the church, which had had its tower filled with a concrete inner tower which formed an observation post for the Germans. The fields around the village had been good agricultural land before the war but were now marked by breastworks and communication trenches, shell holes and mine craters, dugouts and concrete emplacements, unexploded ordnance and bodies of British, Australian and German soldiers.

Temporary huts were constructed for the civilians and a church was built in Rue Sotte under the guidance of the parish priest, Abbé Dahiez. The foundation stone of the new church was laid on 2 March 1924 and it was consecrated on 10 April 1927. Other priorities included the rebuilding of the *Mairie* in Rue de Verdun and of the adjacent school. A co-operative was set up to manage the building work, and despite shortages of local labour and materials, gradually Fromelles rose again from the rubble to become a thriving village amid the agricultural region to the south-west of Lille.

A further feature that marked this period here in Fromelles as well as in countless communities around the world was the unveiling of the war memorial, which bears the names of forty-two soldiers and six civilians '*morts pour la France*' during the Great War. In addition to community memorials there are dozens of memorials to military units dotted all along the Western Front, but it is in Warwickshire that the 61 (South Midland) Division has one of its memorials located, in a recess in the east wall of St Peter's Chapel in the south transept of the Collegiate Church of the Holy Trinity, on the banks of the river in Stratford-upon-Avon.[2] The reasons for the choice of Stratford are given in editions of *The Shakespeare Pictorial* published around the time of the memorial's unveiling. The book says:

> It has been asked why Stratford Church has been chosen for the site of Memorial, rather than one of the great Churches of Gloucester, Worcester, Birmingham or Coventry, all of which cities are within the area of the South Midland Division. The choice of any one of those churches, however, would have aroused honourable jealousy in other counties. Besides being situated in Warwickshire, the county which furnished the Division with an entire Brigade, Stratford is within a short walk of the boundaries of Worcestershire and Gloucestershire. Apart from that, as the birthplace and burial-place of Shakespeare it has more than local claim, which of all England makes it the fitting site for a memorial to South Midland Territorials who fell fighting in her cause.

On the tablet the following inscription can be found:

> To the glory of God
> And in grateful memory of the
> officers, non-commissioned officers and men
> of the Sixty-First South Midland Division
> Who fell in the Great War

The division raised in 1914 comprised units recruited in the counties of Berks, Buckingham, Gloucester, Oxford, Warwick and Worcester, and was placed under the command of James Fourth Marquis of Salisbury K.G. The division proceeded in 1916 under Major-General Sir Colin Mackenzie K.C.B. to France, where it served with conspicuous valour on all parts of the British front in that country, and in Belgium from Ypres to St. Quentin. In 1919 the division was disbanded at the close of the Great War, and the glorious victory of the allies to which it had contributed by the sacrifice of many valuable lives and by continuous and gallant services.

Ypres Laventie Arras Ancre Cambrai St. Quentin
1914   Act well your part, there all the honour lies.   1919

Around the edge of the memorial are carved the badges of the regiments represented in the Division, described in *The Shakespeare Pictorial* as 'the antelope of the Royal Warwicks at the top of the column on the right (the onlooker's left); below it the Sphinx of the Gloucesters, and then the Lion and the Crown of the Worcesters. The Light Infantry Horn of the Oxford and Bucks comes in order of seniority at the bottom of the column, and the Swan of the Bucks battalion at the head of the opposite column. Below it is the Dragon of the Berkshires...' More details are then given of the remainder of this tablet:

Within the wreath at the top of the monument is the sign of the 61st Division, adopted before the Division set out for France in May, 1916, the first of the second line Territorial Divisions to proceed overseas.[3] The device is really a cipher, made of the number of the Division, L.X.I., in Roman numerals. The other badges are those of the Divisional troops – the Royal Artillery, the Royal Engineers, the Duke of Cornwall's Light Infantry [which furnished a battalion of pioneers], the Royal Army Service Corps, the Royal Army Medical Corps and the Machine Gun Corps.

At a parade on Saturday, 16 November 1929, veterans of the Division and the next of kin of many who had died in the Great War gathered in Bridge Street, Stratford-upon-Avon, in the presence of a guard of honour provided by 7 Worcesters, representatives of the 48 (South Midland) Division and the local cadet corps. At 2.25p.m., Lieutenant-General Sir Ivor Maxse KCB, KCVO, DSO arrived, accompanied by Major General Sir Colin Mackenzie KCB, Major-General Lord Salisbury KG, GCVO, CB, TD, and a host of other dignitaries. A flag of the 61 Division, made by a Mrs Newdigate, was carried by VC winner C.S.M. Brooks of 2/4 OBLI. Maxse made a speech to the assembled people prior to the parade processing to the church, where they were joined by the mayors of a number of towns that had contributed men to the Division. After prayers and hymns, Maxse unveiled the tablet which was then dedicated by the Lord Bishop of Coventry followed by the sounding of the 'Last Post' and 'Reveille' by buglers of 7 Worcesters. After the service, tea was served in the Town Hall for the municipal guests and officers of the Division; ex-servicemen marched to the British Legion Headquarters in Bull Street for tea, and at the Yeomanry Drill Hall regulars were served tea by the Girl Guides.

A second memorial to the 61 Division can be found in Laventie, on the wall of the *Gendarmerie* and Town Hall adjacent to the church. It is a bronze panel also bearing the badges of the various units within the Division below a wreath encircling the Divisional sign. To the left is the text: 'This tablet was erected by the British 61st Division to commemorate fallen comrades – The Division first served during the Great War in the neighbourhood of this town of Laventie and is proud to leave its dead sleeping in the sacred soil of France'. The same text in French is to be found to the right of the tablet. By coincidence the Division was back in the area in 1918 when it helped to stem the German offensive on the Lys front. The plaque was unveiled in April 1935 in the presence of Sir Colin Mackenzie, 200 veterans and Brig-Gen A. Spooner CB, CMG, DSO and Bar, who had succeeded Brig-Gen Stewart in July 1916, Col Sir Seymour Williams, formerly CRE in the Division, and Lt Col L. Bilton CMG, a former CO of 2/8 Worcesters.

No memorial to the 5 Australian Division can be found in the area, but it is a short trip across the Franco-Belgian border to Polygon Wood to find the obelisk that commemorates this formation. A large tablet on the face of the monument bears 'Fromelles' as their first battle honour; many more are displayed too, providing clear evidence of the distinguished service given by the Division.

In addition to the Memorial Park at Fromelles there is also a marble tablet on a wall in the village declaring that the location is 'The Square of the Battle of Fromelles', while a CWGC-style headstone in the local museum also commemorates the attack.

In keeping with the vision of Fabian Ware and others, the British cemeteries around Fleurbaix, resembling English gardens, are to this day maintained to the highest standards by the gardeners of the Commonwealth War Graves Commission. VC Corner is the best known, and is unusual for cemeteries on the Western Front as it contains graves but no headstones. The register not only refers to VC Corner Australian 'Cemetery', but the map inside also shows four plots of forty-one rows containing a total of 410 graves of 'unknown soldiers'. In the light of this, the decision was taken to record all the names (1,299) of those 'missing' Australians from the battle on panels on the screen wall behind the cross (though there is a mysterious batch of 31 Btn men mysteriously recorded on the Villers-Bretonneux Memorial, all with 21 July dates, when the battalion was out of the line). It is now a tranquil place in what had been No Man's Land, looking across at the Sugar Loaf Salient.

Other cemeteries in the area include the delightful Le Trou Aid Post a few yards along Rue Delvas, and the nearby Rue Petillon which is entered via an impressive gateway shaded by large willow trees. In the expanse of lawn are the headstones, including long rows consisting solely of 19–20 July casualties, among them some, such as Major Roy Harrison, found well after the war. Y Farm and Croix du Bac are both plots located next to farm buildings that would have been used by the medical services; the large plots at Anzac Cemetery and Canadian Cemetery at Sailly-sur-la-Lys were extensively used in July 1916. In nearby Rue du Bois, plot I, row B contains a group of nine headstones each with two names; the central stone bears a cross but no name. This plot marks a site of a single, closely packed burial that left insufficient room for individual commemoration. Plot II, row A has an unusual stone bearing the inscription, 'To the memory of several Australian soldiers of the Great War buried in this grave. Known unto God.'

In 61 Division sector, Laventie Military Cemetery contains burials from this period, as does Estaires Communal Cemetery Extension. Many other cemeteries containing graves from the battle can be plotted, not only along the route used for the evacuation of the wounded to the Channel Ports but also back in England near hospitals. Others are scattered across the British Isles, as the bodies of soldiers who died in Great Britain were taken close to home for burial. Those who died in German hands, whether soon after the battle, in their hospitals or as POWs in Germany, are buried in plots across northern France and parts of Germany. Burials by the British can be found far from the battlefield: Cabaret Rouge, in the Souchez Valley near Vimy, contains graves of Fromelles casualties, the cemetery being a concentration plot when the battlefields were cleared in 1918–21. Aubers Ridge British Cemetery was another which was created specially to accommodate bodies found on the battlefield, and it was laid out with a plot for 61 Division and another for 5 Australian Division.

A large proportion of Mackenzie's men who died are commemorated on memorials to the missing. It was Ware's idea that all those killed would be commemorated, even if they had no known grave. A large number can correctly be found on the Loos Memorial to the south, which serves an area from the river Lys to the old southern boundary of the First Army, east and west of Grenay; it continues from the Le Touret Memorial period, that is, from the first day of the Battle of Loos to the end of the Great War. Some can be found on the Ploegsteert Memorial, passed as you begin the climb from Armentières to Messines. It serves an area from the line Caestre–Dranoutre–Warneton in the north to the line Haverskerque–Estaires–Fournes in the south. It covers a period from the arrival of III Corps in the area in 1914 to the Armistice is 1918. It therefore embraces the Lavantie–Fleurbaix area at the time of the attack at Fromelles. At least one man was erroneously recorded on the massive Thiepval Memorial on the Somme.

The Germans also buried their dead. In the 'Deutscher Soldatenfriedhof' at Fournes-en-Weppes (150 burials), Laventie (1) and Beaucamps (317) can be found the graves of many German casualties from Haking's attack. Fournes cemetery is tucked away at the end of a lane and contains a variety of headstones, crosses and mass grave markers laid out among the trees, whilst at Laventie the solitary cross bearing a 19–20 July date is among the many black crosses that fill the plain lawn by the side of the road. Beaucamps, the most picturesque of the three, contains both mass graves and individual burials; there are no German casualties from the battle buried in Illies or Wicres, both a short distance to the south of Aubers Ridge.

For many veterans who returned home, the post-war years were not at all easy, and there was no guarantee, having survived the war, of longevity. Various associations were established for veterans; typical of the groups of old soldiers were the Sydney and Melbourne sections of 14 Field Coy Association. They met for Anzac Day marches and developed a strong support network for families, especially during the Great Depression years when help was provided for those in need. They also held reunions on 19 July each year, such was the significance of that date.

Some high-profile characters died prematurely, among them 'Pompey' Elliott, whose misfortunes started during the war when his business in Victoria collapsed with debts of £5,000. Election as a Senator after the war enabled this popular figure to publicise and seek redress for his wartime grievances about the handling of troops and being overlooked for promotion. This latter point was also pursued in correspondence with McCay, Hobbs and Monash but to no avail. His own health deteriorated, and after a spell in hospital he committed suicide on 23 March 1931. Elliott's grave in Burwood Cemetery, Melbourne, bears a bronze tablet showing him in his slouch hat; the artist's impression certainly captures the spirit of 'bull-headed pugnacity' that Bean attributed to him.[4]

The battlefields of France and Flanders are very easy to reach from the United Kingdom. Many families make a trip to visit the locations where relatives fought and, in so many instances, their grave or the memorial bearing a name. Those making the short trip across the English Channel find countryside not too dissimilar from that found at home. For travellers from Australia, meanwhile, the pleasant, green fields may well be in stark contrast to the landscape at home. The distance between the opposing lines may also be a shock – from one side of a field to the other, a patch of ground from which it took months or years to dislodge the enemy at a massive cost.

In 1995 Ray and Ruth Hopkins from Bendigo made this long journey from Australia to Fromelles. They visited the battlefield and the grave of a relation, Capt Clive Hopkins. An account of their trip was published in a local Bendigo paper:

It is one thing to read of things and be shocked by them; it is another experience entirely to come face to face with the actual reality of them as we did. On
the first evening… we visited Clive's grave – no member of Clive's family had
visited his grave since he died.

Nearby, farmers were loading hay onto a truck, birds were whistling and
though aware of the carnage once there, it all looked so serene that our
knowledge of the past seemed slightly unreal.

Clive is buried in his own grave with a cross marking the spot in the
well-tended Australian war cemetery, Rue de Bois. Some of the inscriptions
nominated by the next of kin even held a grim, quite unintended I am sure,
kind of humour.

We decided to visit… the misleadingly-named VC Corner. It is a different
burial ground… for the first thing which strikes you is that there is not one
standing cross nor grave marker. We knew the reason but the stark reality is
overwhelming. There are 410 Australians buried here and their remains were not
gathered in until two or three years after this battle took place. Though neatly
grassed over now, this cannot mask the awfulness of this place… as we studied
the cemetery and read the names of 1299 unknown Australian soldiers… we
found ourselves weeping uncontrollably.

As I stood there I imagined I heard the staccato of weapons and these young
men running, running so futilely across No Man's Land many writhing in
agony, until mercifully released by death. I thought of the people in Australia…
never made aware of the picture now revealed to us. I have no wish to glorify
it, merely to ask that the great suffering and endeavour of these Australians
might not be forgotten; 'lest we forget' now has much greater meaning
for me.[5]

Visitors today can still take a tour of the July 1916 battle area and hardly meet
a soul. There are plenty of concrete structures to be found in both the British
and German sectors; some are built to resemble cottages, while others are stark
intrusions on the landscape. An observation post can be seen in a garden on the
main road through Aubers, and the route of the narrow-gauge line from Fournes
can still be traced. In Fromelles itself the visitor should leave some time to visit the
superb museum created by the Association Souvenir de la Bataille de Fromelles
(ASBF). As well as a museum it is a memorial to the experience of the villagers,
including those serving in the French army, and to the troops of both sides who
were in the area during the Great War.

The ASBF has also excavated several tunnels, dugouts and other features on the
battlefield. The work has been undertaken in controlled circumstances with the
permission of landowners, with care and attention on the part of those conducting
the work and methodical recording of artefacts. Battlefield archaeology can be a
controversial matter but the ASBF have gone about it in an exemplary manner.

Charles Bean visited the Fromelles battlefield after the Armistice, not only to gain a better appreciation of the area but also to identify relics for the future Australian War Memorial. There was a BEF sub-section of the Australian War Records Section headed by Lt S.W. Gullett, formerly of 28 Btn, assisted by Lt W.W. Anderson, ex-23 Btn, and with 15184 Spr T.H.E. Heyes (3 Divisional Signal Company) as Clerk, 11914 Pte A.E. Arscott, Corps Salvage Section as Storeman and 3896 Pte S.H. Morris, also from 23 Btn, acting as Batman and Assistant Storeman. The day after the Armistice, Bean wrote to Gullett informing him that he had visited the battlefield the previous day and commenting:

> There are hundreds of interesting relics there still, in No Man's Land especially SW of the River Laies where 15 Bde went over, poor chaps. The Graves Registration Units are being put onto it at once... what we saw would be I think intensely interesting to you. You could bring back the box car full of old kit, waterbottles, hats etc. [6]

Charles Bean would no doubt have thoroughly approved of the work of the ASBF.

Another mandatory stop for visitors must be the Memorial Park close to VC Corner. The area now occupied by the park has been transformed from a patch of a farmer's field, rough ground punctuated with a row of partially demolished German concrete pillboxes, into a most fitting memorial to the Australians who fought here. At least one pillbox was thoroughly cleared out by Martial Delebarre and ASBF members. In August 1991, once the water had been pumped out, a tunnel running 40 yards or so out under No Man's Land was discovered. Hundreds of artefacts have been found by the ASBF in these dugouts including some excellent pumps, tools and other paraphernalia of daily trench life. The tunnel itself was well constructed with stout timbers and was a remarkable feat of engineering by the German pioneers.

Nowadays there is a lay-by for motorists from which paths lead past the pillboxes to a splendid statue entitled *Cobbers*. This impressive work was commissioned by the Office of Australian War Graves, sculpted by Peter Corlett and cast by Meridian Sculpture Founders of Melbourne in 1998. The design is wholly appropriate for a memorial at Fromelles, consisting as it does of a soldier bringing a wounded man from the battlefield. It depicts 3101 Sgt Simon Fraser, 57 Btn, a farmer from Byaduk, Victoria; the soldier on his back is from 60 Btn and the colour patches and original 'Australia' shoulder titles add a further degree of accuracy.

In the park is one of the battlefield commemoration plaques that have been placed on Australian battlefields around the world by Dr Ross Bastiaan. This is another remarkable personal initiative to commemorate Australian forces. This particular plaque has been repositioned from its original location on the site of Nephew Trench (the British name for this German trench) and it records some of the essential facts about the battle as well as the overall AIF presence on the Western Front.

At the unveiling of the *Cobbers* statue, on a windy day in July 1998, a couple of veterans were present. It is not known when the final 61 Division veteran of the attack died, but the last Australian veteran appears to have been 6066 Driver Augie Band who served with 15 Field Company, Australian Engineers.

Still to this day, 'In Memoriam' notices appear in newspapers remembering 19–20 July casualties. In the early days it was the veterans themselves who produced them, and the phrases they used reflected their pride and sorrow. Typical examples referred to a mate 'Gone into the great rest camp', or read 'In loving memory of my dear pal' or 'To the memory of my brave soldier friend'; the latter included 'Inserted by their sorrowing mates'.

The next of kin were invited after the Great War to select an inscription to be added to the headstone on a soldier's grave. Many biblical quotations were chosen, as well as some inspired, original words. One very apt inscription on a headstone – that of 523 Pte M.N. Smith, 53 Btn – can be found in Ration Farm Cemetery. It reads, 'These deeds which should not pass away names that must not wither'.

Capt W.H. Zander, in his unpublished account,[7] left his memory of the battle:

Fromelles! What memories that word brings back to our minds. Our first scrap – and what a bitter one!

Another soldier who recorded his abiding impression of the trenches at Fromelles was Capt V.C.R. Hood, 29 Btn, who described them as 'a sight never to be forgotten – trenches blown to pieces – killed and wounded everywhere'.[8] Despite its scale, 'Fromelles' was not to be regarded, officially at least, as a 'battle'. The report of the Battles Nomenclature Committee in 1921 simply listed it as 'Battle of Bazentin Ridge – with Subsidiary Attack at Fromelles', with a footnote to remind readers that this was on Aubers Ridge.[9]

The troops may not have had a very high opinion of Haking, but much later in the war General Gomes da Costa of the Portuguese army encountered him during the fighting on the Lys. In his book on the Battle of the Lys, da Costa wrote of 'the esteem in which I held General Haking… under whose command I served, and who always showed himself through his knowledge of the Portuguese language, extremely intelligent and clever, a fine soldier and a loyal friend'.[10]

Finally, another veteran with a clear recollection of his experience of the battle was Arthur Ebdon, interviewed at his home in Bendigo in 1992. Arthur was posted to 57 Btn as a signaller whilst in Egypt in 1916. He was one of the fortunate troops who, instead of leading the attack, was switched around due to the bad weather delaying zero hour. The descriptions given by Arthur of the scenes in the front line area complement any number of written accounts, and he spoke with undisguised dislike for his Divisional General: 'he was called Butcher McCay'.[11]

Arthur Ebdon was subsequently transferred to 15 Bde Engineers. Utilising his skills as a sign-writer, he produced many 5 Division trench signs and memorial crosses. Many years after the war, in 1992, Arthur Ebdon returned to the Western Front and commented on his recollections of the events of 19–20 July 1916 and the contrast between the battlefield and the green fields and neat cemeteries he saw decades later. He concluded by saying, 'it's hard to believe that I came out of it alive'.[12]

The clock cannot be turned back for the benefit of those who did not come out alive, and the responsibility for subsequent generations to 'remember' also cannot be removed.

APPENDIX A:

Order of Battle

General Sir Douglas Haig, Commander-in-Chief
General Sir Charles Monro, GOC First Army
General Sir Richard Haking, GOC XI Corps
General Sir William Birdwood, GOC I Anzac Corps
General Sir Alexander Godley, GOC II Anzac Corps

61 DIVISION

GOC Major-General Colin Mackenzie CB
ADC Capt W.M. Baird (Argyle and Sutherland Highlanders, TF)
ADC Lt T. Coats (Royal Highlanders, TF)
GSO1 Lt Col Sir H. Wake Bt. DSO (KRRC)
GSO2 Major C.G. Stansfield (8 Gurkhas)
GSO3 Capt R. Mostyn Owen (Rifle Brigade)
AA & QMG Lt Col C.C. Marindin (RA)
DAA & QMG Major C.L. Porter (East Kent Regiment)
DAQMG Major E.P. Blencowe DSO (ASC)
CRA Brig-Gen R.C. Coates DSO
CRE Lt Col Seymour William

182 INFANTRY BRIGADE

Brig-Gen A.F. Gordon CMG DSO
Brigade Major Maj J.R. Heelis
Staff Captain Capt P.A. Landon
2/5 Royal Warwickshire Regt Lt Col P.L. Coates
2/6 Royal Warwickshire Regt Lt Col J.J. Shaunnessy
2/7 Royal Warwickshire Regt Col H.J. Nutt
2/8 Royal Warwickshire Regt Lt Col E.C. Cadman
Brigade Machine Gun Company
Brigade Trench Mortar Battery

183 INFANTRY BRIGADE

Brig-Gen C.G. Stewart CMG DSO
Brigade Major Capt M.M. Parry-Jones
Staff Captain Capt R.B. Stevenson
2/4 Gloucestershire Regt Lt Col J.A. Tupman
2/6 Gloucestershire Regt Lt Col F.A.C. Hamilton
2/7 Worcestershire Regt Lt Col L.C. Dorman
2/8 Worcestershire Regt Maj L.L. Bilton
Brigade Machine Gun Company
Brigade Trench Mortar Battery

184 INFANTRY BRIGADE

Brig-Gen C.H.P. Carter CB CMG
Brigade Major Maj E.C. Jepp DSO
Staff Captain Maj R.W. Harling
2/4 Ox and Bucks LI Lt Col W.H. Ames
2/1 Royal Berkshire Regt Lt Col P. Balfour
2/4 Royal Berkshire Regt Lt Col J.H. Beer
2/5 Gloucestershire Regt Lt Col M. Wheeler
2/1 Bucks Lt Col H.M. Williams
Brigade Machine Gun Company
Brigade Trench Mortar Battery

61 DIVISIONAL ARTILLERY

305 Bde RFA (Lt Col H.A. Koebel)
306 Bde RFA (Lt Col F.G. Willcock)
307 Bde RFA (Lt Col F. Hilder)
308 Bde RFA (Lt Col E.W. Furze)[1]

ROYAL ENGINEERS

3/1 Field Company (South Midland) RE (Major O.S. Davies)
2/2 Field Coy (S. Midland) RE (Major O.R. Langley)
1/3 Field Coy (S. Midland) RE (Major C.B. Hosegood)
476, 478, 479 Field Coys RE

FIELD AMBULANCES

2/1 Field Ambulance (Major G. MacKie)
2/2 Field Ambulance (Lt Col G.W. Craig) and 2/3 Field Ambulance (Lt Col P. Moxey)

OTHER UNITS

Divisional Signal Company
Divisional Train (ASC) (Lt Col J.M. Harrison – Senior Supply Officer Major J.R.M. Ball,
Adjutant Lt Hon J.W. French, No. 1 Coy Major J.A.C. Wright, No. 2 Coy Capt R.H.
Butcher, No. 3 Coy Capt R.B. Stanley, No. 4 Coy Capt L.M. Humphries)
521, 522, 523, 524 Coys ASC
61 Division Sanitary Section (Capt W.H. Davison)
Mobile Veterinary Section, 61 Veterinary Section (Capt E.J. Laine)
Pioneer battalions – 1/5 DCLI (Lt Col W.A. Bawden) and the Hampshire Yeomanry (Major
J.F.N. Baxendale)
61 Division Cyclist Company (Capt G. Du S. Atthill)

5 AUSTRALIAN DIVISION

GOC Major-General Hon J.W. McCay CB
ADC1 Lt Hamilton (AIF)
ADC2 Lt Moore (AIF)
GSO1 Lt Col C.M. Wagstaff CIE DSO
GSO2 Major D.M. King (King's Liverpool Regt)
GSO3 Capt A.J. Boase (AIF)
AA & QMG Lt Col P.J. McGlinn CMG (AIF)
DAA & QMG Major R.P. Varwell (Royal Irish Regt)
DAQMG Capt G.D. Smith (AIF)
CRA Brig-Gen S.E. Christian CMG (RA)
CRE Lt Col A.B. Carey CMG (RE)
ADMS Col C.H.W. Hardy
ADVS Major Henry

8 AUSTRALIAN INFANTRY BRIGADE

Brig-Gen E. Tivey DSO
Brigade Major Maj C.S. Davies (Leicestershire Regt)
Staff Captain Capt J.F. Wootten
29 Btn Lt Col A.W. Bennett VD
30 Btn Lt Col J.W. Clark
31 Btn Lt Col F.W. Toll
32 Btn Lt Col D.M.R. Coghill
8 Machine Gun Company Capt T.R. Marsden
8 Field Company Major V. Sturdee
Brigade Trench Mortar Battery

14 AUSTRALIAN INFANTRY BRIGADE

Col H. Pope CB
Brigade Major Maj N.K. Charteris (Royal Scots)
Staff Captain Capt G.A. Street
53 Btn Lt Col I.B. Norris

54 Btn Lt Col W.E.H. Cass CMG
55 Btn Lt Col D.M. McConaghy CMG
56 Btn Lt Col A.H. Scott DSO
14 Machine Gun Company Lt C.M. Spier
14 Field Company Major H. Bachtold
Brigade Trench Mortar Battery

15 AUSTRALIAN INFANTRY BRIGADE

Brig-Gen H.E. Elliott
Brigade Major Maj G.F. Wieck
57 Btn Lt Col J.C. Stewart
58 Btn Lt Col A. Jackson (Major C.A. Denehy took over on 18 July)
59 Btn Lt Col E.A. Harris
60 Btn Major G.G. McCrae
15 Machine Gun Company Lt S. Neale
15 Field Company Major H. Greenway
Brigade Trench Mortar Battery

5 DIVISIONAL ARTILLERY

13 Brigade Australian Field Artillery (Lt Col H.O. Caddy)
14 Brigade AFA (Lt Col O.F. Phillips)
15 Brigade AFA (Lt Col Lucas)
25 (Howitzer) Brigade (Lt Col H.J. Cox-Taylor)
5 Brigade AFA (Lt Col H. Cox-Taylor)
5 Divisional Ammunition Column (Capt McClean)
5 Divisional Trench Mortar Battery

ENGINEERS

5 Divisional Engineers
3 Australian Tunnelling Company (Major L.J. Coulter)
Pioneer Battalion – 5 Australian Pioneer Btn (Major Carter)

FIELD AMBULANCE

8 Australian Field Ambulance (Lt Col A.E. Shepherd)`
14 Australian Field Ambulance (Lt Col A.H. Tebbutt)
15 Australian Field Ambulance (Lt Col A. Horne)

OTHER UNITS

10 (HQ) Coy AASC
18 Coy AASC (for 8 Infantry Brigade)
28 Coy AASC (for 14 Infantry Brigade)

29 Coy AASC (for 15 Infantry Brigade)
Divisional Train (Lt Col Francis) – 757,758, 759, 760 Coy AASC
5 Divisional Signal Company (Major R.A. Stanley)
5 Australian Division Salvage Company
5 Australian Divisional Mobile Veterinary Section (Capt Walters)
5 Divisional Sanitary Section (Capt Mattei)

The 61 Division and 5 Australian Division faced their Bavarian counterparts as follows (from the British left to right):

Division	Brigades	Assaulting Battalions	German unit
5 Australian Division	8 (WA/Qld/Vic)	32 (WA)	21 Bavarian RIR
		31 (Qld/Vic)	
	14 (NSW)	54	
		53	
	15 (Vic)	60	16 Bavarian RIR
		59	
61 Division	184	2/1 Bucks	
		2/4 Berks	
	183	2/4 Glos	
		2/6 Glos	
	182	2/6 Warks	17 Bavarian RIR
		2/7 Warks	

The specific sections of the German line to be taken by the Maj-Gen Mackenzie's brigades were detailed in XI Corps Order No. 58 (amending No 57):

> N.19.a.3.3 – N.13.d.6½.2½ (near Devil's Jump by the Fauquissart-Trivelet lane
>   to the Wick Salient inclusive)
> N.14.c.1½.5½ – N.14.a.8.2 (section in front of Deleval Farm)
> N.8.d.7½.½ – N.14.b.8¼.9¾ (Sugar Loaf to a point opposite the brigade
>   boundary in front of Picantin)

The Australian assault was stated as aiming to capture the German front and support line from where the Laies cuts the German front line at N.8.d.9½.1 to a trench running north–south past Delangre Farm (N.10.c.9.6), and to hold and consolidate the support line N.14. b.8¼.9¾ – where it crosses the Laies – N.14.b.8½.9 – N.15.a.7½.8 – N.15.b.5.9 – N.10. c.8.3½.

APPENDIX B

Artillery Details

In readiness for the attack at Fromelles, considerable preparation had to be made by the artillery. An example of an instruction for the redeployment of artillery can be found in XI Corps Order No. 56, dated 14 July, which states:

2. Following moves will therefore take place:
a) 14th July. 8th Div. Art. via Chocques – Hinges – cross-roads Q.28.b. – cross-roads Q.30.b – Fosse and move to positions in readiness to be selected by 61st Div. to whom instructions have been issued.

These few, simple lines in a corps order would have meant a period of major activity for these gunners, packing their equipment, moving limbers out onto country lanes and then getting organised for their part in the forthcoming attack. Moves might take place solely at night to avoid immediate detection by enemy aircraft, but this corps order states, 'heavy artillery may move by day where considered safe by GOC Heavy Artillery, XIth Corps'.[1]

Attached to the 5 Australian Division from 31 Division were three batteries, A171, B171 and C171 Batteries RFA. From 4 Australian Division (Brig-Gen C. Rosenthal CRA) came 37, 38, 39, 40, 41, 42, 43, 44, 45, 46, 47 and 48 Batteries AFA in addition to 110, 111 and 112 Howitzer Batteries AFA, all belonging to 9, 10 and 11 AFA Brigades.

Consequently, the following was the organisation of 5 Division's artillery:

8 Aust Inf Bde Left Group: Lt Col H. Cox-Taylor	14 Aust Inf Bde Centre Group: Lt Col H.O. Caddy	15 Aust Inf Bde Right Group: Lt Col O.F. Phillips
25 AFA Bde 52 Bty 56 Bty 60 Bty 115 (How) Bty	13 AFA Bde 49 Bty 50 Bty 51 Bty 113 (How) Bty	14 AFA Bde 53 Bty 54 Bty 55 Bty 114 (How Bty)

11 AFA Bde	24 AFA Bde	10 AFA Bde
41 Bty	40 Bty	37 Bty
42 Bty	44 Bty	38 Bty
43 Bty	48 Bty	39 Bty
45 Bty	47 Bty	46 Bty
111 (How) Bty	112 (How) Bty	110 (How) Bty
171 Bde RFA	171 Bde RFA	171 Bde RFA
B Bty	A Bty	C Bty
15 AFA Bde	15 AFA Bde	15 AFA Bde
57 Bty	59 Bty	58 Bty

Additional heavy artillery was also provided to strengthen the barrage on German positions. This was 28 Heavy Artillery Group (Lt Col C.S. Taylor) which comprised 5 Siege Battery and 138 Heavy Battery (from I Corps), 110 Siege Battery and 120 Heavy Battery (from IV Corps), 115 and 118 Siege Battery (from Second Army); 2 Anzac Heavy Artillery, 2 Army, commanded by Brig-Gen Howell Jones, provided 31, 87, 117 and 119 Siege Batteries plus 146, 147, 150, 155 and 156 Heavy Batteries and 2/1 Lancs Heavy Battery. The XI Corps Heavy Artillery provided yet more firepower in the form of 64 Siege Battery from Second Army plus 52, 63 and 92 Siege Battery and No. 1 Armoured Train from First Army, though in the case of 52 and 92 Siege Batteries only half their establishment of guns were sent to this sector for the attack.

The total guns and mortars of the Divisional artillery available for the direct support of the 5 Australian Division comprised 114 18-pounder guns, twenty-four 4.5-inch howitzers and twenty 2-inch medium trench mortars. The heavy artillery supporting the attack was under XI Corp's direction, and was provided by XI Corps Heavy Artillery, 11 Anzac Corps Heavy Artillery and 20 Heavy Artillery Group. Medium and heavy guns from these sources were: thirty-two 60-pounders, two 6-inch guns, twenty-eight 6-inch howitzers, seven 9.2-inch howitzers, and five 12-inch howitzers. The allocation to 5 Division front (under corps control) consisted of twenty-four 60-pounders, ten 6-inch howitzers and four 9.2-inch howitzers.

On top of preparations for Haking's battle a further minor reorganisation of the Divisional artillery was completed six days before these artillery units entered the line on 13 July, a source of disruption and perturbation in the build-up to the battle. Now they had to demonstrate that what training they had would enable them to achieve a satisfactory performance. As well as the structural changes, the original idea for a 'left' and 'right' artillery group was amended on 14 July at a conference at Divisional Artillery HQ,[2] when 13 Australian Field Artillery Brigade plus additional batteries were ordered to move between the other two groups and become the 'centre' group. Consequently, a 'right group' under Lt Col Phillips supported the 15 Brigade, the 'centre group' (Lt Col Caddy) supported the 14 Brigade and on the left Lt Col Cox-Taylor's group was in support of the 8 Brigade. These gunners recorded that the flat terrain hindered selection of concealed positions and observation posts but this does not appear to have prevented them all being ready by the evening of 15 July, though during the night nine batteries relocated to new positions. Their brigade headquarters moved to Croix du Lescornex. These movements attracted some enemy fire and one officer, Lt McNamara (117 Bty) was wounded. Repeated gas alarms were also experienced during the night and two batteries, 40 and 49, were unable to establish communications with their Forward Observation Officer as telephone lines were cut by shrapnel.

The fire plan for the attack had been issued with HQ 5 Australian Divisional Order No. 31. The fire plan provided for seven hours' registration, wire cutting and bombardment from zero hour, which had been confirmed as 11a.m., until 6p.m., the time of the assault. No. 16 Squadron RFC was allocated to co-operate with 5 Divisional Artillery. The timings of the fire plan were:

11a.m.–11.30a.m.	Registration by Divisional Artilleries and Trench Mortars
11.30a.m.–1p.m.	Registration and bombardment by Heavy Artillery (9.2" howitzers[3] and upwards). Registration only by 6inch howitzers was included in this period.
1p.m.–3p.m.	Wire cutting by 18 pdrs.
3p.m.–6p.m.	Wire cutting by 18 pdrs continued. Wire cutting by Trench Mortar Batteries. Bombardment by 18pdrs, 4.5" howitzers, and 6" howitzers.
4p.m.–6p.m.	Heavy Artillery (9.2" howitzers and upwards) slow bombardment.
6p.m.	Artillery lift to barrage lines.

During the bombardment there were 'lifts' to barrage lines for the following periods:

from 3.25p.m . to 3.29p.m.
from 4.00p.m. to 4.04p.m.
from 4.29p.m. to 4.34p.m.
from 5.20p.m. to 5.31p.m.

Between 9a.m. and 11a.m. on 19 July 5 Divisional and attached artillery carried on with registration and wire cutting commenced on 14 July. The fire plan on the 5 Division's front also complied with an order issued by HQ 5 Australian Division on 15 July, 1916, to destroy enemy machine guns.

During the bombardment phase, i.e. from 3p.m. to 6p.m., 18-pounder batteries were ordered to use high explosive with about thirty per cent shrapnel and to burst as low as possible, and immediately short of the support line, to destroy wire behind the front line. The normal rate of fire was not to exceed one round per gun per minute for 18-pounders, one round per gun per minute for 4.5-inch howitzers and the rate of fire for wire cutting was not to exceed one round per gun per four minutes.

During the barrage phase rates of fire were laid down as follows, with the proviso that should the tactical situation demand an increased rate then Group Commanders would order it, resuming the rate laid down when the tactical situation permitted.

Timings	18-Pounders Guns	4.5-Inch howitzers
6p.m. – 7p.m.	Battery fire 15 seconds	Battery fire 60 seconds
7p.m. – 8p.m.	Battery fire 20 seconds	Battery fire 90 seconds
8p.m. – 10p.m.	Battery fire 30 seconds	
8p.m. – 9p.m.		Battery fire 120 seconds
9p.m. onwards		Battery fire 150 seconds
10p.m. onwards	Battery fire 30 seconds	

Direction for the field artillery was published in 5 Australian Divisional Artillery Order No. 9 issued on 15 July allocated to Groups' tasks. This required them to fire on the following areas: the German front line; German wire; German support line system (including communication trenches from front line to support line for 150 yards in depth) and German communication trenches in rear.

Group commanders then allocated these tasks to batteries. Registration was ordered to be carried out on 16 July and wire cutting continued. Wire cutting batteries were confined to wire cutting and registration of wire and the German front line. Batteries deployed close to one another were not to carry out wire cutting and registration at the same time. Where the British and German trenches were close together, battery commanders were ordered to arrange with battalion commanders in turn to clear their trenches while wire cutting was in progress.

As far as the trench mortars were concerned, 5 Australian Divisional Artillery Order No. 10 issued on 16 July directed that the five trench mortar batteries bombard German wire and front line trenches from 4p.m. to 6p.m. during the pre-assault phase; they were ordered to cease during the lifts.

A 5 Divisional Artillery instruction issued to Group Commanders on 18 July defined the targets and the number of batteries in each group that were to engage them during the pre-assault phase and the barrage phase. Artillery Order No. 9 required:

Right Group	
11a.m.–11.30a.m.	Registration as required.
1p.m.–3p.m.	Wire cutting by batteries already allotted.
3–6p.m.	4 x 18-pounder batteries front line and support system 5 x 18-pounder batteries front line and support system 1 x 4.5" howitzer battery enfilade front line until 5.55p.m. then support line to 6p.m. 1 x Section of 4.5" howitzers, front line. 1 x Section of 4.5" howitzers, support line At 5.55p.m. wire cutting batteries lift to front line. At 6p.m. all batteries lift to barrage line.

6p.m.	*Barrage* 7 x 18-pounder batteries on a specified line beyond the objective. 1 x 18-pounder battery on a specified communication trench. 1 x 18-pounder battery (A171) on specified communication trench and Delaporte Farm 1 x 4.5" howitzer battery on specified communication trench and Delaporte Farm 2 x sections of 4.5" howitzers on specified communication trenches.

Centre Group	
11a.m.–11.30a.m.	Registration as required.
1p.m.–3p.m.	6 x batteries wire cutting (18-pounder batteries as allotted by Group Commander).
3p.m.–6p.m.	3 x 18-pounder batteries, wire cutting. 3 x 18-pounder batteries front trench 3 x 18-pounder batteries support system (the above already allocated by Group Commander). 1 x 4.5" howitzer battery 1 x Section on specified section of front line. 1 x Section on specified section of support system. 1 x 4.5" howitzer battery. 1 x Section on specified section of front line. 1 x Section on specified section of support system. At 5.5p.m., 3 wire cutting batteries above lift to front line. At 6p.m. all batteries lift to barrage line.
6p.m.	*Barrage* 8 x 18-pounder batteries on a specified line beyond the objective. 1 x 18-pounder battery search specified communication trench. 1 x 4.5" howitzer battery on specified target beyond the objective. 3 x sections of 4.5" howitzers on specified targets beyond the objective.

Left Group	
11a.m.–11.30a.m.	Registration as required.
1p.m.–3p.m.	3 x 18-pounder batteries wire cutting already allotted.
3p.m.–5.55p.m.	3 x 18-pounder batteries wire cutting on front as specified.

3p.m.–6p.m.	6 x 18-pounder on front line and support system as specified. 2 x 4.5-inch howitzer batteries on front line and support system. At 5.55p.m., 3 wire cutting batteries above lift to front line. At 6p.m., all batteries lift to Barrage Line.
6p.m.	*Barrage* 8 x 18-pounder batteries on a specified line beyond the objective. 1 x 18-pounder battery on two specified communication trenches. 1 x 4.5-inch howitzer battery on Delangre Farm. 1 x 4.5-inch howitzer battery on two specified communication trenches.

Finally, to provide additional firepower a 12-inch howitzer was moved into Laventie, earning the nickname 'Laventie Liz'. Its positioning, fifty yards from the HQ of the Royal Berks and 100 yards from Brigade HQ, and the accurate retaliatory fire from the Germans whenever it fired, did not endear it to the troops.[4]

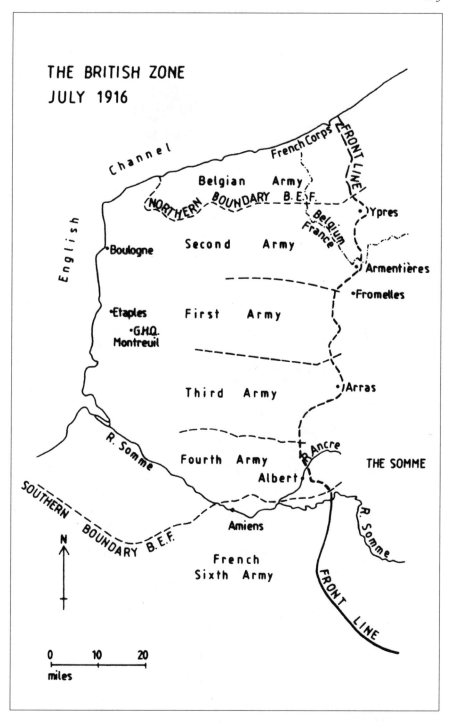

THE BRITISH ZONE
JULY 1916

1 The British Zone, July 1916

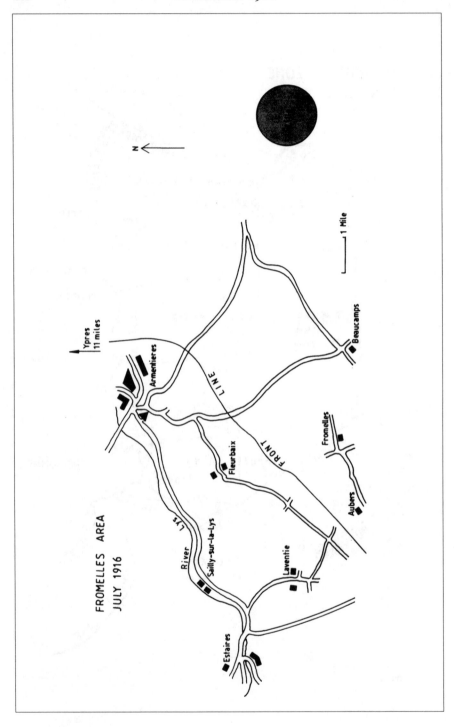

2 Fromelles area, July 1916

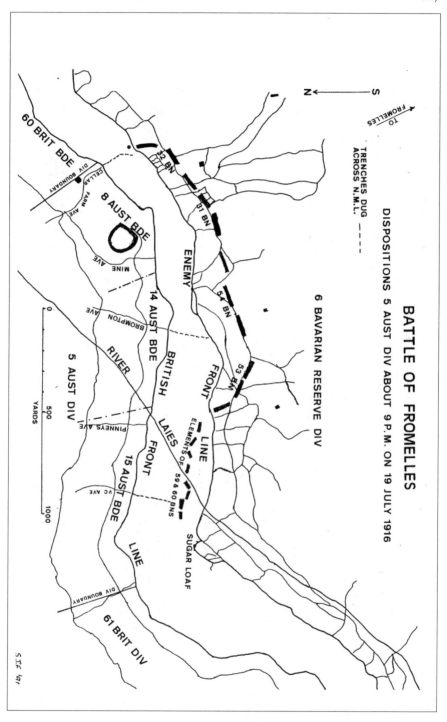

3 Battle of Fromelles: dispositions of 5 Australian Division about 9p.m. on 19 July 1916

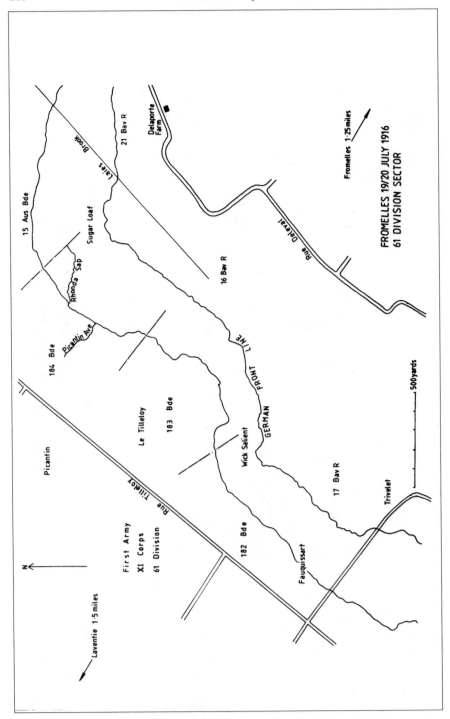

4 Fromelles 19–20 July 1916: 61 Division sector

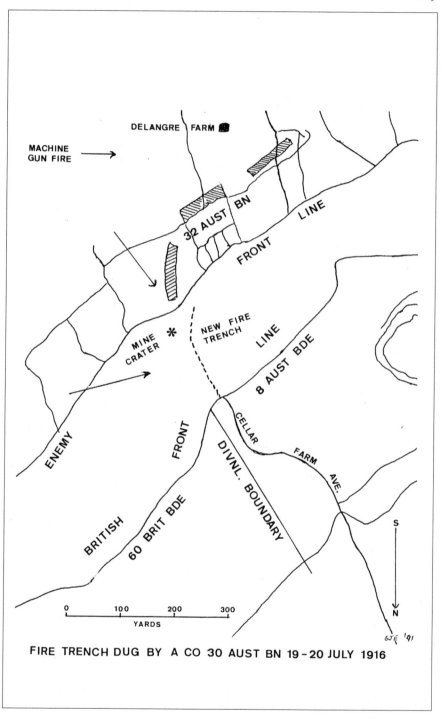

MACHINE
GUN FIRE →

DELANGRE FARM

32 AUST BN

FRONT LINE

MINE CRATER ✳ NEW FIRE TRENCH LINE

8 AUST BDE

ENEMY FRONT

CELLAR FARM AVE.

DIVNL. BOUNDARY

BRITISH 60 BRIT BDE

0   100   200   300
YARDS

S
N

FIRE TRENCH DUG BY A CO 30 AUST BN 19-20 JULY 1916

5 Fire trench dug by A Company of 30 Australian Btn, 19–20 July 1916

Bibliography

Adam-Smith, Patsy, *The Anzacs* (Melbourne: Thomas Nelson, 1978).

Austin, Ron *A Soldier's Soldier: The Life of Lieutenant-General Sir Carl Herman Jess* (Slouch Hat Publications 2001).

Austin, Ron, *Black and Gold: The History of the 29th Battalion 1915–18* (Slouch Hat Publications, 1997)

Australian Dictionary of Biography, Vol. 8: 1891–1931 (Melbourne University Press, 1981)

Barnes, A.F., *The Story of 2/5th Gloucestershire Regiment 1914–18* (Crypt House Press, 1930).

Bean, C.E.W., 'Cass at Krithia and Fromelles', *Reveille*, 30 November 1931.

Bean, C.E.W., *Official History of Australia in the War of 1914–18, Vol. I: The Story of Anzac* (Sydney: Angus & Robertson, 1921).

Bean, C.E.W., *Official History of Australia in the War of 1914–18, Vol. III: The AIF in France 1916* (Sydney: Angus & Robertson, 1940).

Bishop, Bert, *Soldier Solomon*; subsequently published as *The Hell, The Humour and The Heartbreak: A Private's View of World War I* (Kangaroo Press, 1991).

Bristow, Adrian, *A Serious Disappointment: The Battle of Aubers Ridge 1915 and the Munitions Scandal* (London: Leo Cooper, 1995).

Bruno, 'A Story of Fleurbaix', *The Duckboard*, 2 April 1934.

Bullock, Alan, *Hitler: A Study in Tyranny* (Oldhams Press, 1954).

Butler, Col A.G., *Official History of the Australian Army Medical Services, Vol. 2: Western Front 1914–18* (Canberra: AWM, 1940).

Campbell, Maurice, and Hosken, Graeme, *Four Australians At War: Letters to Argyle 1914–1919* (Kangaroo Press, 1996)

Chidgey, H.T. *Black Square Memories: An account of the 2/8th Battalion the Royal Warwickshire Regiment 1914–1918* (Oxford: Basil Blackwell, 1924).

Citizen Soldiers of Buckinghamshire: Second Bucks Battalion (publisher unknown).

Clark, Col J.W., 'A Battalion's Baptism of Fire: The 30th Btn at Fromelles', *Mufti*, 1 July 1937.

Clout, Hugh, *After the Ruins: Restoring the Countryside of Northern France after the Great War* (University of Exeter Press, 1996).

Colley-Priest, L.W., *The 8th Field Ambulance On Active Service* (unpublished AWM).

Crank, Ron, *A Short History of 53rd Battalion AIF (Whale Oil Guards)* (AWM 234 MS 1801181).

Da Costa, Gen Gomes, *O corpo de exército português na Grande Guerra: A batalha do Lys*.

Davies, Frank, and Maddocks, Graham, *Bloody Red Tabs: General Officer Casualties of the Great War 1914–1918* (Pen & Sword, 1995).

Derum, John, and Denis C.J., *More than a Sentimental Bloke.*

Downing W.H., *To The Last Ridge* (Melbourne, 1920).

Edmonds, Brig-Gen Sir James E., *Official History of the Great War: Military Operations France and Belgium 1915* (London: IWM/Battery Press, 1995).

Elliott, H.E., *The Battle of Fleurbaix*, reprinted from *The Duckboard*, 1 September 1930.

Ellis, Capt A.D., *The Story of the Fifth Australian Division* (London: Hodder and Stoughton)

Evans, Stan, 'The Trench: A Small and Futile Sacrifice', *Stand To! Journal of The Western Front Association* 34, April 1992.

Evers, Major S.W., 'Fromelles-Fleurbaix', *Reveille*, 1 November 1941 (AWM 234 MS 1801181).

Gammage, Bill, *The Broken Years* (Penguin, 1974).

Godley, Gen Sir Alexander, *Life of an Irish Soldier* (London: John Murray, 1939).

Graves, Robert, *Goodbye to All That* (Jonathan Cape, 1929).

Green, James, 'Fleurbaix: The Mystery Battle of the AIF', *Sydney Morning Herald*, 19 July 1919.

Hancock, Edward, and Cave, Nigel, *Aubers Ridge* (Pen & Sword, 2005).

Histories of 251 Divisions of the German Army which Participated in the War (1914–1918) (London Stamp Exchange, 1989).

History of the Warwickshire Regiment 1914–19 (IWM 02/41 442 13033).

Hunter, Doug, *My Corps Cavalry: A History of the 13th Australian Light Horse Regiment 1915–1918* (Slouch Hat Publications, 1999).

James, Brig E.A., *British Regiments 1914–18* (Samson Books, 1978).

Kennedy, J.J., *The Whale Oil Guards* (Dublin: James Duffy and Co., 1919).

Kerr, Greg, *Private Wars: Personal Records of the Anzacs in the Great War* (Oxford University Press, 2000).

Kidd, Neville, *An Impression Which Will Never Fade: The True Story of an Original Anzac* (privately published, 2000).

Knyvett, Capt R. Hugh *Over There with the Australians* (London: Hodder & Stoughton, 1918).

Laffin, J., *Guide to Australian Battlefields on the Western Front* (AWM/Kangaroo Press).

Liddle, Peter, *The Soldier's War 1914–1918* (Blandford Press, 1988).

List of British Officers Taken Prisoner in the Various Theatres of War Between August 1914 and November 1918.

MacLaurin, Lt Col G., 'Fleurbaix', *Sydney Morning Herald*, 26 July 1919.

Martin, John, 'Battle of Fromelles 1916', *Reveille*, 1 July 1958.

Matthews, E.C., *With the Cornwall Territorials on the Western Front* (Cambridge: W.P. Spalding, 1921).

McMullin, Ross, *Pompey Elliott* (Melbourne: Scribe Publications, 2002).

McMullin, Ross, 'Pompey Elliott and the Butcher of Fromelles', *The Australian Magazine*, 20/21 July 1996.

McMullin, Ross, 'The Butcher of Fromelles', *Wartime* (AWM magazine) 27.

McQuilton, John, *Rural Australia and the Great War* (Melbourne University Press, 2001).

Middlebrook, Martin, *The First Day on the Somme 1 July 1916* (Allen Lane, 1971).

Middlebrook, Martin, *The Kaiser's Battle 21 March 1918: The First Day of the German Spring Offensive* (Penguin, 1983).

Miles, Capt Wilfred, *Official History of the Great War: Military Operations France and Belgium 1916*, 2 vols (London: IWM/Battery Press, 1992).

Noble, Roger, 'Raising the White Flag: The Surrender of Australia Soldiers on the Western Front', *International Review of Military History* 72 (1990).

Officers Died in the Great War 1914–1919 (HMSO, 1919).

Pedersen, P.A., 'Bringing the Past to Life', *Battlefields Review* 25 (2003).

Powell, Geoffrey Plumer, *The Soldier's General* (Leo Cooper, 1990).

Preston, Sgt H., 'Early Raids in France: 9th Btn's Coup at Fleurbaix', *Reveille*, 1 January 1935.
Purser, Lt Col M., 'Memories of Fromelles: 5 Division Launches First Battle for AIF in
    France', *Reveille*, 1 July 1935.
Rose, Capt G.K., *The Story of the 2/4th Oxford and Bucks Light Infantry* (Oxford: Blackwell).
Rule, Edgar, *Jacka's Mob: A Narrative of the Great War* (Melbourne: Military Melbourne,
    1999).
'Sir Richard Haking', obituary, *The Times*, 11 June 1948.
Sloan, H., *The Purple and Gold* (Sydney: Halstead Press, 1938).
Smith, W., 'Leaves from a Sapper's Diary', *Reveille*, 1 July 1936.
Soldiers Died in the Great War 1914–1919 (various sections) (HMSO, 1919).
Stars in a Dark Night: The letters of Ivor Gurney 2/5 Glos 1914–19 (IWM 23(41)/387/6).
Swann, Maj-Gen J.C., *The 2nd Bucks Battalion*.
Terraine, John, 'Artillery' (Lecture to Thames Valley branch, Western Front Association, 26
    May 1994).
'The Australians Battle in France', *Sydney Morning Herald*, 29 September 1916.
The Battle of Fromelles 19/20 July 1916 (Notes of RUSI of NSW Seminar, 5 November 1997).
'The Brum Ration', newsletter of the Birmingham branch of the WFA.
*The Official Names of Battles and Other Engagements Fought by the Military Forces of the British
    Empire During the Great War of 1914–1919 and the Third Afghan War 1919: report by the
    Battles Nomenclature Committee 1921.*
Tiveychoc, A., *There and Back: The Story of An Australian Soldier* (Sydney: RSSILA, 1935).
Whiteside, Elizabeth, *A Valley in France*, 1999
Who's Who in Australia, 1922.
Williams, H.R., *The Gallant Company: An Australian Soldier's Story of 1915–18* (Sydney: Angus
    & Robertson, 1939).
Williams, J.F., 'Words on "a lively skirmish": Fromelles in contemporary and foreign reports',
    Journal of the AWM 23 (Oct 1993), pp. 21–28.
Williams, John F., *German Anzacs and the First World War* (UNSW Press, 2001).
Wilson, G.H., 'Medium Trench Mortars at Fromelles', *Reveille*, 1 May 1937.
Wilson, G.H., 'The First AIF Battle in France', *Sydney Mail*, 2 July 1931.
Wray, Christopher, *Sir James Whiteside McCay: A Turbulent Life* (Oxford University Press,
    2002).
Wrench, C.M., *Campaigning with the Fighting 9th* (Boolarong Publications, 1985).
Wyatt, E., *The Gloucester Regiment in the War 1914–1918* (IWM 02(41) 442 13 941).

NEWSPAPERS

Bendigo Advertiser; Central News (Amsterdam); *Hamilton Spectator* (Western Victoria area);
    *North German Gazette; Somerset Standard; Sydney Morning Herald; The Age; The Argus; The
    Australian; The Berliner; The Canberra Times; The Register; The Times; The West Australian;
    Vetaffairs.*

Archival Sources

NATIONAL ARCHIVES (UK)

AIR1 1343/204/19/21	16 Squadron Record Book – Summary of Work
AIR1 1344/204/19/26	Daily Routine Orders 16 Squadron
AIR1 1361/204/22/8	10 Squadron Record Book July 1916
AIR1 1365	10 Squadron Summary of Work
AIR1 1373/204/22/33	10 Squadron Record Book 25 July 1915–17 November 1917
MH106 394	Record Book No. 3 Casualty Clearing Station
WO95 5	General Headquarters General Staff
WO95 26	GHQ Adjutant General
WO95 30	GHQ Quartermaster General
WO95 43	GHQ Deputy Adjutant General
WO95 45	Director General of Medical Services
WO95 57	Director Army Signals
WO95 59	Director Ordnance Services
WO95 60	Army Ordnance Corps
WO95 61	Assistant Director Gas Services
WO95 64	Director Railway Transport Royal Engineers
WO95 67	Director Veterinary Services
WO95 71	Deputy Assistant Director of Transport
WO95 72	Deputy Assistant Director of Transport
WO95 76	Director of Supplies
WO95 123	Carrier Pigeons and Dogs
WO95 164	First Army General Staff
WO95 165	First Army General Staff
WO95 182	First Army Adjutant and Quartermaster General
WO95 196	Director Medical Services – 61 Division
WO95 199	Deputy Director of Signals
WO95 200	Deputy Director of Ordnance Services
WO95 201	Deputy Director of Veterinary Services
WO95 202	Deputy Director of Supply and Transport
WO95 237,	230 and 568 Army Troops Royal Engineers
WO95 238	1 Army and 2 Army Troop Company Canadian Engineers
WO95 243	10 Army Tramway Company Royal Engineers

WO95 244	172/176 and 179 Tunnelling Companies Royal Engineers
WO95 245	255 Tunnelling Company Royal Engineers
WO95 245	1 Canadian Tunnelling Company
WO95 245	197 Land Drainage Company Royal Engineers
WO95 881	XI Corps General Staff
WO95 3033	61 Division General Staff
WO95 3035	61 Division
WO95 3036	Adjutant and Quartermaster General – 61 Division
WO95 3037	61 Division Artillery
WO95 3038	Assistant Director Medical Services – 61 Division
WO95 3039	Commander Royal Engineers – 61 Division
WO95 3041	Deputy Assistant Director Ordnance Services – 61 Division
WO95 3041	Assistant Director Veterinary Services – 61 Division
WO95 3042	305 and 306 Bde Royal Field Artillery
WO95 3043	307 Bde Royal Field Artillery
WO95 3044	308 Bde Royal Field Artillery
WO95 3045	Divisional Ammunition Column – 61 Division
WO95 3046	476 Field Coy, Royal Engineers
WO95 3047	478 Field Coy, Royal Engineers
WO95 3048	479 Field Coy, Royal Engineers
WO95 3049	Divisional Signal Coy – 61 Division
WO95 3050	5 DCLI (Pioneers)
WO95 3051	2/1, 2/2 and 2/3 South Midland Field Ambulance
WO95 3052	61 Division Sanitary Section, Mobile Veterinary Section
WO95 3052	Divisional Train (521, 522, 523, 524 Coy Army Service Corps
WO95 3054	HQ 182 Infantry Brigade
WO95 3056	2/5, 2/6 and 2/7 Btn Royal Warwickshire Regiment
WO95 3057	2/8 Btn Royal Warwickshire Regt, Brigade Machine Gun Company and Brigade Trench Mortar Battery
WO95 3058	HQ 183 Infantry Brigade
WO95 3060	2/4 and 2/6 Btn Gloucestershire Regt
WO95 3060	2/7 and 2/8 Btn Worcestershire Regt
WO95 3062	183 Brigade Machine Company and Trench Mortar Battery
WO95 3063	HQ 184 Infantry Brigade
WO95 3065	2/4 Btn Royal Berkshire Regt
WO95 3066	2/5 Btn Gloucestershire Regiment
WO95 3066	2/1 Btn Oxfordshire and Buckinghamshire Light Infantry
WO95 3067	2/4 Btn Oxfordshire and Buckinghamshire Light Infantry
WO95 3067	184 Brigade Machine Gun Company and Brigade Trench Mortar Battery
WO95 3527	HQ Branches and Services General Staff
WO95 3555	Adjutant and Quartermaster General – 5 Australian Division
WO95 3558	Commander Royal Artillery 5 Australian Division
WO95 3565	Assistant Director Medical Services 5 Australian Division
WO95 3568	5 Australian Division Engineers
WO95 3572	Assistant Director Veterinary Services 5 Australian Division
WO95 3573	13 Brigade Australian Field Artillery
WO95 3573	5 Australian Division Cyclist Company
WO95 3576	14 Brigade Australian Field Artillery
WO95 3579	15 and 25 Brigades Australian Field Artillery
WO95 3586	5 Australian Division Ammunition Column

WO95 3587	8 Field Company Australian Engineers
WO95 3590	14 Field Company Australian Engineers
WO95 3592	15 Field Company Australian Engineers
WO95 3595	5 Australian Division Signal Company
WO95 3597	5 Australian Pioneer Battalion
WO95 3605	8 Australian Field Ambulance
WO95 3606	14 Australian Field Ambulance
WO95 3608	15 Australian Field Ambulance
WO95 3609	5 Australian Division Salvage Company/Mobile Veterinary Section
WO95 3610	5 Australian Division Divisional Train
WO95 3611	8 (Australian) Infantry Brigade
WO95 3614	29 Btn AIF
WO95 3617	30 Btn AIF
WO95 3619	31 Btn AIF
WO95 3621	32 Btn AIF
WO95 3622	8 Australian Machine Gun Company
WO95 3623	14 (Australian) Infantry Brigade
WO95 3628	53 Btn AIF
WO95 3629	54 Btn AIF
WO95 3631	55 Btn AIF
WO95 3633	56 Btn AIF
WO95 3635	14 Brigade Machine Gun Company and Trench Mortar Battery
WO95 3636	15 (Australian) Infantry Brigade
WO95 3645	57 Btn AIF
WO95 3648	58 Btn AIF
WO95 3651	59 Btn AIF
WO95 3653	60 Btn AIF
WO95 3655	15 Australian Machine Gun Company
WO95 3657	15 Brigade Trench Mortar Battery

IMPERIAL WAR MUSEUM, LONDON

IWM 69/25/1	Papers re Capt G. Donaldson 2/7 Btn Royal Warwickshire Regt
IWM 80/32/2	Papers Col Sir Geoffrey Christie Miller DSO MC TD 2/1 Bucks Btn
IWM 83/12/1	Diary Lt J.D. Wyatt Northamptonshire Regt attd 2/4 Btn Gloucester Regt
IWM 87/26/1	Papers re Lt Col A.V Spencer 2/4 Btn OBLI
IWM 90/37/1	Papers re Lt W.G. Shipway 2/4 Btn Gloucestershire Regt

AUSTRALIAN WAR MEMORIAL, CANBERRA

AWM/1DRL 0428	Red Cross correspondence re 3333 Pte C. King 53 Btn (file 1510811)
AWM/1DRL 0428	Red Cross correspondence re 3367 Pte W.S. Outlaw 53 Btn (file 2070412)
AWM/1DRL 0206	Papers re Lt C.T. Collier 53 Btn
AWM/1DRL 0300	Sgt Simon Fraser 57 Btn

AWM 1DRL/0427	McCrae papers
AWM 1DRL/0477	Papers re 4929 Pte H.A.B. Maning 60 Btn
AWM 1DRL/0483	Papers re 1296 Sgt L.J. Martin 8 Machine Gun Company
AWM 2DRL/171	Papers re Capt W.H. Zander 30 Btn
AWM 2DRL/0176	Papers re 3239 Pte A.F. Bell 59 Btn
AWM 2DRL/0286	Papers re 5363 Pte C.P. Ashdown 14 Field Company Australian Engineers
AWM 2DRL 0712	Papers re Pte S.K. Donnan 14 Field Company Australian Engineers
AWM 2DRL/0775	Papers re Lt J.G. Ridley MC 53 Btn
AWM 3DRL/2872	Papers re Major T.P. Elliott 60 Btn
AWM 3DRL/3856	Diary Brig Gen H.E. Elliott
AWM 3DRL/6428	Letters Lt J.G. Ridley MC 53 Btn
AWM 28	Honours and Awards 5 Australian Division 18.7.16–22.7.16
AWM 30	POW Reports
AWM 38	Diary 243B Letter from Pte H.E. Williams
AWM 229/2	Court of Inquiry Proceedings
AWM25 1013/2	Papers re BEF Subsection Australian War Records Section
AWM38 243a	Bean Collection
AWM MSS1365	Draft manuscript *A Soldier Looks Back* 2148 Bdr A.J. Williams 53 Battery Australian Field Artillery
AWM PR84/307	Diary Capt V.C.R. Hood 29 Btn
AWM PR89/163	Diary of 3402 Sgt A.T. Winter DCM 55 Btn
AWM PR90/115	Papers re Major E. Lister Australian Artillery
AWM PR00503	Papers T.M. Pflaum 32 Btn
AWM PR01453	Papers C. Ward 30 Btn

Notes

1. LAWYERS, BAKERS AND DRAPERS

1 The 3 Australian Division went straight to England, where it spent several months training on Salisbury Plain before moving to the Western Front in late November 1916.

2 Kiggell was the officer who, on a visit to the Ypres Salient later in the war when the Passchendaele campaign was getting stuck in the mud, was credited with the certainly apocryphal question 'Did we really send men to fight in this?'.

3 AWM DRL 28 12/11/198

4 *Reveille*, 30 June 1931.

5 Robert Graves, when writing about his battalion's time under Haking's command, commented upon his divisional commander in 'Goodbye To All That'; the occasion was after the 9th May 1915 attack on Aubers Ridge. He wrote: 'Haking commands this division… He came round this morning to an informal inspection of the battalion, and shook hands with the survivors. There were tears in his eyes. Sergeant Smith swore, half aloud: "Bloody lot of use that is: busts up his bloody division, and then weeps over what's bloody left… " It's said that Haking told General French that the division's morale has gone completely. So far as I can see that is inaccurate; the division will fight all right, but with little enthusiasm.'

6 It was while the units to form 61 Division were on Salisbury Plain that the divisional sign and colour patches were selected. The divisional mark adopted was the number of the division in Roman numerals (LXI) but moved so that they touched, making a three-sided box with an X in the middle.

7 Barnes, A.F., *The Story of 2/5th Gloucestershire Regiment 1914–18*.

8 Chidgey, H.T., *Black Square Memories: An account of the 2/8th Battalion the Royal Warwickshire Regiment 1914–1918*.

9 Christie Miller papers IWM 80/32/2

10 Crank, R., *The Whale Oil Guards*.

2. AN ADEQUATE SUPPLY OF GUNS

1 WO95 881

2 Address to the Canberra branch of the Returned Soldiers and Sailors Imperial League of Australia (RSSILA) in 1930, later printed in *The Duckboard*.

3   The Returned Soldiers and Sailors Imperial League of Australia. See Scott, Ernest, *Australia During the Great War: Vol. XI Official History of Australia in the War of 1914–18*, 9th ed (Angus & Robertson, 1943), pp 850, 857; formation, objects, and work of, 497n, 853–6; advocates granting war gratuity, 497–8, 499; gatherings 'twenty years after', (plates) 838, 839.

4   Major-General Sir Charles Harington had been brought to Second Army by Plumer very recently. He was well regarded but with modest experience having been commissioned into King's Liverpool Regiment in 1892, and had had a spell at the War Office after attending Staff College. His appointment to Second Army marked a remarkable leap from Major to Major-General in fourteen months.

5   WO95 881

6   Maj-Gen Sir G. Franks KCB, Second Army.

7   Brig-Gen C.W. Gwynn RE, II Anzac Corps.

8   WO95 881

9   Ibid.

10   WO95 3527

11   Ibid.

12   WO95 3558

13   WO95 881

14   WO95 3595

15   Ellis, Capt A.D., *The Story of the Fifth Australian Division*.

16   IWM 80/32/2

17   GHQ Order GS420(A) 17 July 1916.

18   Miles, Capt W., *Military Operations France and Belgium 1916*, p.124.

19   AWM 45, 27 January–27 June 1916.

20   WO95 5

21   AIR 1/1343/204/19/21. 16 Squadron Record Book reported that the weather was 'heavily overcast' on 16 July, 'very heavy mist with low clouds' the following day and 'clouds 500 feet, clearing towards evening' on 17 July.

22   WO95 881

23   Ibid.

24   WO95 3576

25   IWM 80/32/2

3. INTO A STREAM OF LEAD

1   The origin of this name is unclear, and Capt R. Hugh Knyvett's comment in 'Over There with the Australians' is patently wrong. He says, 'VC Ave which was supposed to be built on the spot where Michael O'Leary won the first Victoria Cross of the war'; Pte Michael O'Leary, 1 Btn Irish Guards, did win a VC to the south at Cuinchy on 1 February 1915, but Pte Henry May of 1 Btn Cameronians (Scottish Rifles) won his VC nearby, at La Boutillerie, on 22 October 1914. Three others were also won in the vicinity, at Rouges Bancs, in late December 1914, none of which were the first of the war.

2   AWM 38 Diary 243B

3   Sgt W.H. Downing MM, b. Portland, Victoria, 10 December 1893, educated at Scotch College and University of Melbourne. Enlisted in 57 Btn on 30 September 1915. Barrister 1922, Lt Col 1931, d. Melbourne 1965.

4   Miles, Capt W., *Military Operations France and Belgium 1916*, p.121.

5   An appreciation of the ability of the Germans to see activity in the British lines and to shell it with impunity can be found much later in Lt Col Cass's notes on the battle. He expressed the view that 'the Germans have some very accurate system of observing the

rear of our position. It could be done by a telescope periscope (similar to a submarine's periscope) about 20 feet long and placed in a tree'. He reports his experience on retiring after the hostilities ceased on the morning of 20 July: 'on returning to Rue Petillon via York Avenue I had no sooner reached our 300 line with about 12 or 15 men than heavy shells rained on us and searched the avenue for about 50 yards. This could not have been done by chance as there had been no fire on this point for over 15 minutes prior to my arrival there'. Many roads were clogged with vehicles, 'mostly artillery limbers, and columns of traffic often stood for hours without movement'. Major Christie-Miller, 2/1 Bucks, thought that 'the concentration must have been obvious and why it was not interfered with… by enemy artillery I have never understood'. IWM 80/32/2

6   Present-day visitors to the battlefield can see examples on the site of Nephew Trench, now in part occupied by the Memorial Park, as well as many others dotted around the countryside. Some no doubt were used in July 1916 but others, such as the trench mortar post at Delangre Farm, appear to be later constructions, though with or without concrete structures the German line was well defended. Again writing to Bean in 1926, 'Pompey' Elliott expressed the view, obtained on the occasion of his visit to the battlefield immediately after the Armistice, that 'the enemy thus had the apex of a triangular field of fire… pointed towards us and from the appearance of the bodies which lay along the bank of the Laies and along the edge of the road it is evident that the different waves in these localities walked into a stream of lead'. AWM 38 Diary 243B.

7   WO95 3611

8   Downing, W.H., *To The Last Ridge.*

9   WO95 3623

10   AWM 38 Diary 243B

11   WO95 881

12   It is worth mentioning, purely for the sake of curiosity, that among the Bavarian troops was one by the name of Adolf Hitler. As leader of Nazi Germany, Hitler returned to Fromelles after the fall of France in 1940 and visited bunkers on Aubers Ridge where he had been based at various stages of his time on the front. To mark his visit to the area a plaque was unveiled on a billet used by him in Fournes, just to the south of Fromelles. Later this was replaced by a concrete plaque which can now been viewed in the museum in Fromelles. Hitler had joined 1 Company of the 16 Bavarian RIR, sometimes referred to as the List Regiment after its original commander, very early in the war. Among his contemporaries in his regiment were Rudolf Hess and Max Amann, the latter becoming a business manager in the Nazi party's publishing activities. Hitler's role was as a messenger – *Meldeganger* – taking messages between Company and Regimental headquarters, and it was in this capacity that he served at Fromelles. The rest of his life's story is history.

13   WO95 3623

14   'The Australians Battle in France', *Sydney Morning Herald*, 29 September 1916.

15   WO95 881

16   AWM 2 DRL 171

17   Interview with author, 1992.

18   IWM 80/32/2

19   Bean also wrote a note to accompany the many private accounts submitted to the Australian War Memorial's archives: 'The private diaries in this collection furnish some of its most valuable historical records, but, like all private memoirs which were not compiled with any historical purpose, they should not be regarded as first hand evidence except where it is certain that they are so. The diarist is almost always sincere in his desire to record accurately, but he is subject to no obligation or inducement to indicate whether he is recording his own observations or incidents told him by friends or heard at third or fourth hand at the mess-table.'

4. SENDING FRITZ IRON RATIONS

1   Spr W. Smith 14 FC (later Lt 53 Btn), *Reveille*, 1 July 1936.
2   AWM 2 DRL 171
3   WO95 881
4   AIR1/1361/204/22/8
5   WO95 3655
6   WO95 3636
7   The establishment of 15 MGC was ten officers and 143 other ranks, of which eight officers and 109 other ranks were available at zero hour, the remainder being away on other duties or in hospital.
8   WO95 3655
9   Ibid.
10 Wilson, G.H., 'Medium Trench Mortars at Fromelles', *Reveille*, 1 May 1937.
11 WO95 3587
12 WO95 3590
13 WO95 3568
14 WO95 3592
15 WO95 3590
16 Ibid.
17 IWM 80/32/2
18 WO95 3587
19 WO95 3590
20 WO95 3592
21 WO95 3623
22 WO95 3645
23 Williams, H.R., *The Gallant Company: An Australian Soldier's Story of 1915–18*.
24 Downing, W.H., *To The Last Ridge*.
25 Diary Major E. Lister PR 90/115
26 WO95 3619
27 Elliott papers AWM 3DRL 3856
28 Capt E.H. Mair 58 Btn.
29 AWM 3DRL 6428
30 WO95 3037

5. ANNIHILATING FIRE

1   *Citizen Soldiers of Buckinghamshire: Second Bucks Battalion.*
2   Page papers via Cleve Page.
3   WO95/881
4   *Citizen Soldiers of Buckinghamshire.*
5   Chidgey, H.T., *Black Square Memories.*
6   IWM 80/32/2
7   WO95 3056
8   WO95 165
9   Ibid.
10 Ibid.
11 Ibid.
12 2/1 Bucks previously incurred their four casualties in the line from the troops' own weapons: two men were wounded by defective rifle grenades, one NCO was accidentally killed inspecting weapons, and one man shot by a sentry when he did

not respond to a challenge when returning from a listening post. (IWM 80/32/2 Col Christie-Miller papers)

13   WO95 3033
14   2/1 Bucks Companies were commanded by Capt H. Church (A), Capt R.F. Symonds (B), Capt H.S.G. Buckmaster (C) and Capt I. Stewart-Liberty (D).
15   Major Christie-Miller's papers record it as being a German HE shell. IWM 80/32/2.
16   IWM 80/32/2
17   The correct name for a 'pipe-pusher' was a Barratt hydraulic jack. It pushed a pipe filled with ammonal forward at a depth of four or five feet. When required, this was exploded and provided a very basic communication trench.
18   *Citizen Soldiers of Buckinghamshire.*
19   *Citizen Soldiers of Buckinghamshire.* If 265388 L/Cpl A.F. Stevens did reach the enemy line he did not live to tell the tale and his name is on the Loos Memorial. (IWM 80/32/2)
20   Beer had originally come to France as second-in-command of 2/8 Royal Warwicks.
21   WO95 165
22   *Citizen Soldiers of Buckinghamshire.*
23   WO95 165
24   WO95 881

6. I'LL BE ALRIGHT

1   WO95 3651
2   The whole matter of communication was a critical aspect of command and control throughout the Great War. Indeed, one reason for so many daylight attacks was to enable the position of troops or the fall of shells to be observed.
3   WO95 3573
4   WO95 165
5   WO95 3576
6   AWM 2DRL 176. Pte Bell was born in Traralgon, Victoria in 1891 and educated at Lakes Entrance State School. He was employed as a firemen when he enlisted in the AIF on 21 July 1915.
7   WO95 3653
8   WO95 3651
9   McCrae's successor, appointed on 22 July, was Major H.M. Duigan.
10   AWM 3DRL 3856
11   Elliott suffered personal loss in the war when his brother, Capt George Elliott, a medical officer attached to 56 Btn, died of wounds on 25 September 1917 at Chateau Wood in the Ypres Salient. He is buried in The Huts British War Cemetery, Belgium (VII D 20).
12   AWM 3 DRL 3856
13   AWM 3 DRL 2872
14   WO95 3576
15   WO95 3592
16   Ibid.

7. SOME GHASTLY SIGHTS

1   WO95 3623
2   Ibid.
3   Ibid.

4   Evers, Major S.W., 'Fromelles-Fleurbaix', *Reveille*, 1 November 1941 (AWM 234 MS 1801181).

5   WO95 3623

6   AWM 3 DRL 6428

7   Ibid.

8   Ibid.

9   Williams, H.R., *The Gallant Company*.

10 Capt, Clive Hopkins, 14 LTMB, served in the Gallipoli campaign where he was wounded and had a fortunate escape when a bullet smashed his revolver. He was mentioned in despatches by Sir Ian Hamilton and by 10 August 1915 had been promoted to Captain. Hopkins crossed to France as a Staff Captain with 14 Bde. On the eve of the fighting at Fromelles he volunteered to transfer to the brigade's trench mortar battery.

11 Hopkins's grave can now be found, marked with the usual CWGC headstone, in Rue du Bois Military Cemetery near Fleurbaix, plot 1 row F grave 18. Hopkins papers via Ray Hopkins.

12 Knyvett, Capt R. Hugh, *Over There with the Australians*.

13 WO95 3611

14 Association Souvenir de la Bataille de Fromelles (ASBF).

15 AWM 38 Diary 243B

16 WO95 3623

17 Oswald Croshaw had previously served in the British army. Whilst in Egypt he became tired of a desk job and grabbed the opportunity to join 53 Btn. After the battle, Major Croshaw took over command of the battalion. Later awarded the DSO, Croshaw died of wounds at Polygon Wood on 26 September 1917 as 14 Bde advanced across what is now the Buttes New British Cemetery, Polygon Wood, Belgium. He is buried in Bedford House, Zillebeke, enclosure 21, row A, grave 21. Details of Croshaw's death can be found in the *Official History of Australia in the War 1914–18* Volume IV, page 827.

18 54 Btn's company commanders were Capt Taylor (A Coy), Capt Hansen (B Coy), Major Holman (C Coy) and Capt Jack (D Coy).

19 Bishop, Bert, *Soldier Solomon* (subsequently published as *The Hell, The Humour and The Heartbreak: A Private's View of World War I*).

20 Ibid.

21 AWM 2 DRL 712

22 WO95 3633

23 AWM PR89/163

8. TWISTED HEAP OF KHAKI

1   'A. Tiveychoc', *There and Back: The Story of An Australian Soldier*.

2   Col Toll's son had already been killed in the war. 1908 Pte Frederick Vivian Toll, 15 Btn, died on 8 August 1915 aged twenty and is commemorated on the Lone Pine Memorial, Gallipoli.

3   WO95 3619

4   'Forgotten Hero of the Somme', *Somerset Standard*, 6 November 1992; Keeling papers via Brian Dyer.

5   WO95 3605

6   WO95 3619

7   WO95 3576

8   WO95 3619

9   WO95 3611

10   WO95 3621

11   WO95 3611

12   AWM 1DRL 483

13   Ibid.

14   AWM 2DRL 171

15   Ibid.

16   WO95 3619

17   Bean, C.E.W., *Official History of Australia in the War of 1914–18, Vol. III: The AIF in France 1916*, p.374.

18   WO95 3611

19   AWM 1 DRL 483

20   In his epic work *The First Day on the Somme*, Martin Middlebrook relates a story of a soldier chained to his gun. Sgt Les Martin wrote to his family, 'the Germans treat their soldiers in a most brutal fashion, especially in the case of machine gunners. In this particular case there were seven men to a gun crew, and they were all chained to the gun… to prevent them deserting their gun.'

21   WO95 3611

22   WO95 3621

23   WO95 3619

24   WO95 3611

25   Bean, C.E.W., *Official History of Australia in the War of 1914–18, Vol. III: The AIF in France 1916*, p383.

26   WO95 3619

27   AWM 2DRL 171

28   Ibid.

29   WO95 3611

30   Letter, 11 July 1916: Ross papers via T. Denny.

31   Ibid.

32   Purser, Lt Col M., 'Memories of Fromelles: 5 Division Launches First Battle for AIF in France', *Reveille*, 1 July 1935.

33   Clark, Col J.W., 'A Battalion's Baptism of Fire: The 30th Battalion at Fromelles', *Mufti*, 1 July 1937.

34   In September 1918 at Bellicourt, Wark won the VC. His name is listed on Pymble station roll of honour, New South Wales.

35   Story repeated by Lt Col M. Purser in *Reveille*, 1 July 1935.

36   Among the 30 Btn troops was a group of ex-RANR men from Port Fairy including 1067 Pte S.G. Evans, a fisherman, 1080 Cpl F. Hanley, eldest son of the owner of the local paper, the *Port Fairy Gazette*, 1163 Pte D.J. Lane, a farmer's son, and 1073 Pte R.W. Goldie, also a farmer's son, but who, as a Leading Seaman in the RANR, had been a member of the AN&MEF which went in pursuit of the Germans in September 1914. The majority of A Coy, 30 Btn, were Victorian ex-RANR men. At Seymour Camp in May 1915 these naval men were drafted into what became known as the Victorian Naval Unit and the intention was that they would proceed overseas for service on minesweepers. Several weeks passed and they remained firmly on dry land but moved to Broadmeadows. On parade they were positioned at the rear of the parade until one named Tosh Ridley requested that etiquette be observed and the naval men be repositioned at the front. The Camp Commandant agreed to this change! After some weeks in Broadmeadows Camp, they travelled by train to Liverpool and created what was probably a unique event in the AIF's history when, wearing their blue uniforms, they marched into camp while the band played 'Sons of the Seas'. In due course their blue was exchanged for khaki and they fought as part of 30 Btn for the duration of the Great War. (Evans papers via S. Evans.)

37 WO95 3619
38 Ibid.

9. DESTRUCTION AND HAVOC

1   WO95 5
2   WO95 165
3   IWM 83/12/1
4   Chidgey, H.T., *Black Square Memories*.
5   WO95 3648
6   WO95 165
7   WO95 881
8   Ibid.
9   WO95 3636
10 WO95 3576
11 WO95 3623 report by Capt S.B. Pope.
12 WO95 3623
13 Elliott, H.E., 'The Battle of Fleurbaix', reprinted from *The Duckboard*, 1 September 1930; Ellis, Capt A.D., *The Story of the Fifth Australian Division*.
14 WO95 881
15 WO95 165
16 It is noteworthy that Lt Reginald George Scrase is commemorated on the Thiepval Memorial; 'James' has not been identified. The only likely officer is 2/Lt Donald Croft James from Bristol, serving with 2/4th Gloucesters, killed in action on 19 July 1916 and commemorated on the Thiepval Memorial. *Officers Died...*and the CWGC details concur, but the former does not indicate that he was attached to another unit, hence being on a memorial that covers another geographical area. It is possible that a simple error has caused him to be listed on the wrong memorial.
17 IWM 83/12/1

10. CONSPICUOUS GALLANTRY

1   The Grashof was most probably the 'strong and important enemy position... protected in front by high, heavy barbed wire entanglements some five feet high and would have been a difficult position to storm and was intact from our own gunfire' reported by Col Toll in his account of the battle. WO95 3619.
2   AWM 2DRL 171
3   This award proved useful in 1917 when Col Cass provided a reference for Capt Gunter, as he then was, who was about to be discharged as a consequence of wounds received in action and was seeking employment training troops.
4   Sloan, H., *The Purple and Gold*, p.80.
5   WO95 3631.
6   Wilson, G.H., 'Medium Trench Mortars at Fromelles', *Reveille*, 1 May 1937.
7   Freirat was Swedish by birth and was typical of the mix of nationalities within the AIF.
8   AWM 38 Diary 243 B
9   Bean, C.E.W, *Official History of Australia in the War of 1914–18, Vol. III: The AIF in France 1916*, p.408.
10 Bishop, Bert, *Soldier Solomon*
11 Ibid.

12   Williams, H.R., *The Gallant Company*.
13   WO95 3655
14   AWM PR89/163
15   Bean, C.E.W., *Official History of Australia in the War of 1914–18, Vol. III: The AIF in France 1916*.
16   WO95 3633

11. THE FINAL STAGES

1   The circumstances of Capt Mills's capture are related by Ellis, in his history of 5
     Australian Division: 'his right hand was suddenly shattered, the air was filled with
     bursting grenades, and a German hand seized him roughly, saying "Officer, why do you
     not put up your hands?" He was dragged into a communication trench and hurried to
     the rear as a prisoner of war.' Mills, with his arm in a sling, is readily identified in some
     of the well known German photographs taken on 20 July.
2   Lt Trounson was singled out for special mention in Toll's report. WO95 3619.
3   WO95 3611
4   Ibid.
5   AWM1 DRL 483
6   AWM 2 DRL 712
7   WO95 881
8   Ibid.
9   WO95 3619
10   Middlebrook, Martin, *The Kaiser's Battle 21 March 1918: The First Day of the German
     Spring Offensive*.
11   AWM 2DRL 171
12   WO95 3619
13   WO95 3635
14   Williams, H.R., *The Gallant Company*.
15   WO95 3623
16   AWM PR89 163
17   663 Pte D. Low DOW 4 August 1916, buried Tottenham Cemetery.
18   AIR1/1343/204/19/21

12. A FEARFUL PRICE

1   AWM 2 DRL 171
2   Chidgey, H.T., *Black Square Memories*.
3   In addition to Spencer Maxted, Fr John Kennedy served with distinction in this division,
     as did Chaplain James Green. Green was born in Newcastle, England, in 1864; he settled
     in Australia in 1889 and served as a correspondent in the Boer War. He was wounded
     and returned to Australia but re-enlisted, went back to South Africa and was captured
     by the Boers. In the Great War he served firstly at Gallipoli and then on the Western
     Front, in 14 Bde. It was not just in the battle zone that he was inspirational; Green was
     instrumental in the establishment of the AIF Recreational Centre in Horseferry Road,
     London. For his valuable work he was awarded a DSO and later the CMG. After the war
     he continued to work for the Methodists in Sydney; he retired in 1934 and died in 1948.
4   'The Australians Battle in France', *Sydney Morning Herald*, 29 September 1916.
5   WO95 3597
6   Bishop, Bert, *Soldier Solomon*.

7   Arthur Ebdon and Tom Brain, interviews with author 1992.
8   Bishop, Bert, *Soldier Solomon*.
9   Ibid.
10   Pte R.C. Bishop is on the Red Cross list of names which the Germans compiled when burying the dead at Pheasant Wood, Fromelles. Sheet 36SW2 map reference N17c.35.08.
11   Lt Col Herbert Thomas Layh CMG DSO and bar.
12   Williams, H.R. *The Gallant Company*.
13   Barnes, A.F., *The Story of 2/5th Gloucestershire Regiment 1914–18*.
14   WO95 3527
15   Ibid.
16   AWM 38 Diary 243 B
17   Ibid.
18   Bean, C.E.W., *Official History of Australia in the War of 1914–18, Vol. III: The AIF in France 1916*, p.442
19   WO95 3636
20   Page papers via Cleve Page.
21   Downing, W.H., *To The Last Ridge*.
22   WO95 3573
23   Knyvett, Capt R. Hugh, *Over There with the Australians*.
24   AWM 1DRL/300
25   Sgt Fraser was mistaken in thinking that Marshall was awarded the VC.
26   Downing W.H., *To The Last Ridge*.
27   Williams, H.R., *The Gallant Company*.
28   IWM 80/32/2
29   AWM 2DRL 171
30   Clark, Col J.W., 'A Battalion's Baptism of Fire'.

13. CASUALTIES

1   *The Duckboard*, 1 June 1934
2   Butler, Col A.G., *Official History of the Australian Army Medical Services, Vol. 2: Western Front 1914–18*.
3   Wrench, C.M., *Campaigning with the Fighting 9th*.
4   Butler, Col A.G., *Official History of the Australian Army Medical Services Vol. 2 Western Front 1914–18*.
5   WO95 3565
6   WO95 881
7   WO95 3038
8   Colley-Priest, Pte L.W., *The 8th Field Ambulance On Active Service*.
9   Ibid.
10   Ibid.
11   Ibid.
12   WO95 3605
13   WO95 3536
14   WO95 3565
15   AWM 2DRL 171
16   Butler, Col A.G., *Official History of the Australian Army Medical Services, Vol. 2: Western Front 1914–18*.
17   WO95 881
18   WO95 3565

19 MacLaurin, G., 'Fleurbaix', *Sydney Morning Herald*, 26 July 1919.

20 WO 95 3003

21 WO95 196

22 WO95 5

23 Miles, Capt Wilfred, *The Official History of the War, Military Operations France and Belgium 1916 II*, states 79 officers and 1468 other ranks respectively (p133) and 178 and 5355 for the Australians.

24 WO95 165

25 Ibid.

26 WO95 3527

27 Interview Bob Cleworth 2001.

28 WO95 3623

29 George Rankin interview with Randall King 1991.

30 WO95 3623

31 IWM 80/32/2

32 WO95 3033

33 WO95 3572

34 WO95 3609

35 WO95 3555

36 Ibid.

14. CAPTIVITY

1 AWM 30 series.

2 Carter papers via Len Carter.

3 If these two men were from 53 Btn like Mitchell, they were possibly 3337 L/Cpl B. Kent – though there was a 2835 Cpl R.S. Kiss, 54 Btn, in Munster POW camp – and 3235 Cpl L.F.J. Bailey.

4 Noble, Roger, *Raising the White Flag: The Surrender of Australia Soldiers on the Western Front*.

5 Ibid.

6 Ibid.

7 Smith papers via Peter Smith.

8 Fromelles POWs were held at the following camps: Osnabruck, Clausthal in the Hartz Mountains, Blankenburg Mark, Diepholz, Dulmen, Minden, Heestenmoor, Rethemer Moor, Soltau, Gutersloh, Crefeld, Swarnistedt, Holzminden, Hamelburg, Friedeichsfeld, Schneidenuhl, Stargard.

15. FIRST VIEW OF HEAVEN

1 Jack Ridley was born on 8 September 1896. It is thought that he ran one of very few Bible study groups in the AIF, if not the only one. He was commissioned and returned to 53 Btn, and for gallantry between 30 September and 2 October 1918 was awarded the MC. He died on 26 September 1976. Jack Ridley's brother Alec was wounded at Gallipoli.

2 AWM 3DRL 6428

3. Ibid.

4 Ibid.

5 Ibid.

6 Ibid.

7 Ibid.

8 T.C. Whiteside was the son of a Presbyterian Minister who emigrated to California and then to Gippsland, Victoria, Australia. He was known as 'Clair' rather than Thomas. See Whiteside, Elizabeth, *A Valley in France*.

9 3867 Pte W. O'Sullivan and 2768 Pte A.J. Russell. In August 1916, Whiteside received news that Russell had died of wounds.

10 Bill Mair was a veteran of both the Boer War and the Australian Naval & Military Expeditionary Force to Rabaul in German New Guinea. Born in Gulgong in 1874, he worked as a shearer and wool-classer; having been discharged from the AN&MEF, he joined the AIF in search of further soldiering. On 16 July 1917 Sgt Mair embarked from Sydney on HMAT A16 Port Melbourne as part of 8 Reinforcements to 33 Btn. Despite a bout of influenza in late November 1918, he returned to Australia and was discharged on 22 March 1921.

11 Campbell, Maurice, & Hosken Graeme, *Four Australians At War: Letters to Argyle 1914–1919*.

12 Field papers via Delma Rich.

13 Inglis papers via Elsie Teede.

14 AWM 1DRL 206

15 AWM PR90/115

16 In all cases their date of death is erroneously given as 18 July 1916.

17 AWM MSS 1365 draft manuscript, *A Soldier Looks Back*. 2148 Bdr A.J. Williams, 53 Battery, Australian Field Artillery.

18 Sam Yeates' story was again published in the *Bairnsdale Advertiser*, 19 April 2002.

19 1DRL 428 12/11/1587 Red Cross POW Dept: Individual Case Files of Australian POWs 1914–18. Pte Outlaw's file ref 2070412.

20 Pte Shark appears to be 4872 Pte E. Sharkey.

21 Lt C.T. Collier, 53 Btn, solicitor of Roseville, NSW. Born Geurrie, NSW, 24 August 1893; enlisted AN&MEF 18 August 1914; served German New Guinea 9 Reinforcements 8 Btn; 2 May 1916 to 53 Btn.

22 Cleworth papers via Bob Cleworth.

23 Pte R.E. Arbon was not a casualty of the battle. He died on 19 July 1916 in England and is buried in Nottingham General Cemetery.

24 *Hamilton Spectator*, 15 August 1916.

16. BITTER LEGACY

1 Bishop, Bert *Soldier Solomon*.

2 Miles, Capt Wilfred, *Official History of the War: Military Operations France and Belgium 1916*, vol. II, p.134.

3 WO95 881

4 WO95 165

5 AWM 3DRL 6428

6 *Sydney Morning Herald*, 28 July 1916.

17. BETTER THAN I EXPECTED

1 WO95 881

2 Ibid.

3 George Rankin interview with Randall King, 1991.

4 Bishop, Bert, *The Hell, The Humour and The Heartbreak*, p.61.

5 WO95 3022

6   WO95 3037

7   WO95 165

8   WO95 165

9   Cleworth papers via Bob Cleworth. The soldier was 1572A Dvr William Demeral.

10   WO95 3576

11   WO95 3576

12   WO95 3611

13   WO95 3576

14   WO95 3558

15   WO95 3056

16   IWM 80/32/2

17   Presumably in an error, Capt L.W. Crouch, Lt J.P. Chapman, 2/Lts C.G. Abrey and W.C. Trimmer are recorded as having been killed on 21 July.

18   Arthur and Ralph Brown were two of nine men, serving with the same battalion, from the Chiltern village of The Lee lost in this single attack. The others were Sydney Dwight, Harry Harding, Arnold Morris, Charles Phipps, Harry Pratt, Percy Price and Edward Sharp.

19   Swann, Maj-Gen J.C., *The 2nd Bucks Battalion*.

20   AWM PR90/115

21   WO95 3623

22   Elliott's speech to Canberra RSSILA, 1930.

23   WO95 3611

24   Clark, Col J.W., 'A Battalion's Baptism of Fire'.

25   WO95 3619

26   Ibid.

27   AWM 3DRL 3856

28   WO95 3595

29   WO95 3495

30   WO95 3587

31   WO95 3590

32   WO95 3592

33   Clark, Col, J.W., 'A Battalion's Baptism of Fire'.

34   WO95 3611

35   Green, James, 'Fleurbaix: The Mystery Battle of the AIF', *Sydney Morning Herald*, 19 July 1919.

36   H.E. Elliott letter to Bean, 17 August 1926; AWM 38 Diary 243 A.

37   Returned Services League.

38   AWM PR84/307

39   WO 95 881

40   In May 1915 Haking was GOC 1 Division in Monro's I Corps. In both the May 1915 and again in July 1916 Monro was Haking's immediate commander.

41   AWM 45 27/1 – 27/6

42   WO95 165

18. THE DISMISSAL OF HAROLD POPE

1   IWM 80/32/2

2   Australian War Records Section papers; biographical details of Pope.

3   Col Pope papers via Rob Gray.

4   Having Charteris as his Brigade Major must have been a difficult experience for Harold Pope. Charteris, at 38, was a professional soldier in the Royal Scots who had

served in South Africa and in the Dardanelles and Egypt and was part of the British Establishment, his grandfathers being earls (Wemyss and Albemarle). Moreover, Pope having been a citizen soldier in Australia, Charteris may have been placed in his brigade to keep an eye on him; if so, who monitored Elliott and Tivey? According to Charteris, there had been an incident before the battle in which Charteris indicated to Pope that he did not approve of his behaviour and would feel bound to report any further instance. Pope may have missed an opportunity to sack Charteris for insubordination and disloyalty, if indeed the event ever took place.

5   AWM 38 3/8042 item 109

6   WO95 3623

7   'Memo regarding the case of Colonel Pope', Col Pope papers via Rob Gray.

8   *Who's Who 1922*: 'Charteris Bt Lt Col Nigel K CMG 1918 DSO 1916, b 10 March 1878 son of Capt the Hon FW Charteris RN younger son of 9th Earl of Wemyss and Lady Louisa Keppel of 6th Earl of Albemarle, educated Winchester and Oxford, commissioned Royal Scots 1899 served SA War 1899–1902 (MiD twice), served GW 1914–18 MEF, 1915 EEF, 1916 BEF, France 1916 and 1918 (MiD three times, DSO Bt Lt Col CMG). Recreations – hunting, shooting, cricket, golf, motoring. Club – Cavendish.'

9   Col Pope papers via Rob Gray.

10   Ibid.

11   Ibid.

12   Ibid.

13   The quick appointment of Hobkirk was to be a sore point for Pope, but giving preference to British officers when making appointments in the AIF was quite common during the Great War. This occurred at various levels including battalion command and corps level. There were other instances of British officers finding a niche in the AIF, though, Oswald Croshaw being one such example. Monash was perhaps the highest profile personality, from within the AIF, to break the mould when he became commander of the Australian Corps in May 1918 in succession to Birdwood, a British officer, who moved to head the Fifth Army. This practice of favouring British officers did not end with the Armistice; a later example would be the controversial appointment, in June 1938, of Eton educated Major-Gen E.K. Squires who was then Director of Staff Duties at the War Office, London, as Inspector-General of the Australian Military Forces.

14   Col Pope's diary, Col Pope papers via Rob Gray.

15   Col Pope papers via Rob Gray.

16   Whatever Bean's personal view of these events, he mentions Pope again in the Official History only twice, both instances being in Vol. IV, once in a footnote and once when Pope was seriously wounded. After the Great War Pope certainly loaned Charles Bean some of his papers, presumably in the hope of ensuring that a favourable verdict was published; clearly he was not successful, and a more equitable epitaph was not recorded. However, in May 1929 Bean informed Pope that he would shortly be handing over his papers to the Australian War Memorial but on condition that they would not be for general inspection 'during present lifetimes'. He offers to remove the notes he extracted from Pope's diaries covering July 1916, but recognised that the donor might wish them to remain. Naturally, Pope preferred it to go 'exactly as it is – whatever may be in it represents exactly the fact of actual happenings'. (AWM 38 3/8042 item 109)

17   Bean, C.E.W., *Official History of Australia in the War of 1914–18, Vol. III: The AIF in France 1916*. Changes in the 5 Australian Division: Major R.H. Beardmore had replaced Lt Col Coghill (wounded), Major C.J. Holdorf had been promoted to succeed Col Cass invalided home via England, Major C.A. Denehy now commanded the 58 Btn in place of Lt Col Jackson, also wounded, and Major H.T.C. Layh now led the 59 Btn in succession to Lt Col E.A. Harris, now recovering from wounds. In addition, Major

Oswald Crowshaw was promoted to fill the gap created by the death in action of the gallant Lt Col I.B. Norris of 53 Btn, and Major H.M. Duigan took over from the late Major G.G. McCrae in Elliott's 60 Btn.

18 Rt. Hon. Sir George Pearce, Minister for Defence 1914–21 and Acting Prime Minister 1916.
19 Col Pope papers via Rob Gray.
20 Ibid.
21 Ibid.
22 Ibid.
23 Will Harris served with distinction at Fromelles, being recommended for a DSO but awarded an MC.
24 Col Pope papers via Rob Gray.
25 Ibid.
26 Ibid.
27 Ibid.
28 Ibid.
29 Ibid.
30 Ibid.
31 Ibid.
32 Ibid.
33 Ibid.
34 Ibid.
35 Ibid.
36 Ibid.
37 Ibid.
38 Ibid.
39 Ibid.
40 Ibid.
41 Ibid.
42 Ibid.
43 Ibid.
44 AWM 38 Diary 237
45 Col Pope papers via Rob Gray.
46 Ibid.
47 National Library of Australia, Monash papers MSS 1884, folder 921 box 124 Personal Correspondence April–Aug 1916.
48 National Library of Australia, Monash papers MSS 1884, Corres B folder 943, series 4, Private letters, book 5 7 6 6.12.15–3.8.16.
49 National Library of Australia, Monash papers MSS 1884, folder 921 box 124 Personal Correspondence April–Aug 1916.
50 Col Pope papers via Rob Gray.
51 Ibid.
52 Ibid.
53 Ibid.
54 Ibid.
55 Ibid.
56 Ibid.
57 AWM 38 Diary 237
58 History books will always record 'Pope's Hill' on maps relating to the Gallipoli campaign, named in honour of Pope after his battalion captured this position on 25 April 1915.

19. REMEMBERING

1   Other members of the population took advantage of the concrete structures built by the British or Germans, and close to Fromelles, at Festubert, one lady lived in a British blockhouse until around 1980.

2   This memorial was designed by Capt R.B. Saunders ARIBA who served with the Division from the outset. He was gazetted to the 2/6 Warwicks as signalling officer in October 1914, he attained the rank of Captain in December 1916 and served as a regimental officer throughout the war, being awarded the Military Cross in September 1917 after service in the Ypres Salient. Saunders was educated at St. Edwards High School, Birmingham, and was an early student at the Birmingham School of Architecture. Subsequently, he was articled to Messrs. Peacock and Bewlay, of Birmingham, and in 1912 had the good fortune to be assistant to an architect synonymous with Western Front memorials, Sir E.L. Lutyens RA. The memorial itself is made from Hopton Wood stone by a Capt Broadbent of Fulham.

3   In fact the 45 (2 Wessex) Division was the first second line division to go overseas, to India in December 1914.

4   Bean, C.E.W., *Official History of Australia in the War of 1914–18, Vol. 1: The Story of Anzac*, p.133

5   *Bendigo Advertiser*, 25 April 1996

6   AWM 25 1013/2

7   AWM 2 DRL 171

8   AWM PR 84/307

9   *The Official Names of Battles and Other Engagements Fought by the Military Forces of the British Empire During the Great War of 1914–1919 and the Third Afghan War 1919: report by the Battles Nomenclature Committee 1921.*

10 Da Costa, Gen Gomes, *O corpo de exército português na Grande Guerra: A batalha do Lys.*

11 Interview with author, 1992.

12 Interview with author, 1992.

APPENDIX A: ORDER OF BATTLE

1   WO95 3033

APPENDIX B: ARTILLERY DETAILS

1   WO95 881

2   WO95 3573

3   The 9.2-inch howitzer employed at this time was an impressive piece. The final design had been approved in July 1914 and the first examples saw action in October 1914, just four months later. The movement of the gun and carriage entailed a 36-hour operation to dismantle and transport it using three purpose-built carriages pulled by horses or traction engines. The gun and fittings weighed 15 tons, it had a range of 10,060 yards and it fired a shell weighing 290lb.

4   IWM 80/32/2

Acknowledgements

In addition to a special word of thanks to my wife Tessa, who typed much of the manuscript, sincere thanks are offered to the following who willingly contributed family papers, photographs, stories and other material in the course of my researching this book:

Arthur Millwood (Pte F.W. Millwood 30 Btn); Barbara Robertson (Pte B.J. Watson 57 Btn); Bea Burke (Sgt M. Burke 29 Btn); Bill Townsend (Pte P.W. Townsend 54 Btn); Bob and Edna Levy (Sgt G. Downer 1 Btn); Col Terry Cave CBE; Bob and Gwen Cleworth (Pte J. Cleworth 29 Btn); Bob Antrobus (W. and A. Antrobus 29 Btn); Bob Clark (Pte W.J. Clark and Pte R. Clark 54 Btn); Brian Dyer (Pte Thomas Keeling 30 Btn); Bruce Cobb (Gnr Ormuz Cobb 113 Bty AFA); Bruce Lees (Lt J. Benson DCM 32 Btn); Cleve Page (Sgt Page 14 FC); Col John Healy; Dave Joseph (Pte J. Joseph 31 Btn); David and Helen Harris (Lt W.D. Harris MC 54 Btn); Delma Rich (Sgt F. Field 30 Btn); Diana Cousens (Col Cass); Dorothy and Mervyn Dunk (Pte K. Dunk 32 Btn); Elizabeth Morey (NZ units); Elizabeth Whiteside (Pte T.C. Whiteside 59 Btn); Elsie Teede (Pte J. Inglis 32 Btn); Erma O'Donnell and Elaine Tallais (Lt Gunter 54 Btn); Frank Thexton and Betty Shepherd (Thexton family); Fred Allen (Spr F. Sainty 14 FC); Geoff Flowers (Pte F. Flowers 60 Btn); Geoff Luck (Pte W. and Pte E. Plater 54 Btn and Pte R. Plater 5 MG Btn); Glenville Mitchelson (Sgt J.G. Shepherd 30 Btn); Gordon Rae; Grant Lee (Pte J. Lee 32 Btn); Joe Walker (Pte W. Landy 58 Btn); John and Hazel Watters (Spr A. Findlay 14 FC); John Battersby; Len Carter (Pte H. Carter 54 Btn); Len Western (Pte L.C. Western 59 Btn); Lt Col Paul Simidas; Major Bruce Munchenberg AO; Major Lawrie Hindmarsh (artillery material); Maree Hahn (Pte C.A. Barr 59 Btn and Pte R.A. Wallis 59 Btn); Necia Forster (Pte H. Hollingsworth 5 Div Signal Coy); Neville Kidd (Major R. Harrison 54 Btn); Pam Goesch (Bert Bishop papers); Peter Jones; Peter Smith (Pte G.W. Smith 55 Btn); Randall and Cheryl King (Pte C. King and Pte W.S. Outlaw 53 Btn); Ray and Ruth Hopkins (Capt C.B. Hopkins 14 LTMB); Robert Gray (Col H. Pope CB); Ron Hansard (Pte Robert Fulton 53 Btn); Ron James (Pte A.H. James 30 Btn); Ross St. Claire (54 Btn information); Roy Hewitt (Pte G. Eamans 53 Btn); Stan and Alma Evans (Pte S. Evans 30 Btn); Steve Knight; Stewart Smith (Pte A.E. Smith 53 Btn); Ted Ecclestone (Pte W.C. Ecclestone 59 Btn); Thelma Denny (Pte J.V. Ross 8 MGC and Pte J. Cairns 53 Btn); Thomas Welch (Pte A. Welsh 31 Btn); Tony Spagnola; Trish Lesina (Gnr W. Webb 5 AFAB); Richard Jeffs (OBLI); Lin Collier (maps); the staff of the AWM Research Centre; and finally to Martial Delebarre of Fromelles, who has done so much to commemorate the events of 19–20 July 1916.

List of Illustrations

All photographs are from the author's collection unless otherwise stated.

1   Maj-Gen the Hon Sir J.W. McCay. Reproduced by permission of the Australian War Memorial.
2   Brig-Gen Harold Elliott. Reproduced by permission of the Australian War Memorial.
3   The Armistice Commission in Spa; Lt-Gen Sir Richard Haking. Reproduced by permission of the Australian War Memorial.
4   Aerial view of the Sugar Loaf Salient. Reproduced by permission of the Australian War Memorial.
5   Australian prisoners of war with German soldiers. Reproduced by permission of the Australian War Memorial.
6   Officers of 2/1 Bucks Battalion at Parkhouse Camp. Courtesy of Richard Jeffs.
7   Gen Sir Alexander Godley.
8   Maj-Gen Sir Colin Mackenzie.
9   Brig-Gen E. Tivey.
10   Col Harold Pope CB.
11   Col Pope with his family. Courtesy of Robert Gray.
12   Col Pope at an Anzac Day parade after the war. Courtesy of Robert Gray.
13   Lt-Col W.E.H. Cass. Courtesy of Diana Cousens.
14   Major Geoff McCrae.
15   Grave of Major McCrae.
16   Captain Will Harris, 54 Btn. Courtesy of David and Helen Harris.
17   Captain Clive Hopkins. Courtesy of Ray and Ruth Hopkins.
18   Pte Billy Outlaw.
19   Pte Chris King.
20   Pte Aubrey Antrobus. Courtesy of Bob Antrobus.
21   Pte Walter Antrobus. Courtesy of Bob Antrobus.
22   Father Louis Dahiez with the remains of a soldier killed at Fromelles.
23   Pte Kenneth Dunk. Courtesy of Dorothy and Mervyn Dunk.
24   Wedding of Jim and Ethel Cleworth, with Charlie Peters MM and Rose. Courtesy of Bob and Gwen Cleworth.
25   Eaglehawk Boys (C Company 29 Btn) at Seymour. Courtesy of Bob Cleworth.
26   Villagers in front of Fromelles church before the Great War.

27   The main street of Fromelles before the war.
28   Men of 53 Btn immediately prior to the attack on 19 July 1916. Reproduced by
          permission of the Australina War Memorial.
29   German trench railway in the damaged village of Fromelles, 1916.
30   The *Cobbers* statue in Fromelles Memorial Park.
31   British and Australian prisoners marching through Fournes.
32   Australian dead lying in the German front line, 20 July 1916.
33   VC Corner at Fromelles.
34   Commemorative plaque, Fromelles village.
35 & 36   German mass grave from 19–20 July 1916 in Beaucamps German cemetery.
37   Memorial to 61 Division at Laventie.
38   Australian POWs in Fromelles, 20 July 1916.
39   A contemporary sketch of Winchester Trench in 61 Division sector.
40   A German observation post at Aubers, as seen today.
41   Pte W.C. Ecclestone. Courtesy of Tes Ecclestone.
42   Pte H. Carter. Courtesy of Len Carter.
43   Sgt Maurice Burke. Courtesy of Bea Burke.

MAPS

1   The British Zone, July 1916.
2   Fromelles area, July 1916.
3   Battle of Fromelles: dispositions of 5 Australian Division about 9p.m. on 19 July 1916.
4   Fromelles 19–20 July 1916: 61 Division sector.
5   Fire trench dug by A Company of 30 Australian Btn, 19–20 July 1916.

Index

Ames Col W.H. (2/4
    OBLI) 181
Antrobus Pte A. (29 Btn)
    118
Antrobus Pte W. (29 Btn)
    118
Arblaster Capt C. (53 Btn)
    53, 57, 79, 81, 83, 84,
    170
Australian Imperial Force
    II Anzac Corps 12, 16,
    72, 94, 104, 105
    3 Australian Division 11,
    13, 189
    4 Australian Division 12,
    13, 15, 17, 18, 19
    5 Australian Division 12,
    13, 14, 17, 19, 25, 33,
    41, 69-72, 90, 94, 104,
    108, 111, 196
    5 Pioneer Btn 34, 35, 36,
    96
    8 Australian Bde 13, 14,
    24, 39, 43, 49, 56, 59,
    61, 63, 66, 73, 74, 78,
    83, 87, 90, 91, 108, 117,
    119, 163, 167, 169
    29 Btn 65, 66, 78, 87, 88,
    104, 118, 171
    30 Btn 36, 61, 64, 65, 66,
    67, 68, 78, 79, 83, 104,
    127, 171
    31 Btn 36, 39, 49, 60, 61,
    63-65, 67, 68, 77, 83,
    87, 90, 172, 196
    32 Btn 49, 60, 62, 63, 65,
    67, 68, 77, 78, 83, 87,

88, 90, 117, 172
    8 Field Ambulance 60,
    106-108
    8 Field Company 35, 36,
    66, 174
    8 Machine Gun
    Company 64, 65
    14 Australian Brigade 43,
    51, 63, 73, 74, 77, 80,
    83, 86, 87, 90, 91, 117,
    163, 171, 182
    53 Btn 53-55, 57, 62, 77,
    79-81, 84, 85, 114, 116
    54 Btn 53, 54, 57, 62, 77,
    78, 80-82, 86, 92, 117,
    171
    55 Btn 57, 64, 78, 82, 86,
    91, 92, 117, 171
    56 Btn 53, 55, 83, 84, 86,
    90, 91
    14 Field Ambulance 106,
    108
    14 Field Company 35,
    36, 55, 64, 174
    14 Machine Gun
    Company 53, 80
    15 Australian Brigade 19,
    32, 33, 43, 46, 47, 49,
    52, 69, 70, 72, 74, 77,
    83, 89, 101, 108, 109,
    169, 173
    57 Btn 33, 37, 43, 49, 74
    58 Btn 19, 33, 43, 49, 70,
    71, 74
    59 Btn 36, 49, 50, 51, 70,
    71, 152
    60 Btn 36, 49, 50, 51, 70,

71, 74, 77, 79, 152, 163,
    173
    15 Field Ambulance 106,
    110, 126
    15 Field Company 35,
    36, 52, 70,174
    15 Machine Gun
    Company 33
    3 Australian Tunnelling
    Company 36, 37, 46

Bachtold Maj H. (14 FC)
    35, 57, 58, 94
Barrow Maj-Gen Sir G.
    16, 89
Bean C. 12, 25, 29, 61, 82,
    100, 157-159, 160, 176,
    178, 184, 186, 198, 200
Beardsmore Maj R.H. (30
    Btn) 66, 67
Beer Lt Col J.H. (2/4 R
    Berks) 47
Birdwood Gen Sir W. 129,
    183-185, 188, 189, 191,
    192
Bishop Pte R.C. (55 Btn)
    96, 97, 157, 158
Bishop Pte W.H. (54 Btn)
    97, 130, 157
Bishop Pte W.H. (Bert) (55
    Btn) 38, 57, 82, 97, 130,
    157, 158, 174
Brain Pte T. (60 Btn) 29, 96
British Army
    First Army 11, 12, 15, 16,
    20, 36, 112, 165
    XI Corps 12, 15, 18, 20,

21, 27, 42, 71, 158
61 (2 South Midland)
    Division 12, 13, 17, 25,
    26, 39, 41, 71, 73, 89,
    90, 111, 157, 160, 165,
    175, 176, 179, 194, 196
182 Bde 13, 43, 69, 70
2/5 Warwicks 45
2/6 Warwicks 44, 45, 169
2/7 Warwicks 43, 45-47,
    70, 71, 115, 116, 167
2/8 Warwicks 13, 43, 70
183 Bde 13, 46, 69, 70
2/4 Gloucesters 69, 75
2/6 Gloucesters 46
184 Bde 13, 32, 33, 46,
    69, 70, 73, 169, 178
2/5 Gloucesters 13, 99
2/1 Bucks Btn (OBLI)
    41, 43, 46, 47, 70, 104,
    114, 169
2/4 OBLI 70, 73
2/4 Royal Berks 46, 47
Second Army 11, 12, 15-17,
    20, 36
60 Brigade 17, 18, 43, 60,
    67, 68, 73, 88, 113
6 Btn OBLI 19
1 Field Ambulance 106
2/1 (SM) Field
    Ambulance 106
2/3 (SM) Field
    Ambulance 106
3 Field Ambulance 106
94 Field Ambulance 106
No.2 Motor Ambulance
    Convoy 106, 111
No.13 Motor Ambulance
    Convoy 111
1/3 South Midland FC
    RE 46
173 Tunnelling Company
    37
181 Tunnelling Company
    37
255 Tunnelling Company
    37
10 Squadron 18, 32
16 Squadron 18, 32
British Cemeteries and
    Memorials 23, 50,

88, 95, 98, 102, 115,
    116,130, 152, 196, 197,
    199, 201
Brown CSM A. (2/1 Bucks)
    19, 169
Brown CSM R. (2/1
    Bucks) 169
Buckmaster Capt. H.S.G.
    (2/1 Bucks) 114, 169
Butler Maj-Gen Sir R. H.
    K. 16, 20, 21, 176

Caddy Lt Col H.O. 49
Carter Brig-Gen C.H.P.
    (184 Bde) 13, 46, 73,
    181
Carter Pte H. (54 Btn) 118
Cass Lt Col W.E.H. (54 Btn)
    27, 56, 57, 61, 63, 77,
    78, 80, 81, 84, 85, 86,
    89, 90, 92, 170, 171,
    185, 186
Charteris Maj N.K. (R
    Scots) 182, 183,186-
    190, 191
Christie-Miller Maj G. (2/1
    Bucks) 13, 22, 29, 35,
    45, 46, 104, 169, 181
Church Capt H. (2/1
    Bucks) 19, 46, 47, 69,
    169
Clark Lt Col J.W. (30 Btn)
    67, 104, 171, 174
Cleworth Pte J. (29 Btn)
    113, 167
Coghill Lt Col D.M.R. (32
    Btn) 60, 68, 189
Colley-Priest Pte L.W.
    (8FA) 107
Collier Lt C.T. (53 Btn)
    154, 170
Coulter Maj L.J. (3ATC)
    36, 37
Crank Lt R. (53 Btn) 55
Crowshaw Maj O.M. (53
    Btn) 57, 114

Delebarre M. 200
Denehy Maj C.A. (57 Btn)
    21, 74, 104
Denoon Lt W. (55 Btn)

85, 86
Donnan Spr S. (14 FC) 57,
    58, 89
Downing Lt R.G.(54 Btn)
    79, 170
Downing W.H. Pte (57 Btn)
    24, 25, 28, 38, 102
Drayton Lt F. (31 Btn) 63,
    87
Dunk K.A. (32 Btn) 93, 94

Eamons Pte G. (53 Btn) 116
Ebdon Pte A. (57 Btn) 96,
    201
Eckersley Maj P.A.M.
    (31Btn) 63, 172
Edmonds Brig-Gen Sir J.E.
    178
Elliott Brig-Gen H. E. (15
    Bde) 15, 18, 19, 23, 25,
    26, 33, 38, 39, 45,49,
    50, 51, 70, 72-74, 96,
    98, 101, 112, 157, 173,
    175-9,188, 198
Elliott Maj T.P. (60 Btn)
    51, 74
Ellis Capt A. D. 18, 73, 100,
    163
Evans Lt S.E.(15 FC) 36,
    52, 74

Farlow Pte S. (29 Btn) 121
Farmer Lt E.N. (55 Btn)
    79, 80
Field Sgt F. (30 Btn) 151
Findley Spr A. (14 FC) 55
Folkard Lt G. (55 Btn) 120,
    122
Forbes Cpl A. (32 Btn) 88,
    89
Fraser Sgt S. (57 Btn) 102,
    200
Fulton R. Pte (53 Btn) 13,
    55

Gaylor CSM J. H. (5 Pnr
    Btn) 36, 96
German Cemeteries 198
German Units 12, 26, 39-
    41, 44, 77, 80, 100,
    114-5

Gibbins Capt N. (55 Btn) 78, 79, 82, 91-94

Godley Gen Sir A. 12, 16, 183, 185, 188,189, 192

Gordon Brig-Gen A.F. (182 Bde) 13, 43, 178

Greenway Maj H. (15FC) 35, 52, 70

Gunter Lt A.C. (54 Btn) 79, 121

Haig Sir D. 11, 12, 16, 20, 21, 158, 176, 183

Haking Lt-Gen Sir R. 12, 15, 16, 17, 19-22, 26, 27, 42, 69, 71, 73, 74, 89, 90, 100, 104, 165, 166, 167, 176, 177, 180, 201

Hamilton Lt Col F.A.C. (2/6 Glos) 46

Hammond Pte J.H. (55 Btn) 120, 123

Hardy Col C.H.W. 108

Harington Maj-Gen C. 16, 19

Harris Lt Col E.A. (59 Btn) 50, 51

Harris Lt W.H. (54 Btn) 185, 186

Harrison Maj R. (54 Btn) 57, 170, 197

Higgon Maj J.A. (32 Btn) 61

Hobbs Lt Gen Sir T. 192, 198

Hobkirk Lt Col C.J. 183, 190

Hoddle-Wrigley 2/Lt T. (14MGC) 91

Holman Maj R. (54 Btn) 170

Hood Capt V.C.R. (29 Btn) 179, 201

Hopkins Capt C.B. 55, 91, 198

Horne Lt Col A. (15FA) 110, 184, 185

Hospitals 97, 121, 123, 126-129, 130, 151, 152, 154

Howard Maj H. 16, 19, 20, 176

Hughes Maj J.J. (32 Btn) 62, 65, 120, 123

Hutchinson Maj A.J.S. (58 Btn) 71, 72, 74, 175

Inglis Pte J.L.F. (32 Btn) 151

Keane Maj Sir J. (5 Div TMB) 34

Keay Capt R.A. (32 Btn) 122

Keeling Pte T. (30 Btn) 59

Kennedy Fr J.J. 15, 179, 180

King Maj D.M. 66

King Pte C. (53 Btn) 97, 98

Knyvett Capt R. H. (59 Btn) 56, 102

Krinks Capt F.L. (32 Btn) 78, 88, 89

Layh Maj H. (59 Btn) 51, 98

Lees Lt J.S. (30 Btn) 67

Liddelow Capt A. (59 Btn) 51, 102

Lillecrapp Lt M.A. (8MGC) 65

Lloyd Capt F. (32 Btn) 93

Lording Cpl R.E. (30 Btn) 59, 127, 128

Lovejoy 2/Lt H.R. (54 Btn) 93, 120, 122, 123

Lowe Capt M.J. (54 Btn) 93,185, 186

Luly Sgt A.E. (32 Btn) 119, 120, 123

Mackenzie Maj-Gen C. 13, 15, 45, 47, 69, 71-73, 89, 90, 114, 178, 195, 196

MacLaurin Lt Col C. 110, 173

Marsden Capt T.R. (8 MGC) 64

Marshall Capt N. (57 Btn) 37, 103

Martin Sgt L. (8 MGC) 60, 89, 151

Maxted Rev S.E. 95

McCay Maj-Gen Sir The Hon J.W. 13, 15-17, 41, 42, 51, 65, 70, 72-74, 78, 89, 90, 92, 98, 99, 103, 113, 165, 166, 176-178, 181, 182, 184, 185, 187, 189, 190-192, 198, 201

McCloughay (15 FC) 36, 52

McConaghy Lt Col D. (55 Btn) 79, 81, 83, 85, 92, 171, 185, 186

McCrae Maj G.G. (60 Btn) 51, 74, 98

Merkel Lt L.G. (14FC) 35, 121

Miles Pte W. (29 Btn) 99-101

Mills Capt C. (31 Btn) 63, 68, 87, 118

Mills Lt S.E.G. (32 Btn) 88

Mitchell Pte C.A. (53 Btn) 80, 84, 119

Moffit Lt H.L. (53 Btn) 57, 170

Monro Gen Sir C. 12, 15, 16, 20, 21, 89, 90, 100, 176, 177

Mortimer Capt K.M. (29 Btn) 88, 99

Murdoch Maj (29 Btn) 99-101

Murray Capt J.J. (53 Btn) 53, 79, 119

New Zealand Division 12, 17, 35, 43, 106, 113

Noedl Lt L. (15FC) 36, 52

Norris Lt Col I.B. (53 Btn) 57, 170, 171, 187

Nutt Lt Col H.J. (2/7 Warks) 45

Outlaw Pte W.S. (53 Btn) 97, 98, 153

Page Spr R. (14 FC) 42, 101

Pearce Sen G. 184, 188, 189, 190, 191

Pitcher 2/Lt (2/1 Bucks) 19, 169

Plumer Sir H. 12, 16, 20,

114, 165, 183

Pope Capt S.B. 25, 72, 182,
    184, 186, 188
Pope Col H. 90, 181–192
POW Camps 118, 123, 124
Prisoners of War 19, 46, 61,
    69, 72, 111, 115, 117–
    124, 163, 197
Purser Maj M. (30 Btn)
    66, 83

Ranson Capt F.R. (53 Btn)
    123, 170
Ridley Sgt J.G. (53 Btn) 40,
    54, 125, 126, 159
Ross Pte J.V. (8MGC) 66

Sampson Maj V.H.B. (53
    Btn) 53, 57, 170
Scheuermann W. 98, 159,
    161
Scott Lt Col A.H. (56 Btn)
    53
Sheen Capt W.R. (56 Btn)
    84
Shirley Sgt G. (55 Btn) 123,
    124
Simpson Maj A.J. (56 Btn)
    53
Spier Capt C.M. (14 MGC)
    80, 91
Stegga Pte A. (53 Btn) 97,
    98
Stevens L/Cpl A.F. (2/1
    Bucks) 47
Stewart Brig-Gen C.G. (183
    Bde) 46, 196
Stewart-Liberty Capt I. (2/1
    Bucks) 99, 169
Street Capt F. (30 Btn) 66,
    184, 185, 187, 188, 190
Stringfellow Cpl G.H. (55
    Btn) 86, 120, 122
Sturdee Maj V. (8FC) 35

Tebbutt Lt Col A.H. (14FA)
    108, 184, 185
Thomson Capt D. (53 Btn)
    53, 170
Tivey Brig Gen E. (8 Bde)
    61, 78, 99, 127, 168,

171, 172, 188

Toll Lt Col F.W. (31 Btn)
    39, 59, 60, 62, 63, 64,
    68, 77, 87, 90, 91, 168,
    172

Wagstaff Lt Col 73, 90
Wark Capt B.A. (30 Btn) 68
Watts Pte T.L. (30 Btn) 89
Wells L/Cpl S.B. (30 Btn)
    89
Whelpton 2/Lt (15MGC)
    33
White Capt A.R. (32 Btn)
    62, 63, 87
Whiteside Pte T.C. (59 Btn)
    129, 130
Williams Col H.M. (2/1
    Bucks)) 181
Williams H.R. (56 Btn) 38,
    55, 83, 99, 104, 174
Wilson Capt G.H. (5 Div
    TMB) 34, 80
Winter Sgt A.T. (55 Btn) 58,
    85, 93
Woods Capt P.W. (55 Btn)
    185, 186
Wrigley Lt H. (59 Btn) 52
Wyatt Lt J.D. (N'hants) 69,
    75

Yeates Pte F.C. (59 Btn) 152,
    153

Zander Capt W.H. (30 Btn)
    28, 32, 61, 64, 65, 78,
    95, 101, 201

TEMPUS – REVEALING HISTORY

The Defence and Fall of Singapore
1940-42
BRIAN FARRELL
'A multi-pronged attack on those who made the defence of Malaya and Singapore their duty... [an] exhaustive account of the clash between Japanese and British Empire forces' **BBC History Magazine**
'An original and provocative new history of the battle' **Hew Strachan**

£13.99   0 7524 3768 2

Zulu!
The Battle for Rorke's Drift 1879
EDMUND YORKE
'A clear, detailed exposition... a very good read' **Journal of the Royal United Service Institute for Defence Studies**

£12.99   0 7524 3502 7

Paras
The Birth of British Airborne Forces from Churchill's Raiders to 1st Parachute Brigade
WILLIAM F. BUCKINGHAM
£17.99   0 7524 3530 2

Voices from the Trenches
Life & Death on the Western Front
ANDY SIMPSON AND TOM DONOVAN
'A vivid picture of life on the Western Front... compelling reading' **The Daily Telegraph**
'Offers the reader a wealth of fine writing by soldiers of the Great War whose slim volumes were published so long ago or under such obscure imprints that they have all but disappeared from sight like paintings lost under the grime of ages' **Malcolm Brown**

£12.99   0 7524 3905 7

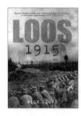

Loos 1915
NICK LLOYD
'A revealing new account based on meticulous documentary research... I warmly commend this book to all who are interested in history and the Great War' **Corelli Barnett**
'Should finally consign Alan Clarke's farrago, The Donkeys, to the waste paper basket' **Hew Strachan**

£25   0 7524 3937 5

The Last Nazis
SS Werewolf Guerilla Resistance in Europe 1944-47
PERRY BIDDISCOMBE
'Detailed, meticulously researched and highly readable... a must for all interested in the end of the Second World War' **Military Illustrated**

£12.99   0 7524 2342 8

Omaha Beach A Flawed Victory
ADRIAN LEWIS
'A damning book' **BBC History Magazine**
£12.99   0 7524 2975 2

The English Civil War
A Historical Companion
MARTYN BENNETT
'Martyn Bennett knows more about the nuts and bolts of the English Civil War than anybody else alive' **Ronald Hutton**
'A most useful and entertaining book – giving us all precise detail about the events, the places, the people and the things that we half-know about the civil war and many more things that we did not know at all' **John Morrill**

£25   0 7524 3186 2

TEMPUS – REVEALING HISTORY

 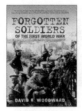 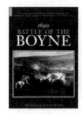 

R.J.Mitchell
Schooldays to Spitfire
GORDON MITCHELL
'[A] readable and poignant story' *The Sunday Telegraph*
£12.99   0 7524 3727 5

Forgotten Soldiers of the First World War
Lost Voices from the Middle Eastern Front
DAVID WOODWARD
'A brilliant new book of hitherto unheard voices from a
haunting theatre of the First World War' *Malcolm Brown*
£20   0 7524 3854 9

1690 Battle of the Boyne
PÁDRAIG LENIHAN
'An almost impeccably impartial account of the most
controversial military engagement in British history' *The
Daily Mail*
£12.99   0 7524 3304 0

Hell at the Front
Combat Voices from the First World War
TOM DONOVAN
'Fifty powerful personal accounts, each vividly portraying the
brutalising reality of the Great War... a remarkable book' *Max
Arthur*
£12.99   0 7524 3940 5

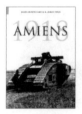   

Amiens 1918
JAMES MCWILLIAMS & R. JAMES STEEL
'A masterly portrayal of this pivotal battle' *Soldier: The
Magazine of the British Army*
£25   0 7524 2860 8

Before Stalingrad
Hitler's Invasion of Russia 1941
DAVID GLANTZ
'Another fine addition to Hew Strachan's excellent *Battles
and Campaigns* series' *BBC History Magazine*
£9.99   0 7524 2692 3

The SS
A History 1919-45
ROBERT LEWIS KOEHL
'Reveals the role of the SS in the mass murder of the Jews,
homosexuals and gypsies and its organisation of death squads
throughout occupied Europe' *The Sunday Telegraph*
£9.99   0 7524 2559 5

Arnhem 1944
WILLIAM BUCKINGHAM
'Reveals the real reason why the daring attack failed' *The
Daily Express*
£10.99   0 7524 3187 0

If you are interested in purchasing other books published by Tempus, or in case you have difficulty finding any
Tempus books in your local bookshop, you can also place orders directly through our website
www.tempus-publishing.com

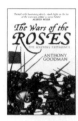

The Wars of the Roses
The Soldiers' Experience
ANTHONY GOODMAN
'Sheds light on the lot of the common soldier as never before' *Alison Weir*
'A meticulous work' *The Times Literary Supplement*
£12.99   0 7524 3731 3

D-Day
The First 72 Hours
WILLIAM F. BUCKINGHAM
'A compelling narrative' *The Observer*
A *BBC History Magazine* Book of the Year 2004
£9.99   0 7524 2842 2

English Battlefields
500 Battlefields that Shaped English History
MICHAEL RAYNER
'A painstaking survey of English battlefields... a first-rate book' *Richard Holmes*
'A fascinating and, for all its factual tone, an atmospheric volume' *The Sunday Telegraph*
£25   0 7524 2978 7

Trafalgar Captain Durham of the Defiance: The Man who refused to Miss Trafalgar
HILARY RUBINSTEIN
'A sparkling biography of Nelson's luckiest captain' *Andrew Lambert*
£17.99   0 7524 3435 7

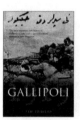
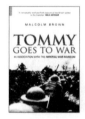

Battle of the Atlantic
MARC MILNER
'The most comprehensive short survey of the U-boat battles' *Sir John Keegan*
'Some events are fortunate in their historian, none more so than the Battle of the Atlantic. Marc Milner is *the* historian of the Atlantic Campaign... a compelling narrative' *Andrew Lambert*
£12.99   0 7524 3332 6

Okinawa 1945 The Stalingrad of the Pacific
GEORGE FEIFER
'A great book... Feifer's account of the three sides and their experiences far surpasses most books about war' *Stephen Ambrose*
£17.99   0 7524 3324 5

Gallipoli 1915
TIM TRAVERS
'The most important new history of Gallipoli for forty years... groundbreaking' *Hew Strachan*
'A book of the highest importance to all who would seek to understand the tragedy of the Gallipoli campaign' *The Journal of Military History*
£13.99   0 7524 2972 8

Tommy Goes To War
MALCOLM BROWN
'A remarkably vivid and frank account of the British soldier in the trenches' *Max Arthur*
'The fury, fear, mud, blood, boredom and bravery that made up life on the Western Front are vividly presented and illustrated' *The Sunday Telegraph*
£12.99   0 7524 2980 9

If you are interested in purchasing other books published by Tempus, or in case you have difficulty finding any Tempus books in your local bookshop, you can also place orders directly through our website

www.tempus-publishing.com

   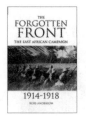

Private 12768 Memoir of a Tommy
JOHN JACKSON

'Unique... a beautifully written, strikingly honest account of a young man's experience of combat' **Saul David**

'At last we have John Jackson's intensely personal and heartfelt little book to remind us there was a view of the Great War other than Wilfred Owen's' **The Daily Mail**

£9.99   0 7524 3531 0

The German Offensives of 1918
MARTIN KITCHEN

'A lucid, powerfully driven narrative' **Malcolm Brown**

'Comprehensive and authoritative... first class' **Holger H. Herwig**

£13.99   0 7524 3527 2

Verdun 1916
MALCOLM BROWN

'A haunting book which gets closer than any other to that wasteland marked by death'
Richard Holmes

£9.99   0 7524 2599 4

The Forgotten Front
The East African Campaign 1914–1918
ROSS ANDERSON

'Excellent... fills a yawning gap in the historical record'
The Times Literary Supplement

'Compelling and authoritative' **Hew Strachan**

£25   0 7524 2344 4

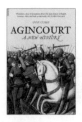  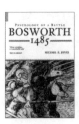 

Agincourt
A New History
ANNE CURRY

'A highly distinguished and convincing account'
Christopher Hibbert

'A tour de force' **Alison Weir**

'The book on the battle' **Richard Holmes**

A **BBC History Magazine** Book of the Year 2005

£25   0 7524 2828 4

The Welsh Wars of Independence
DAVID MOORE

'Beautifully written, subtle and remarkably perceptive' **John Davies**

£25   0 7524 3321 0

Bosworth 1485 Psychology of a Battle
MICHAEL K. JONES

'Most exciting... a remarkable tale' **The Guardian**

'Insightful and rich study of the Battle of Bosworth... no longer need Richard play the villain' **The Times Literary Supplement**

£12.99   0 7524 2594 3

The Battle of Hastings 1066
M.K. LAWSON

'Blows away many fundamental assumptions about the battle of Hastings... an exciting and indispensable read' **David Bates**

A **BBC History Magazine** Book of the Year 2003

£25   0 7524 2689 3

If you are interested in purchasing other books published by Tempus, or in case you have difficulty finding any Tempus books in your local bookshop, you can also place orders directly through our website

www.tempus-publishing.com